MEXICAN BALLADS,
CHICANO POEMS

The New Historicism: Studies in Cultural Poetics
Stephen Greenblatt, General Editor

MEXICAN BALLADS, CHICANO POEMS

HISTORY AND INFLUENCE
IN
MEXICAN-AMERICAN
SOCIAL POETRY

José E. Limón

University of California Press
Berkeley · Los Angeles · Oxford

University of California Press
Berkeley and Los Angeles, California

University of California Press, Ltd.
Oxford, England

© 1992 by
The Regents of the University of California

Library of Congress Cataloging-in-Publication Data
Limón, José Eduardo.
  Mexican ballads, Chicano poems : history and influence in Mexican-
American social poetry / José E. Limón.
    p.   cm. — (The New Historicism ; 17)
  Includes bibliographical references (p.   ) and index.
  ISBN 0-520-06865-3 (cloth : alk. paper). — ISBN 0-520-07633-8
(paper : alk. paper)
    1. American poetry—Mexican American authors—History and
criticism.   2. Ballads, Spanish—Mexico—Appreciation—United
States.   3. Mexican Americans—Intellectual life.   4. American
poetry—Mexican influences.   5. Mexican Americans in literature.
6. Social problems in literature.   I. Title.   II. Series.
PS153.M4L55   1992
811.009′86872—dc20   91-32426
                                                                 CIP

Printed in the United States of America

1   2   3   4   5   6   7   8   9

The paper used in this publication meets the minimum requirements of
American National Standard for Information Sciences—Permanence of
Paper for Printed Library Materials, ANSI Z39.48-1984.

For my father,
                who taught me ballads;

And my mother,
                who taught me books.

Contents

Preface

Clyde Kluckhohn once suggested that anthropology may be nothing more than an intellectual poaching license. As a cultural anthropologist, I must confess at the outset that such license may be my only charter in undertaking this study of Mexican and Chicano poetry. But perhaps a better reason is to be found in the recent disciplinary blurring toward the more holistic intellectual activity now loosely labeled "cultural studies." From this latter perspective, the differences between myth and ritual, on the one hand, and written poetry on the other, may be far less than we thought, particularly as these speak to the social. From this same perspective, the subjects of anthropology are now as likely to be found in the cultural West as in the "third world."

Ultimately, however, the most fundamental reason of all may have more to do with my formation as an intellectual of Mexican descent who was born and raised in the United States. To put it too simply for the moment, I am a product of the various social and poetic worlds explored in this study: race and class domination, patriarchy and the maternal, folk culture and high modernism, the Mexican ballad and Chicano political poetry. This study is my attempt to understand the worlds that I have grown up in over these last forty-odd years and thereby to understand myself. If others profit from this attempt at understanding—even if only in disagreement—I shall be glad of it.

It is often said that defeat is an orphan, while victory has many fathers. (We may as well open on a patriarchal note.) If there is any measure of victory or success in the pages that follow, several fathers have some claim to it.

First and foremost, I thank my own father. Through his hard labor as an agricultural worker, long-haul truck driver, and finally as a meat-cutter (always a union man), he held his family together in tough times. Yet he found and continues to find time and spirit to love, cook Sunday afternoon barbecue, and sing a ballad or two while hunting fresh cilantro in his garden.

Posing as my high school mechanical drawing teacher, Chipman G. Stuart, a covert social philosopher, would periodically hand me books and say, "Limón, read this and tell me what you think of it!" And so I would take Plato, or Nietzsche, or Marx home and up to the room I shared with my brother in the federal housing project where I was raised. Slowly, I would read, dictionary at the ready. Plato was lovely; Nietzsche was exciting; but Marx was right. Looking out my window provided utter confirmation for a high school boy.

My education in modernism began in mechanical drawing, and I shall always be grateful to Chip Stuart. This education continued at the University of Texas at Austin, courtesy of the federal educational loan programs, and no thanks to my high school counselor who, on the eve of Viet Nam, strongly suggested that the army provided good careers for "boys like me." At Austin my undergraduate and graduate studies in modern literature and philosophy were shaped by Irwin C. Lieb, David J. De Laura, Norman K. Farmer, James Ayres, Vartan Gregorian, Joseph Malof, and the late Douglas N. Morgan. Belatedly, I thank them all and hope that what follows speaks well of their teaching.

Literature and philosophy soon blurred into cultural anthropology via the mediation of folklore studies. I also became somewhat of a specialist in Mesoamerica and Mexican-Americans. Here I must acknowledge Roger D. Abrahams, Richard Bauman, Richard N. Adams, and the late Angel Palerm. But a singularly special acknowledgment must be reserved for Américo Paredes, who, in his person and intellectual practice, brought together for me all of my education and my life. His influence and my indebtedness, care, and respect for him are, I trust, evident everywhere in this study and particularly in part 1.

Finally in this list of familial and intellectual father-figures I acknowledge a man who is both: my father-in-law, Professor Nathan Adler of the California School of Professional Psychology in Alameda. He has energetically read and commented on every page of this study and shared with me much of his great store of Freudian and modern thought. His marvelous modernist library, possibly the best north of Berkeley, was indispensable to my writing.

Like my poets, I now veer in the direction of the maternal for an equal kind of sustenance that requires acknowledgment. Here, I must express my care and gratitude to my mother-in-law, Elizabeth, who, with unfailing graciousness, provided her home and her generous care while I wrote some of the key portions of this book.

The strength—political and poetic—of the maternal is, indeed, one of the central proposals of this book, and in all these matters my largest acknowledgment and gratitude belongs to my mother, who started and kept everything going through the darkest adversity. This book, seemingly about men, is really about her.

Belonging on neither list but contributing fundamentally to my thought is my wife and intellectual partner, Marianna Adler. We, and this study, began in 1979 amid glasses of wine, conversation, and love at Les Amis Café in Austin, Texas. We continue, having now added another measure of love in Renata, age five.

I have also profited greatly from other sources of support in this writing. Most recently, I am indebted to the very helpful anonymous reviewers of the manuscript for the University of California Press. Teresa McKenna and José Saldívar provided stimulating conversations and a generous discussion of the manuscript's principal subjects throughout. Extremely helpful critical responses were also provided by a faculty-graduate student seminar organized by Renato Rosaldo at Stanford University. I thank him especially. I participated in this seminar during a 1987–88 fellowship year at the Stanford Humanities Center. For the latter and its generous support, let me thank Bliss Carnochan and Morton Sosna, director and associate director of the center, as well as the center's staff and the Ford Foundation. While I spent most of that year working on another project, they generously provided the necessary logistical support for completing the present study. The latter came principally in the person of Dee Marquez, who provided skillful, invaluable word-processing for this "low-tech" professor. The Academic Services Center of the University of California at Santa Cruz prepared the final version of the manuscript with utmost skill and punctuality. I am also grateful to Amy Einsohn for improving the manuscript as she copyedited.

Other institutional beginnings and intermediary places also deserve acknowledgment. The University of Texas at Austin, University Research Institute provided a 1979 Summer Research Grant that permitted the first sustained reading and reflection for this study. Along the way, I presented several chapters at meetings of the Modern Language Association and at the 1981 Symposium on Chicano Art and Literature at the University of California at Santa Barbara. Finally, sections of chapters 2 and 5 appeared respectively in *The New American Literary History*, edited by La Vonne Brown Ruoff (New York: Modern Language Association, 1990) and *Creativity: Self and Society*, edited by Renato Rosaldo, Kirin Narayan, and Smadar Lavie (Ithaca: Cornell University Press, 1990), as well as in the Working Papers Series of the Stanford Center for Chicano Research.

This book, a study of poetic influence, is itself the result of many sources of influence. My hope is that, in Harold Bloom's terms, it will be a strong poem in its own right and complimentary testimony to all who helped bring it into being. Its faults, however, are my own.

The author wishes to thank Juan Gómez-Quiñones for his generous permission to reprint "Canto al Trabajador" and "The Ballad of Billy Rivera," both of which appeared in *5th and Grande Vista (Poems, 1960–1973)*, published by Colección Mensaje, New York.

The following individuals and publishers have also given permission to quote from copyrighted works: Alfred A. Knopf, Inc., for "An Ordinary Evening in New Haven" by Wallace Stevens, in *The Collected Poems of Wallace Stevens*; Cambridge University Press, for *The Ethnic Revival* by Anthony D. Smith; Cornell University Press, for *Drama, Fields, and Metaphors: Symbolic Action in Human Society* by Victor Turner; *Cultural Critique*, for "Authority (White), Power and the (Black) Critic: Or, It's All Greek to Me" by Henry Louis Gates, Jr.; Farrar, Straus & Giroux, for *The Old Gringo* by Carlos Fuentes; Harcourt Brace Jovanovich for *The Waste Land* by T. S. Eliot and for *World of Our Fathers* by Irving Howe; Houghton Mifflin Company for "Song of Myself" by Walt Whitman, in Walt Whitman, *Complete Poetry and Prose*, edited by James E. Miller, Jr.; Methuen and Company, for *Orality and Literacy: The Technologizing of the Word* by Walter Ong; MIT Press, for "On the Nature and Form of the Essay" by Georg Lukács, in *Soul and Form*, translated by Anna Bostock; W. W. Norton & Company, for *Ecrits: A Selection* by Jacques Lacan, translated by Alan Sheridan; Edward W. Said, for *Beginnings: Intention and Method*, published by Basic Books; The University of Chicago Press, for *Criticism and Social Change* by Frank Lentricchia; University Press of New England for *Life Against Death: The Psychoanalytic Meaning of History* by Norman O. Brown; and University of Texas Press for *Speech Genres and Other Late Essays* by M. M. Bakhtin, translated by Vern W. McGee, for *Chicano Authors: Inquiry by Interview* by Juan Bruce-Novoa, and for *With His Pistol in His Hand* by Américo Paredes.

That is, we consider literature as an order of repetition, not of originality—but an eccentric order of repetition, not one of sameness—where the term *repetition* is used in order to avoid such dualities as "the original versus the derivative," or "the idea and its realization," or "model/paradigm versus example"; and where *eccentric* is used in order to emphasize the possibilities for difference within repetition and to signify that while authors, works, periods, and influences are notions that pertain to writing in specific cases, they are really terms used to describe irregularities of varying degrees and qualities within writing as a whole.

Edward Said,
Beginnings: Intention and Method

Folklore is in general saturated with time; all of its images are profoundly chronotopic. Time in folklore, the fullness of time in it, the folkloric future, the folkloric human yardsticks of time—all of these are very important and fundamental problems. We cannot, of course, discuss them here, even though folkloric time exerted an immense and productive influence on literature.

M. M. Bakhtin,
Speech Genres and Other
Late Essays

How subtle, the old gringo thought in that early hour, is the knowledge a father inherits from all his fathers and transmits to all his sons.

Carlos Fuentes, *The Old Gringo*

Amor matris, subjective and objective genitive may be the only true thing in life. Paternity may be a legal fiction. Who is the father of any son that any son should love him or he any son?

James Joyce, *Ulysses*

The fact that the Father may be regarded as the original representative of this authority of the Law requires us to specify by what privileged mode of presence he is sustained beyond the subject who is actually led to occupy the place of the Other, namely, the Mother. The question, therefore, is pushed still further back.

Jacques Lacan, *Ecrits: A Selection*

INTRODUCTION

This study is an exploration of the social origins, continuity, transformation, and ideological meanings of a particular range of political poetry produced by men of Mexican descent, mostly in the United States. I begin with the oral folk poetic form known as the corrido, or Mexican ballad, produced on both sides of the Mexico–United States border at least since the mid-nineteenth century. Next, I take up the political poetics of one of the most distinguished scholars and intellectuals of Mexican descent in the United States, Américo Paredes. This poetics is examined in an analysis of one of his formal poems and in the textuality of *With His Pistol in His Hand*, Paredes's classic study of the Mexican ballad. I then turn to three long poems generated in the emergent American political culture of the 1960s known as the Chicano movement: José Montoya's "El Sol y los de Abajo," Rodolfo "Corky" Gonzales's "I Am Joaquín," and Juan Gómez-Quiñones's "Ballad of Billy Rivera."

I treat these bodies of poetry as socially symbolic action at three historical moments: The corrido of greater Mexico is most salient during the turn-of-the-century revolutionary period along the U.S.-Mexico border. The work of Américo Paredes has its principal historical significance from the 1930s into the 1960s and serves as a key link between the Mexican ballad tradition and the written poetry of the Chicano political movement in the late sixties and early seventies.

My study proceeds along two dialectically related lines of analysis. First, I am interested in bringing to the surface the dynamic relationship of poetic influence that exists among these poetic works, oral and written. To this end, I draw upon and revise Harold Bloom's theory of poetic influence. However, I simultaneously argue that these bodies of poetry are also responding to the social contradictions of race, class, and gender in their respective historical moments. Here, I appropriate the theoretical work of Fredric Jameson to my interpretive service. But, in a way that the conceptual language of Raymond Williams will help me explain, the diachronic relationship of poetic influence is deeply implicated in and energizes the ability of the later poems to speak to their respective social moments.

In this relationship the Mexican corrido is not a mere "antecedent" or "background" literature but rather, in Bloom's terms, a master poem that, as key symbolic action, powerfully dominates and conditions the later written poetry. In the wake of Paredes's own influenced and influential mediation of the corrido, the three Chicano long poems examined here respond dialectically and ritually both to the precursory corrido and also to their own social moment. Each succeeding poem manifests a more mature and sophisticated poetic relationship to the precursors and subsequently a richer political and cultural apprehension of the present. In my reading, however, this total relationship contains an interesting paradox for this highly patriarchal, highly ethnic lineage. This growing apprehension is predicated on an increasingly sophisticated grasp of a cultural poetics of gender, specifically of women's imagery and voice, principally in the form of the maternal. Equally a paradox, it is also predicated on an appropriation of an Anglo-American modernist poetry.

Through this kind of analysis, I propose to intervene in certain critical debates and issues in contemporary cultural studies. Let me note these, moving from the most specific to the most general.

Specifically, I am interested in historicizing some aspect of the literature of the people of Mexican descent in the United States in two temporal dimensions, a concern I elaborate in my concluding chapter. First, I sense in the current critical study of this literature a general absence of analyses that offer close and extended social readings of a corpus of literature with specific reference to particular historical periods. Here, one looks for, and generally does not find, analyses that work at the intersection of race, ethnicity, class, and gender as each of these is artistically articulated at a specific historical moment. Second, I sense a similar absence of richly diachronic studies that densely link past and present periods in this literary history, rather than treat the former as "background" to the latter. I hope to offer a richer sense of some aspects of this literature, and in large part I propose to do so by bringing current and controversial cultural theory to bear on these poetic materials. In doing so, I hope to address several more general issues.

Among these is the question of gender in culture. However, rather than focus on women (in a way that currently tends to become synonymous with gender analysis), I focus on an all-male tradition as my way of making two interrelated and paradoxical proposals for the study of gender. First, I will, in effect, be arguing for the creative poetic and political impulses that at times, and in specific historical instances, can originate in patriarchy. However, I will also be proposing that these impulses are deeply conditioned by a psychopoetic acknowledgment of the strength of women, principally in the form of the maternal.

The poetic materials I have chosen also permit an intervention in another debate in the study of culture: the relationship of folklore to written literature, and questions of orality and literacy. Generally siding with those who wish to restore the relative cultural importance of oral expression in cultural studies, I offer one case in which a specific oral tradition, the Mexican corrido, takes a kind of poetic primacy over written poetry.

In turn, however, this argument leads me to another paradoxical observation. For even as I make this historically specific claim about the primacy of the oral and of folk culture, I also make a countervailing argument for the written tradition of high modernism: that the most artistically and politically successful of these poets are those who incorporate the full power of oral folk culture and join it to a powerful reading of modernism. In my conclusion, I also draw out some of the pedagogical implications of this model in terms of current "Western" versus "non-Western" curricular debates.

In addressing all these issues, and as befits its inclusion in the New Historicism series, this study also enters—if only tangentially—into an ongoing discussion concerning the critical possibilities and limitations of what has come to be called the "new historicism" in cultural studies. As my general contribution to this discussion, and by way of my particular poetic materials, I want to expand the historical and social horizons of new historicist practice, which seems to me to remain decidedly synchronic and canonical in its focus. I elaborate on this question in my concluding chapter.

Finally, as my most general contribution to cultural studies, I offer this book as an effort to integrate the specific analysis of Mexican culture in the United States with current global cultural theory, and thereby to assist the development of both. Lest they become insular and parochial, local ethnic studies must be consistently exposed to the most globalizing interpretive theory. Lest it lose touch with specific practices that test its validity and lest it become elitist and exclusivist, global theory consistently needs to be questioned and revised in terms of the local. I am also mindful that this particular local—the Mexican people of the United States—is often ignored in global discussions in comparison to, let us say, African American and American Indian cultural poetics. I trust that this study will be of some assistance in bringing this topic before a more general intellectual public even as it also addresses a native intelligentsia.

Such then are the various concerns and arguments of this book. Its plan is as follows. In chapter 1, I offer a discussion of the historical emergence, poetic character, and social evolution of the greater Mexican corrido. My central argument is that by virtue of its history, poetics, and social meaning, the corrido is historically positioned to become, in Bloom's terms, a master poem for subsequent poets.

At this juncture, readers not wholly familiar with Bloom's theory of poetic influence may wish to review his theory and my revisionary reading of it in Appendix A. These revisionary remarks also include an exposition of Fredric Jameson's ideas. Rather than break my narrative of influence from poet to poet and generation to generation, I have placed this theoretical exposition in an appendix where readers may draw on it as they need to.

Chapters 2 and 3 take up the cultural poetics of Américo Paredes and analyze the first struggle of influence between the master poem and its foremost poetic son. Chapters 4 through 7 examine the politics and poetics of the Chicano movement and that generation's struggle of influence with the corrido. These poets, I argue, will struggle against the dominating poetic and political influence of the corrido as they attempt to write their own strong social poems. As part of their armament, the most successful draw on a repressed poetic sense of the maternal and on modernism to counter the corrido's influence. These poets' political and poetic successes and failures also epitomize the ideological phases in the Chicano movement from 1965 to 1972. In my concluding chapter I assess the various theoretical issues generated by my analysis of this poetic data.

PART ONE

POLITICS, POETICS, AND THE
RESIDUAL PRECURSORS, 1848–1958

Oral cultures indeed produce powerful and beautiful verbal performances of high artistic and human worth, which are no longer even possible once writing has taken possession of the psyche.

Walter J. Ong, *Orality and Literacy*

Corrido, the Mexicans call their narrative folk songs, especially those of epic themes, taking the name from *correr*, which means "to run" or "to flow," for the *corrido* tells a story simply and swiftly, without embellishments.

Américo Paredes,
With His Pistol in His Hand

No hay mejor cosa que un buen corrido. [There is nothing better than a good corrido.]

My father (all the time)

Borders, Bullets, and Ballads
The Social Making of a Master Poem

In 1915, as European imperialist powers fought their bloody Great War, and two years before the Bolshevik uprising in Russia, both war and revolution raged in Mexico and briefly on the northern side of the Mexico–United States border. During the initial phase of the Mexican Revolution (1910 to 1911), various allied revolutionary groups had deposed the autocratic, United States–supported dictatorship of Porfirio Díaz. However, this initial unity fragmented when the more conservative groups in the coalition took power but failed to demonstrate a clear commitment to the speedy realization of the Revolution's ideals, principally serious land redistribution. The more liberal and populist forces of leaders such as Pancho Villa and Emiliano Zapata, in alliance, opposed this betrayal and the civil war continued. In April 1915, in "the most famous military engagement of the Revolution—the battle of Celaya," the army of general Alvaro Obregón, in the service of the conservative President Venustiano Carranza, defeated the populist forces of Francisco Villa in a ferocious encounter that presaged the ultimate demise of Villa and Zapata (Meyer and Sherman 1979:539).[1] The Wilson administration's recognition of the Carranza government that same year also signaled the eventual triumph of conservative capitalist rule in Mexico and the continuing impoverishment of the Mexican masses, albeit in the guise of an official rhetoric of "institutional" revolution (Cockcroft 1983:99–116).

The pivotal Battle of Celaya was witnessed in part by a wealthy American adventurer, man of letters, and world traveler, Edward Larocque Tinker, who accompanied Villa's troops as a civilian observer. On the evening following the battle, as he "wandered along the boxcars on which the troops were quartered on the roofs," he heard "singing and the strumming of stringed instruments." Seeking the source of this music, he

came into the light of a campfire around which a crowd of Villa's ragged soldiers were gathered with their *soldaderas*—those amazing Amazons

7

who cooked for their men, and, with pots and pans, and often a baby on their backs, kept up with the regiments on gruelling marches; or, when need arose, snatched a rifle from a corpse and fought as fiercely as any male. This strange motley crowd, most of them showing strong strains of Aztec, was listening in the moonlight like fascinated children to the singing of three men. (1961:7)

As he listened "to the assonance of their voices," Tinker reports,

I too was fascinated and thought they sang some old folk tale. As verse after verse, however, took the same melodic pattern I suddenly realized that this was no ancient epic, but a fresh minted account of the battle of the day before. . . . It was a *corrido*—hot from the oven of their vivid memory of the struggle between Villa and Obregón—the first one I had ever heard. (1961:7)

The context of social conflict; singing in verse with the "same melodic pattern"; a narrated account of a specific powerful incident; male performers and a predominantly male audience (we shall attend to the presence of women later)—all of these enter into Tinker's general but likely accurate account of his first corrido performance. In 1943, when he returned to Mexico "to lecture on North American idealistic literature" at the National University, he "got a chance to study the subject" and also realized that, while "no ancient epic" singers, the corrido performers he had seen,

like the payadores of Argentina and Uruguay, were, in almost every essential, the lineal descendants of the troubadours who performed at the Court of Eleanore of Aquitaine in the middle of the 12th century, and that their songs were the Creole counterpart of the early Spanish *romances*, those Iberian *chansons de geste* in which countless medieval bards sang the famous exploits of Hispanic knights to the accompaniment of the *lira mendicoram—romances* which must have come to America with the Conquistadores. (1961:7–8)

In this chapter I shall examine Tinker's definition of the corrido in much greater detail and set out its relationship to the social history of its most active period. It must be clear from the outset that I am not discussing all corridos but only the epic heroic corrido of greater Mexico. We will see how this song narrative with its long heritage, compelling artistry, and its implication in social conflict became a master precursor poem for at least two generations of male Mexican-descent poets in the United States. For although the corrido had a very limited influence on writers in Mexico (Paredes 1958a:102), it exerted a far more creative influence on Mexican-American writers. It was in the Mexican North and in the U.S. Southwest (hereafter, the Border) with their intimate ties of geography, population, and culture that the Mexican corrido flowered. In that same spring of 1915, as Obregón's machine guns and artillery were cutting down Villa's barbed-wire-entangled infantry like so many British at the Somme, the Texas rural police known as the Texas Rangers, supported by U.S. cavalry, were ruthlessly suppressing an armed rebellion of Mexican-Americans protesting Anglo-American authority in south Texas (Paredes 1958b:25–27; Harris and Sadler 1978; Montejano 1987:117–28). Around campfires in south Texas and in northern Mexico, where the rebels took refuge, they strummed guitars and sang of their violent encounters with the hated *gringos* (Paredes 1976:32–34). They sang in the same verse forms and recurring melodic patterns used by Villa's *norteño* (northern) soldiers, who at that moment were fighting against U.S.-supported domination a few hundred miles south of the border at Celaya.

Before explaining how a medieval poetic form introduced into southern Mexico by the Spanish conquistadors became a distinctive and artistically powerful master cultural poetics of the northern Border, I want to expand and specify Tinker's description of the corrido.

THE GREATER MEXICAN CORRIDO:
AN EXPANDED DEFINITION

Even allowing for the literary license often taken by Anglo-American writers on Mexico (Robinson 1977), it is not difficult to appreciate why the Mexican corridos "fascinated" both Villa's "ragged soldiers" and the urbane, cosmopolitan Professor Tinker. But one must correct Tinker's impression that the corrido is a direct, relatively unchanged descendant of the Spanish romance introduced into Mexico with the Conquest. For the moment, let us note the key differences, which I will historicize later in this chapter. Following Mendoza (1954), Geijerstam (1976:50–51) lists these important differences between the older Spanish romance and the later corrido:

1. The romance has lines of seven or eight syllables; corridos tend to have eight, but may have up to twenty syllables per line. (This is particularly the case with historical corridos from the state of Guerrero.)

2. The romance consists mainly of a nonstrophic series of lines, asso-nantic, with simple rhymes (*monorrimos*) on lines with an even num-ber; the corrido is strophic, with four or six lines in each verse, and has different types of rhyme.

3. The romance is epic, novelistic, and *morisco*, that is, it deals with fiestas, tournaments, love affairs, and so forth. The corrido expands these themes, becoming a kind of local news service.

4. In musical terms, the romance is "serious," modal, and melodically restrained, while the corrido is "overflowing," lyrical, and of wider melodic range, though it retains the metric and rhythmic characteristics of its Spanish ancestor.

5. The romance usually consists of a dialogue between two principals; in contrast, the corrido is a narrative usually in the first or third person, with the troubadour acting as the (hypothetical) witness of the event described.

Contemporary scholars have refined these observations. Almost all scholars agree that the corrido is a male narrative folk song of greater Mexico composed in octosyllabic quatrains and sung to a tune in ternary rhythm and in 3/4 or 6/8 time. The quatrains are structured in an *abcb* rhyme scheme with no fixed number of stanzas for any given song or performance. The opening stanza usually sets the scene, time, and central issue of the narrated events and may, on occasion, carry a request from singer to audience for permission to begin the song. Often the closing stanza offers an overall comment on the narrated events and may also announce that the ballad has ended and express a farewell from the singer to the audience (McDowell 1981; Mendoza 1939, 1954; Paredes 1958b, 1963, 1976; Simmons 1957). Finally, corridos, in the words of their best younger scholar, "focus on events of particular consequence to the *corrido* community," on "events of immediate sig-nificance" that produce a "heightened awareness of mutual values and orientations" (McDowell 1981:46). The variations are sometimes con-siderable, but all scholars posit this basic corrido type.

Tinker heard an early and immediate corrido about the monumental battle at Celaya. Although he provides no text, most likely the ballad he heard resembled the version collected by Vicente T. Mendoza (1954). The first and last stanzas are (the translations are my own):

De Los Combates de Celaya

En mil novecientos quince
Jueves Santo en la mañana
salió Villa de Torreón
a combatir a Celaya

.   .   .   .

Ya no le temo al cañón
ni tampoco a la metralla
aquí da fin el corrido
del combate de Celaya
          (Mendoza 1954:53–56)

Of the Battles of Celaya

In nineteen hundred and fifteen
On a Holy Thursday morning
Villa left from Torreon
To do battle at Celaya

. . . .

I no longer fear the cannon
Nor the machine gun do I fear
and here ends the corrido
Of the battle at Celaya.

We may begin by noting the poem's predominantly octosyllabic lines—"En *mil* nove*cien*tos *quin*ce"—with syllabic stresses on two, five, and seven. From the outset the folk poet has a traditional obligation inherited from the Spanish romance to shape his lines within this rhythmic constraint, especially if we assume that the poem may also be read. There is some validity to this latter assumption, as we shall see.

However, the socially and artistically optimum mode for the corrido is as a sung poem, and in this mode a musical rhythm overrides the poetic meter. As Paredes (1958b:208) and McDowell (1981:65–70) both note, as song, the corrido imposes an additional artistic obligation upon the corridista (the composer-singer): to sing to a rhythm that in all likelihood is not consonant with the meter. To use their own shared example, let us consider the two opening lines from "El Corrido de Gregorio Cortez" (The Ballad of Gregorio Cortez):

En el condado del Carmen
Miren lo que ha sucedido

In the country of El Carmen
Look what has happened

If read as poetry, these lines would be stressed on the first, fourth, and seventh syllables: *En* el con*da*do del *Car*men. But when sung, the lines would have a very strong stress on the second, rather than the first, syllable of each line. When repeated in each line of the ballad, this musical syncopation, which alters the poetic meter, produces a discernible aesthetic effect. The "counterpointing of rhythms," Paredes explains, and the ending of the second line of each quatrain on "the major chord formed on the subdominant," and "high register singing," all add "a great deal of vigor, almost defiant vigor, to the delivery of the *corrido* when it is sung by a good singer" (1958b:209). Already at the level of rhythm, the artistic manipulation of what McDowell calls "two autonomous systems, the poetic and the musical" constitutes the fundamental basis of a strong poem (1981:70).

A contrapuntal relationship is also articulated by the contrast between the corrido's stable rhyme scheme and its stanzaic novelty. In each stanza the second and fourth lines "must be controlled for rhyme or assonance" (McDowell 1981:56). McDowell elaborates on this artistic challenge: "From the composer's point of view, the critical moment in this structural unit are those key words at the end of lines 2 and 4. . . . Spanish, with its tendency to alternate vowels and consonants and even to delete certain unstressed consonants, contains many words which fortuitously end with the same pair of final vowels" (1981:57). As McDowell emphasizes, "it is the task of the *corridista* to exploit these congruences in tailoring his stanzas, while maintaining the semantic integrity of the *corrido*" (1981:57).

However, even as the corridista is maintaining the rhythmic patterns and rhyme scheme, he is also constructing a chain of stanzas in which, according to corrido tradition, there is rarely a repetition of stanzas and there is no refrain. That is, "the content of each successive stanza is new" (McDowell 1981:56), creating the rapidly changing imagistic scenery of the corrido (Paredes 1958b:185). Thus, in the first stanza of the Celaya corrido we imagine Villa, the protagonist, setting out from Torreón to do battle; in the second stanza, we find ourselves riding a troop train, and we are also introduced to General Obregón, Villa's antagonist.

> Corre, corre, maquinita
> no me dejes ni un vagón
> nos vamos para Celaya
> a combatir a Obregón.
>   (Mendoza 1954:53)

> Run, run, little train
> Leave no cars behind
> We are going to Celaya
> To do battle with Obregón.

The imagistic and scenic novelty of each stanza is artistically counterpointed to the recurrent rhyme and rhythm. (Perhaps it was something like this for Francisco Villa's peasant soldiers riding in their troop trains. They must have watched the changing scenes of the landscape from northern Coahuila to south-central Guanajuato even as they heard the repetitive rhythm of the train carrying them down the tracks to their destiny at Celaya.)

Earlier, I spoke of the corrido as a narrative folk song, yet it is not a wholly narrativized discourse in the strictest sense. Rather, as Mc-Dowell points out, the general "narrative" of the corrido is really a structure of alternations. The corrido often alternates between actually narrated (chronologically linear) segments, in which an iconic account of events is presented, and other segments that constitute "the emotional kernel of the *corrido*," verses that "dramatize that most dramatic of human involvements, the face-to-face interaction." The corrido may "expand the greater portion of its energy in presenting dialogue," and when it does so, iconicity is transcended and an "experiential substratum" appears in the ballad with a "relation of identity . . . presumed to obtain between the words spoken in the experiential substratum and the words sung by the *corridista*" (McDowell 1981:47).

"El Corrido de Gregorio Cortez" illustrates the point. At one instant in his flight, Cortez is surrounded by lawmen who have thrown up a corral around him. Under intense gunfire, he jumps the corral, kills a second sheriff and escapes with parting shots from his gun and his lips.

> Allá por El Encinal
> según lo que aquí se dice
> les formaron un Corral
> y les mató otro cherife.
>
> Over by Encinal
> According to what we hear
> They made him a Corral
> And he killed another sheriff.

In the next stanza, Cortez speaks in quietly boasting metaphors:

> Decía Gregorio Cortez
> echando muchos balazos
> —Me he escapado de aguaceros,
> contimás de nublinazos.
>   (Paredes 1958b:156)
>
> Then said Gregorio Cortez
> Shooting out a lot of bullets
> "I have weathered thunderstorms;
> This little mist doesn't bother me."

For McDowell, such a scene is the key to the corrido's artistic power, for it permits a "narrative discourse . . . punctuated by flashes of identification between the narrative and the experiential substratum" (1981: 48); while the corrido "does not favor poetic conceit in its presentation of narrative detail . . . the portions of reported speech . . . provide the *corridista* with ample scope to wax poetic" (1981:61).

Marked and traditional poetic language emerges in the form of ritualized and metaphorical boasts and insults by the central protagonist of the ballad. That Gregorio Cortez uses metaphoric language to compare the lawmen's furious shooting to a "little mist" also reinforces the image of the hero as an accomplished individual who can ride, shoot, and speak, often in "complex and subtle poetic conceits native to the oral tradition of his community." In the final analysis, of course, we are really speaking of the folk poet's ability to be an "accomplished man of words" (McDowell 1981:64).

While being attentive to all these artistic obligations, the folk poet must also respond to certain demands created by his relationship to his community, and these demands also shape his poem. Of particular interest here is what McDowell calls the "reflexive" character of the corrido manifested in its traditional opening and closing stanzas, which place the principal narrative in a metanarrative frame. The opening scene-setting stanza and the formally announced closing and farewell at the end enable the song to refer to itself, to "draw attention to the occasion of performance rather than to the occasion of narrative action" (McDowell 1981:48). Here one might quarrel a bit with McDowell, though. It is not clear, for example, why the opening stanza of the Celaya corrido—describing Villa setting out from Torreón—is not part of the "occasion of narrative action" but rather a reference to the "occasion of performance." Nonetheless, this opening stanza is distinct from those that follow, in that the latter put the audience immediately and imagistically into the movement and din of battle, which is, after all, the central concern of the corrido. In its imagistically unfocused, somewhat more abstract language, the first stanza does have something of a metanarrative quality. The reflexive quality of the final stanza is, in contrast, transparent: for the first and only time the singer at Celaya refers to himself in the first person, implicates himself in the battle, and clearly informs his audience that his song is ended.

Such reflexivity situates the song in an intimate relationship to the audience and, by extension, to society. Whatever the considerable achievement of the individual folk poet, the song also flows from the social and back to it again. This useful fiction, that society is also the author of the song, is also upheld by another artistic convention. While we clearly have the appearance, albeit brief, of the first person in the final stanza of the Celaya corrido, most corridos embrace "the literary fiction of an understood observer, who encases his observations in the impersonal third-person ... the typical case involves an impersonal authorial voice, present but not implicated in the events it depicts" (McDowell 1981:46). The effacement of the author into the impersonal third person precludes the audience from indulging in any easy personal identification with any figure in the poem. Rather, one tends to identify with the public social events depicted and the cultural actions that produce them. Further, the effacement of the corridista reinforces the social, collective nature of the corrido. While most corridos are the work of a single author, any personal point of view manifested in the ballad seems to represent a shared perspective. "Above all," Simmons posits, the composer "must identify himself with the *pueblo* and take care that the opinions he expresses are acceptable to the *pueblo*" (1957:36).

As to the performance itself, the optimum manner for experiencing the corrido as social art is in a face-to-face performance, such as that reported by Tinker. Following Paredes (1976), McDowell notes three traditional principal occasions for the singing of corridos: the solitary setting (when riding the range alone on horseback, for example); the familial context, with both sexes and different ages present; and the all-male group setting. The first is, by definition, not a social performance, while the second makes for a limited repertoire and a subdued rendition (violent corridos might be excluded or censored, for example). The all-male setting, however, places no such limits on the fullest display of the corridista's competence. Both Paredes and McDowell situate such performances in a cantina, or barroom, but they also take place today during men-only barbecues in south Texas. It is in these all-male settings that the full range of corrido aesthetics is on display, both the talents of the singer-composer as well as the skills of the audience, their ability to judge and comment on the form and content of the ballads (McDowell 1981:71).

Today, corridos are also transmitted through the printed page, films, records, and oral recitation without music. But the all-male face-to-face performance still dominates the perception and definition of the corrido, and it too is an ideological act in its own right. Indeed, we must pursue the theme of masculinity a bit further as we now examine the propositional content—the heroic world—of the corrido.

THE HEROIC WORLD OF THE
CORRIDO

The corrido, we noted earlier, focuses on events that are of particular significance to the corridista's community and that capture and articulate this community's values and orientations. Among such classes of events—natural disasters, the election of officials, the untimely death of a child—one theme seems to have struck a special resonance: confrontation, violent confrontation, between individual men who often represent larger social causes but just as often are concerned with their personal honor. In neither case should the issue be petty or small, and in some corridos both concerns are intertwined:

> The fearless man of action, the capacity to die honorably—these are themes characteristic of a heroic world view and the world view of the *corrido* is decidedly heroic. Part of the propositional intent of the *corrido* is to stipulate that a man *should* die honorably, *should* confront death fearlessly.
> The honorable course of action is highlighted by presentation of its opposite, the man who disgraces himself by flinching at impending death. (McDowell 1981:53)

At the height of the battle of Celaya, his soldiers falling around him, rather than retreat, Villa redoubles his courage, according to his corridista:

> Dice Don Francisco Villa:
> —De nuevo voy a atacar,
> me han matado mucha gente,
> su sangre voy a vengar.
> > (Mendoza 1954:55)

> Don Francisco Villa says:
> —I will attack again
> They have killed many of my people
> Their blood I will avenge.

In contrast, as the composer of the ballad of Gregorio Cortez tells us, the Anglos chasing Cortez knew only fear:

Venían los americanos
más blancos que una paloma
de miedo que le tenían
a Cortez y su pistola

The Americans were coming
They were whiter than a dove
From the fear that they had
Of Cortez and his pistol

Cortez then speaks:

Decía Gregorio Cortez
Con su pistola en la mano:
—No corran, rinches cobardes
con un solo Mexicano.
        (Paredes 1958b:156)

Then said Gregorio Cortez,
With his pistol in his hand:
—Don't run, you cowardly rangers,
From just one Mexican.

It is this image of the fearless man defending his right with his pistol in hand that defines the male heroic world of the corrido. To the extent that his personal sense of honor and right are congruent with larger social values and conflicts that concern the entire community, his heroic posture assumes an even more intense social signification. If this latter point is correct, we can begin to understand why the corrido flourished along the Border from the mid-nineteenth century and then declined after 1930.

THE SOCIOHISTORICAL ORIGINS OF
THE HEROIC CORRIDO

Most scholars of the genre agree that corrido-like songs have been composed in Mexico since the Conquest. There is also total agreement on the corrido's general formal and thematic indebtedness to the Spanish romance, although significant differences argue decisively for the corrido's distinctiveness as a genre, as already noted. Therefore, most scholars take their cue from Mexico's leading authority on the history of the corrido and agree that "in its crystallized form, such as we know it today" the Mexican corrido is "relatively modern" (Mendoza

1954:xiii), that is, a product of the late nineteenth and early twentieth century, especially of the intense social change occasioned by the Mexican Revolution. Simmons offers a respected dissenting note and argues that much earlier corrido-like songs are found throughout Latin America, although he also concludes that the corrido "finally evolved or solidified into its modern or definitive form during the last thirty years of the nineteenth century" (1963:1). Mendoza locates the geographical origins of the corrido in southern Michoacán, in deep southwestern Mexico. From there, he believes, it traveled into the northern part of the country, where, he notes, it is also very strong (Mendoza 1939:152–53).

In 1958, however, in conjunction with the publication of his *With His Pistol in His Hand*, Américo Paredes, an American scholar of Mexican descent, suggested a significantly different theory for the historical and geographical origins of the Mexican heroic ballad. In "The Mexican *Corrido*: Its Rise and Fall" (1958a), Paredes puts forth a persuasive and undogmatic case for locating the corrido's temporal origins in the mid-nineteenth century and its geographical origins in southern Texas, where the Rio Grande meets the Gulf of Mexico, an area Paredes calls the Lower Border.

Paredes cautiously and prudently begins to make his argument by noting the inability of scholars to locate a distinctive ballad tradition within Mexico prior to the period of the Revolution. While there are earlier scattered balladlike songs throughout Mexico, none of these are clearly heroic ballads, nor do they constitute a ballad tradition, that is, a group of ballads enduring over time and expressing a focused collective consciousness (1963:233). But, Paredes argues, such a balladry was in existence in the Lower Border at least since, but probably not before, the mid-nineteenth century, long antedating Porfirio Díaz's dictatorship and the first stirrings of revolution in national Mexico. Recently, Luis Leal has affirmed Paredes's thesis in his own work on the border corrido "Leandro Rivera" (1987).

It is at this juncture that we can begin to historicize the differences noted earlier between the Spanish romance and the Mexican corrido. In a phrase, the period's intense social change seems to have produced a condensing, grounded effect on the aesthetics of the romance. The generally looser form of the nonstrophic, metrically diverse romance now becomes strophic, with a regular meter and a more complicated rhyme. The " 'serious,' modal and melodically restrained" music of the romance now becomes the " 'overflowing,' lyrical" energy of the corrido, as though its wider melodic range were musically equipping it to respond to a socially energetic moment. We may also historicize the shift in authorial voice between these two forms. The Spanish romance has a wholly detached, almost silent narrator whose main focus is delineating dialogue between two principals, while the corrido is "a narrative usually in the first or third person, with the troubadour acting as the hypothetical witness of the event described" (Geijerstam 1976:51). This shift to the witnessed event would seem consistent with the need to concretely ground and legitimize the corrido as an ideological instrument in the context of sharp social conflict. And this same sharp sense of conflict would occasion the need for a more direct narrative delineation of events rather than the indirect emergence of the story through dialogue.

Finally, we note a thematic shift from the epic, novelistic Spanish romance, which deals with "fiestas, tournaments, love affairs, and so forth," to what Geijerstam, after Mendoza, believes is an expansion of these themes in the corrido. Geijerstam is only partially correct here, for although corridos on a wide variety of subjects do begin to appear, in the manner of the Spanish romance, nonetheless, the heroic corrido with its thematic of socially significant male confrontation becomes the best known and most popular. We may say that even as the genre expands, it also contracts, with the best-known corridos fixed, as Paredes says, on "one theme . . . conflict; [on] one concept of the hero, the man fighting for his right with his pistol in his hand" (1958b:149).[2]

For most of greater Mexico, the Revolution provided the intense social conditions required for the crystallization of the heroic corrido. But Mexico had undergone at least three major social crises: the war of independence from Spain (1810–1821), the invasions of the U.S. army in the 1840s, and the French occupation in the 1860s. Why did these crises not produce a definitive heroic balladry? And what conditions prevailed along the Lower Border during this same period that did? Paredes does not explicitly answer the first of these questions, but suggests an answer in his discussion of the second.

For Paredes, at least two general social conditions are prerequisite to the emergence of a heroic balladry. First, there must be present a community with a general tradition of balladry, scattered and uncrystallized as the tradition may be. Second, this community must find itself in a fairly sharp adversarial relationship with other groupings in the social order, a relationship based on an unequal distribution of power, status, and resources. Both of these obtained during Mexico's successive conflicts with Spain, the United States, and France, and they were also present in the northeastern corner of Mexico, which historically included much of what is now south Texas. (Before independence, this land was part of the Spanish province of Nuevo Santander, afterwards, part of the Mexican state of Tamaulipas.) Yet the former set of relationships produced only scattered corrido-like songs in the interior of Mexico, while the latter adversarial relationship produced a heroic balladry on the Lower Border. Here we must enter into the more specific conditions that Paredes finds necessary for the crystallization of the Spanish romance tradition, which was part of the Border's oral entertainment, into a truly heroic balladry: relative isolation from "the main currents of world events," a reliance on orality as a primary means of communication, the presence of a patriarchal culture, and the cultural practice of a kind of vernacular democracy in which the local community managed its own political affairs with little interference from the central government. These conditions, Paredes implies, were not present in the interior of Mexico but did define the Lower Border.

THE LOWER BORDER AND THE
BIRTH OF THE HEROIC CORRIDO

Settled in the mid-eighteenth century by the Spanish as part of their northern expansion out of Central Mexico, the Lower Border was home to a relatively isolated folk society. Arid geography and nomadic Indians separated these folk from the developing centrist culture of central New Spain and, after independence, Central Mexico:

> The Lower Rio Grande people lived under conditions in which folk cultures develop. They lived in isolation from the main currents of world events. They preferred to live in small, tightly knit communities that were interested in their own problems. Their type of social organization was the family holding or the communal village, ruled by patriarchal authority under a kind of pre-eighteenth century democracy. (Paredes 1958b:242)

The villages' decision making was done by male elders with, one assumes, the more or less tacit consent of others. Compared to, let us say, Central Mexico, this generally self-subsistent, vernacularly democratic society lacked a sharp sense of social stratification—one might

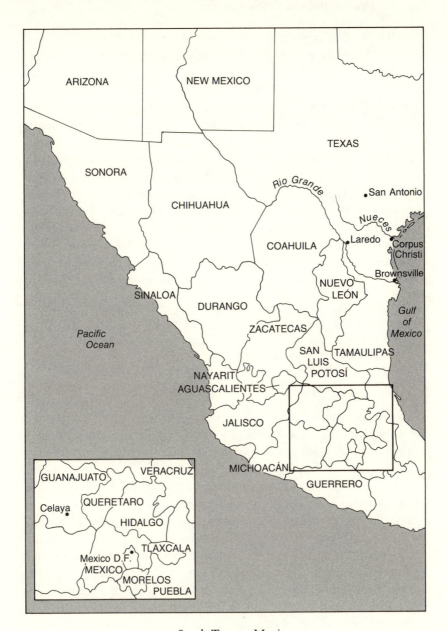

South Texas – Mexico

say that the Border people tended toward a gemeinschaft society and culture.[3] Lastly, Paredes notes, "their forms of entertainment were oral."

These then are some of the specific internal social features that, when joined to an adversarial relationship with an external force, generate a heroic balladry, especially when this adversarial consciousness is widely shared within the community and not overridden by sharp internal factionalism, that is, when the adversarial consciousness itself becomes cultural and historically enduring. The persistent adversary was, of course, the United States. More specifically, in 1826 Mexico decided to permit the regulated settlement of Americans, largely from the South, immediately north of the Lower Border, in what is now central and eastern Texas. For some ten years, these new settlers lived alongside the Lower Border people of Mexican descent, with the Nueces River more or less separating them. But larger political events soon brought those north of the Nueces into direct conflict with those on the Lower Border:

> What subsequently made the balladry of the Lower Border different was the Texas Revolution and the annexation by Texas of the Nueces–Rio Grande part of the old province of Nuevo Santander, one-half of the home area of the Lower Rio Grande people. Thus a border was created, and the bitterness resulting from events between 1836 and 1848 provided the basis for a century of conflict. (Paredes 1958b:243)

The passage requires some elaboration, particularly as it concerns the development of an American hegemony over the Lower Border people on the north bank of the Rio Grande after the United States–Mexico War of 1846–47.

At the conclusion of the war, the Lower Border people on the north bank were legally Americans, their homeland now a part of Texas. They found themselves annexed into a new culture whose racism, religious prejudice, and linguistic xenophobia were directed toward them (de Leon 1983). They had first encountered these attitudes in the reprehensible actions of General Zachary Taylor's army troops, many of whom were southerners. In affirmation of a specious U.S.-Texas claim to southern Texas, Taylor's army was ordered to march from its staging area near Corpus Christi into the disputed territory, thereby initiating hostilities. It met and defeated the Mexican army in a series of battles— the first, north of the Rio Grande—on its way to victory in Mexico City. What is sometimes overlooked is this army's initial encounter with Lower Border guerrillas—the first Mexicans to fight (Paredes

1958b:133)—as well as its indiscriminately violent conduct toward the largely civilian population both along the border and in the interior of Mexico (Montejano 1987:1–99).

Reinforced by the events at the Alamo and at Goliad, Anglo-American antipathy toward Mexicans continued to find sharp expression among the new settlers who began to enter the Lower Border area from central Texas, the site of the initial Anglo core settlement, and the South. The political marginalization, strict social segregation, and racial violence against local "Mexicans" that began at that time have not yet entirely disappeared (de Leon 1983; Foley 1977; Montejano 1987). It is this sustained asymmetrical social encounter—this "conflict of cultures," Paredes calls it—that, in his estimation, provided the prime generative ground for the mid-nineteenth-century emergence and development of the heroic corrido along the Lower Border.

The oldest complete corrido known to scholars also dates from the 1860s and deals with border conflict. "El Corrido de Kiansis" has as its subject the cattle drives from the new Anglo-owned large ranches of south Texas to Kansas. Although organized and financed by Anglo-American ranching entrepreneurs, Mexican *vaqueros* (cowboys) furnished a substantial part of the labor and know-how for this industry and these drives. There is no man-to-man violent conflict in this ballad, but we do find the heroic Mexican vaquero pitting his superior riding and roping skills against those of Anglo cowboys:

> Quinientos novillos eran,
> todo grandes y livianos,
> y entre treinta americanos
> no los podían embalar.
>
> Llegan cinco mexicanos,
> todos bien enchivarrados,
> en menos de un cuarto de hora
> los tenían encerrados.
>
> (Paredes 1976:55)

> Five hundred steers there were,
> All big and quick,
> And thirty American cowboys
> Couldn't keep them bunched together.
>
> Then five Mexicans arrive,
> All of them wearing good chaps;
> And in less than a quarter-hour
> They had those steers penned up.

According to Paredes, there is some fragmentary evidence of another heroic corrido from the early 1860s telling of an armed encounter between Juan Nepomuceno Cortina, a hero of the Lower Border, and the Anglo-American authorities after they mistreated a Mexican. Cortina kills a sheriff, organizes local Mexicans to fight the Anglos, and then, facing superior forces, escapes across the Rio Grande.

From the 1860s until the turn of the century, heroic corridos about such encounters began to appear in large numbers along the Lower Border. The concept of the local hero fighting for his right, his honor, and status against external foes, usually Anglo authorities, became the central theme of this balladry, reaching its social artistic zenith in the most popular of corridos, that of Gregorio Cortez. (We will return to this most famous ballad in some detail in chapter 3.) While focused on the local hero and his right, the heroic corrido consistently places Cortez in relationship to broader social conflict, as in the Kansas ballad, with emphasis on the collective experience of "mexicanos" versus "americanos." We often find this dialectic between self and society, as in one of the late corridos of the period concerning the organized armed uprisings against Anglo-American authority in south Texas in 1915. "Bands of Border men," Paredes tells us, "under the leadership of Aniceto Pizaña and Luis de la Rosa raided as far north as the King Ranch, burning ranches, derailing trains, killing American civilians, and attacking U.S. army detachments." Paredes notes the results of this uprising.

Texas Rangers and sheriff's deputies took out their frustration at not being able to catch the *sediciosos* (the seditionists) by slaughtering as many innocent Mexican farm workers as they could lay their hands on. Hundreds were summarily "executed" without trial, and many hundreds more fled to Mexico to escape the *rinche* terror. The results were that more land in south Texas was cleared of Mexicans so it could be "developed" by Anglo newcomers in the 1920s. (1976:33)

It is in this context that the composer of "Los Sediciosos" (The Seditionists) tells us:

> Decía Aniceto Pizaña
> en su caballo cantando
> —¿Dónde están por ahí los rinches?
> que los vengo visitando.
> —Esos rinches de la Kiñena,
> dicen que son muy valientes,

hacen llorar las mujeres
hacen correr a las gentes.
                    (Paredes 1976:73)

Aniceto Pizaña said,
Singing as he rode along,
"Where can I find the rangers?
I'm here to pay them a visit."

Those rangers from the King Ranch
Say that they are very brave;
they make the women cry,
and they make the people run.

Paredes's account is entirely authoritative and persuasive, but several other factors also contributed to the emergence of the heroic corrido of the Lower Border. First, a prolonged period of social domination does not of itself produce this balladry; this relationship must be mediated. Before such a balladry can exist, there has to be a significant emergence of actual social resistance to domination, a social source of the ballad's heroic thematics. We have already noted examples of such resistance in the armed actions of individuals like Gregorio Cortez and groups like the *sediciosos* of 1915. Other important forms of resistive discourse included militant newspapers in the major towns in south Texas, such as Laredo, Brownsville, and San Antonio; left-of-center labor union activity, which organized numerous strikes, particularly in the agricultural section (Zamora 1986); and organized reformist political activity that sought redress for social grievances through institutional means (Limón 1974). All of these operated within a general ethnic nationalist temper (de Leon 1983) and formed the wider context of the Lower Border corrido.

Second, Paredes clearly suggests that heroic actions are most appealing and most productive of a balladry when they occur in a losing cause. In a brilliant comparison to Scottish resistance to English domination, he argues that while

> the Scot was able to mount a strong attack and score some local victories, he always lost in the end to a superior army from the south. The same situation faced the Mexican border raiders. It was the Scot, usually on the losing side, who produced the most stirring of the British border ballads. On the Rio Grande, it was only the losers in the conflict, the Border Mexicans, who produced ballads. (1958b:244)

As part of a powerful and expanding American capitalist political economy, Anglo-American victory on the Lower Border was, indeed, almost inevitable. From this perspective, Paredes's "conflict of cultures" thesis can be viewed at a much more fundamental level, as can the ideological significance of the corrido. What was fundamentally at issue in the Lower Border was a rapid transformation of a whole cultural mode of production. As Montejano (1987) has demonstrated, racial and cultural oppression were but the overt manifestations and ratifications of the forced transformation of a whole way of life from the generally self-subsistent, vernacularly democratic, political cultural economy keyed on the Spanish language and face-to-face oral communication, to an increasingly mass capitalistic, cash crop agriculture and an English-language print and media cultural economy, all of the latter dominated mostly by Anglo-Americans, who controlled the political state apparatus. With the rapid loss of their small landholdings through legally and morally questionable means, the people of Mexican descent in south Texas either died, became dislocated cheap labor in the new economy, or left for Mexico (Montejano 1987). After 1910 this cheap labor force was replenished by thousands of impoverished refugee Mexicans crossing the Rio Grande into Texas, mostly from the northern Mexican states, leaving behind the chaos and unfulfilled promise of Mexico's thwarted Revolution and bringing with them even more corridos, these from a later experience of social conflict.

THE BORDER HEROIC CORRIDO, THE MEXICAN REVOLUTION, AND GREATER MEXICO

Based on the foregoing argument, Paredes also offers an implied thesis to explain the relative absence of a heroic corrido tradition in Mexico's interior during most of the nineteenth century. At the same time, he implies an explanation for the heroic corrido's relatively sudden emergence in Central Mexico during the period of the Revolution.

Earlier, following Paredes, I suggested that certain enabling sociocultural conditions for the corrido did not obtain in the Mexican interior prior to the Revolution, among these a collective adversarial consciousness, a prolonged social conflict, a sense of a violated communal social order, an orally based culture, heroic actions by local heroes, a sense of a "lost cause" in the face of a fundamental cultural transformation, and, finally, of course, the general if latent sense of a ballad tradition awaiting the appropriate social conditions to foster its emergence. While these conditions did not prevail throughout most of the nineteenth century, they did coalesce during the period of Revolution, set in motion by the same fundamental international political economy that had affected the Lower Border. The same essentially North American capitalist forces had been at work in Mexico since Porfirio Díaz came to power in 1876. The late nineteenth century was a period of intense political centralization and economic development in Mexico, but the development was of questionable benefit to Mexico as a whole. It was a time "in which foreigners, with U.S. entrepreneurs at the forefront, took over much of the economy": "The state did not merely submit to foreign pressures on the debt: it threw open the doors to foreign investment in an attempt to marshall sufficient capital and technical expertise to generate significant economic growth for the benefit of domestic and foreign monopolies" (Cockcroft 1983:87).

With the huge exception of Mexico's poverty-stricken laboring masses, "almost all bourgeois and large-landholder interests prospered from vast increases in production and trade" supported by the Díaz dictatorship, which "institutionalized a repressive apparatus and an ideological system emphasizing political stability, science, technology, and material progress" (Cockcroft 1983:87)—but only for a few and to the massive social detriment of many, particularly the large poor rural sectors. The latter's social condition, always precarious, worsened under the Díaz regime (Meyer and Sherman 1979:458). Through legal coercion and state power, these large sectors lost what remained of their traditional landholdings. In southern Mexico, "by the early twentieth century most of the villages in rural Mexico had lost their *ejidos* [commons] and some 134 million acres of the best land had passed into the hands of a few hundred fantastically wealthy families" (Meyer and Sherman 1979:458).

In the north, traditionally a region of small, individually owned ranch holdings (not unlike those of pre-1848 south Texas), "tendencies to concentration of landed property . . . had been fierce"; in Chihuahua, "by 1910 seventeen persons owned two-fifths of the state," while "95.5 percent of all heads of families held no individual property in land" (Wolf 1969:33). After some postindependence reform, the oppressive hacienda (plantation) system of the Spanish colonial period was reinstituted, in the north and south, and "over one half of all rural Mexicans lived and worked on the haciendas by 1910" (Meyer and Sherman 1979:458). Severe social deprivation also befell the other half, the "free," itinerant, easily exploitable labor force that moved from hacienda to hacienda. And, as might be expected, their urban counterparts fared no better (Cockcroft 1983:88–94).

Such deprivation in complex modern societies goes hand in hand with high rates of illiteracy among the dominated—at least until such time as technological advancement requires an "adequately" literate labor force. Estimates of illiteracy during the Porfiriato range as high as 84 percent (Cockcroft 1983:88). Therefore, one can reasonably assume that among the most deprived social sectors, orality continued to be a primary mode of communication and artistic expression. An important difference between this period of class orality and others earlier in Mexican history was its predominantly Spanish character; that is, by the late nineteenth century Mexico was predominantly a mestizo, Spanish-speaking nation (Heath 1972:53).

During the late nineteenth century, then, Paredes's three initial critical conditions—the political disruption of a rural, communal social order; a period of prolonged and intense social domination; and a predominantly Spanish-language, class-based, mestizo oral culture—came together as never quite before. Politically, they led to the Revolution of 1910; aesthetically, to the emergence of the heroic corrido in the Mexican interior.

Three other important factors also contributed to the emergence of both revolution and balladry. First, in response to the massive scale of oppression under Díaz, the popular participation in rebellion was massive as well, distinguishing this period of revolution from others in Mexican history, when the most deprived sectors of the populace participated on an inconsistent and piecemeal basis. The Revolution of 1910 was truly a popular, peasant rebellion (Wolf 1969:3–50). Second, the vanguard of the Revolution, unlike earlier Mexican leaders drawn from the more elite elements, was composed of men close to the people and to folk traditions like the corrido. Finally, we must note the decisively northern character of the Revolution. With few exceptions, such as Emiliano Zapata of the southern state of Morelos, the strongest leadership and the strongest participation came from the northern Mexican states (Cline 1969, Knight 1986:11–62).

This last point is critical because it lends even greater strength to Paredes's thesis concerning the border origins of the heroic corrido. As he notes, "It would be little short of wonderful if the *corrido* had suddenly come into being at two different places and two different times. Either the Lower Border *corrido* owes its existence to the Greater Mexican form, or the Greater Mexican *corrido* is indebted to the more localized Texas-Mexican ballad" (1958b:105). The latter option seems more likely. As Villa's *norteño* soldiers sang their ballad around the evening campfire near Celaya in April 1915, it is likely that they were singing in a form they had learned in their home region of Chihuahua, across the Rio Grande from Texas. It was a form that their regional neighbors in the Lower Border states and likely their kinfolk, the Texas-Mexicans, had been employing in their struggle against Anglo domination since the 1850s. A parallel set of social conditions in central Mexico later in the century provided further nurturance for this poetic form, which, like much of the revolutionary energy, came down into Mexico from the north. Formed through an earlier experience with social domination along the Lower Border, the heroic corrido became an expressive form for all of greater Mexico during the Revolution.

The United States continued to support the Porfiriato, and early on the Mexican Revolution "in terms of the key interests of peasants and workers ... was *defeated*" (Cockcroft 1983:112). This defeat added the final ingredient to the forging of the corrido on the southern side of the border—the sense of a lost, though just, cause. After the war many of Mexico's poor went north, crossing the border and making their way principally to the Southwest but also to the Midwest and to Pennsylvania. Most of these immigrants were from the northern Mexican states, where the fighting had been particularly harsh. They established permanent residence in the United States and joined earlier generations of Mexicans who had settled here. As they moved beyond Texas, they introduced the heroic corrido into California, New Mexico, and Arizona, as well as the Midwest.

In this amalgamation of greater Mexican peoples, we also find an amalgamation of many distinct, though closely related, cultural forms, among them the heroic corrido. For the corrido continued to be sung wherever Mexican people traveled and settled. The corrido corpus now included ballads of Lower Border conflict and those newer ones from the Revolution. A corridista singing in the central market area of San Antonio, Texas, in the 1930s would sing of both Celaya and Cortez, as would his counterpart in a plaza in Guadalajara, Jalisco, for people and songs also moved south when workers returned home. North and south of the border, audiences continued to be fascinated by the theme of strong men fighting for their rights and for their people, a theme cast in a complex poetics. It is this imagistically powerful unification of the personal, the artistic, and the social that appealed to the predominantly male corrido community and made the corrido a master poem of social struggle.

SOCIAL STRUGGLE AND THE POLITICAL UNCONSCIOUS: THE MAKING OF A MASTER POEM

It is not difficult to see how the greater Mexican corrido becomes an expressive instrument of social struggle. Much of its imagery unequivocally speaks in these terms. However, we can strengthen this reading if we probe beyond the corrido's manifest significations and toward what Fredric Jameson calls the "political unconscious" of Western narrative forms, an unconscious politics that Jameson finds registered at three distinct levels in such narratives. (For a more detailed exposition of Jameson's ideas, see Appendix A.) We are partially anticipated in this approach by Richard Flores (1987), who offers just such an analysis of "Los Sediciosos," a corrido mentioned earlier in this chapter.[4]

Taking Jameson's first level of analysis, that of chronological political history, Flores suggests that corridos may be seen as the repositories of the essential "facts" of social struggle; for example, the passed-on knowledge of 1915, of a real living man named Gregorio Cortez, of oppressive Mexican dictators and Texas Rangers. The importance of this primary level of political efficacy and social struggle must not be diminished, for such a condensed repository of basic knowledge is essential for any resistive consciousness. Yet, as McDowell has noted, the corrido is not primarily intended to be such a repository, and, indeed, assumes a wider field of knowledge already present in the corrido community and gained from other sources (1981:47).

Given this limited, autonomous contribution to the community's knowledge of chronological political history, it is at Jameson's second and, most fundamentally, at his third level of signification and interpretation that the full articulation of the corrido's political unconscious must be sought. For the corrido of border conflict, and here we continue to follow Flores's lead, the second level of analysis would see the chronological figures of the first level not as literal representations but as what

Flores, after Jameson, calls *ideologemes*, minimal units of symbolic discourse in a discourse of class relations. In this second-level reading, the opposing figures of border Mexican hero and the Anglo authorities must be seen in the full social context of the antagonistic class relations: "the Texas-Mexicans, reduced to peones in a class system, construct an ideological discourse to resist the forces . . . that have dehumanized them" (Flores 1987:17). Thus the corrido, with its surface, first-level projections of ethnic difference "also reflects a deeper conflict based on class difference and the emerging agricultural industry. In this context, the ideologemes of Ranger–bandit and rinche–hero reflect the ensuing class conflict around the shared code of the land: the control and ownership of the means of production on the border" (Flores 1987:15).

Like the corrido of border conflict, the corrido of the Mexican Revolution can also be seen as a repository of basic historical data for a public with minimal access to the official written word. Again, the historical particulars transmitted by the corrido are important but not as socially significant as the reproduction of class relations and consciousness. For example, an overwhelming number of folk corridos speak admiringly of those figures most closely associated by historians with the interest of the Mexican masses, principally Villa and Zapata. Other figures in the Revolution do not fare as well. Not too surprisingly, there are almost no corridos about Porfirio Díaz (Simmons 1957:70), and those few concerning such figures as Carranza, Madero, and Obregón are at best ambivalent in their attitudes and at worst reproving of men who ultimately betrayed the Revolution (Simmons 1957). The corridos of the Mexican Revolution thus also speak of oppressive class relations and resistance through the concrete ideologemes of the true revolutionary hero and the apostates who supported a return to the class-dominant status quo. As in the corridos of border conflict, in these later corridos the shared code of struggle is the rightful ownership of the land.

In speaking interpretively of the corrido as a signifier of class relations, one is forced to acknowledge the perhaps too easy applicability of a notion like the political unconscious to this material. Unlike the modernist texts from which Jameson derived his theory—texts in which political content is largely repressed—the corridos display the political unconscious in a way only too manifest. In the corridos about Celaya and Cortez, for example, the sociopolitical dimensions and class relations are immediately accessible. Other corridos, however, depict confrontations between men as a matter of personal honor rather than as representations of social causes. To understand how such a corrido expresses class relations, we must recall the corrido's historical context. The ballads' depiction of personal duels in the name of honor is occurring at a time (1890–1930) when bourgeois society no longer subscribes to such a code and now directs and practices violence on the mass scale of Celaya, south Texas, and the Somme. Only the subaltern classes of greater Mexico, the corrido seems to say, have maintained the courage and personal sense of honor to settle their disputes face-to-face and not through the mass, anonymous, industrialized violence of machine guns, tanks, and poison gas. Only in this context can we understand one corridista's paradoxical appreciation of face-to-face violence:

> ¡Qué bonitos son los hombres
> que se matan pecho a pecho
> Cada uno con su pistola
> defendiendo su derecho!
> (Paredes 1976:78)

> How admirable are men
> Who fight to the death face to face,
> Each of them with his pistol,
> Defending his right.

It is not the violence in itself that matters, the corrido seems to say, but its form. For if men must fight, the form of violence can provide some large degree of redemption.[5]

Having thus evoked the notion of form—here, the social form of violence—we approach Jameson's third level of interpretation, in which we look to the *form* of symbolic acts to grasp their role in the articulation of social conflict and change at the highest level or broadest sphere. For Jameson, this is the inherent conflict that constitutes any social formation, the latter understood as the social arrangements of any given historical period where distinct modes of production overlap and come into conflict. Here symbolic acts may speak to this conflict by articulating, principally in their form, the sedimented ideological traces of older modes of production in conflict with the present or the anticipatory messages of a future mode of production. Thus, quite apart from its function as a record of political history and as a carrier of the ideologemes of class relations, the corrido of greater Mexico, in its formal florescence from about 1890 to 1930, formally articulates the antagonistic modes of production. It is a formal expression of a self-subsistent, vernacular, democratic political economy. Here I add to Flores's fine beginning.

We have already noted the political economic domination of greater Mexico by a world capitalist economy led by the United States. It is equally important to highlight the cultural component of this domination. For example, even as the Anglo-American capitalists reorganized the economic life of the border Mexicans and imposed a new political order, they also began the systematic effort (almost completed) to culturally assimilate this population even while maintaining it as socially subordinate. This new cultural reeducation entailed a two-front strategy and a host of weapons. First, it was necessary to delegitimize native culture, indeed at times to render it odious to Mexicans themselves. These efforts included the institutional purveyance of denigrating stereotypes; the disciplined expulsion of Spanish from public life, particularly the schools; and, most effective of all, the socially produced construction of "Mexican" as synonymous with "poor" and the socially ostracized; indeed, strict social segregation became the order of the day in many parts of the Southwest until well into the 1950s (de Leon 1983; Montejano 1987). Second, while maintaining Mexicans in a low status, the Anglo-American authorities saw to it that Mexican youngsters were taught English and basic American civic culture, at least through their earlier years of schooling. Some minimal amount of such learning was absolutely necessary if this labor force was to be well disciplined and integrated into the lower end of the new political economy, particularly as the latter shifted away from agriculture to an urban industrial identity (Barrera 1979). The school system served as a locus for both broad strategies: Mexican youngsters learned the English language and American civic culture in schools that were consistently segregated at least until the 1950s in some parts of the Southwest (San Miguel 1987).

This broad two-part strategy was in full swing by 1911, in the middle of the corrido period, as is evident in discussions within the Mexican-American community at the time. Members of this community resented the purveyance of denigrating stereotypes and upheld their right to maintain Spanish, yet they grudgingly recognized that they must learn English if they were to have any mobility in the new social order (Limón 1973, 1974). As we shall see in the next chapter, to the degree that such linguistically keyed mobility occurred, it led to the emergence of an ambivalent, small, middle class whose solidarity with the mass working classes was at best tenuous. It is against these discourses of domination that, in Foucault's terms, we must see other increasingly subjugated discourses of resistance such as the struggle of the Spanish-language press and, in our present case, the florescence of the corrido (Foucault 1980). We have already argued this case at two levels, primarily levels of content, but here we are interested in positing the notion of form and its sedimented ideology of conflict and resistance.

For at a historical moment when Mexican culture, as well as its political economy, was being reorganized and "Anglicized" in the interest of domination, it is just possible that the sheer music, the strict predictable measured poetics, the Spanish language of the corrido, indeed, the strong sensory quality of the male performance context constituted a point of resistance at the level of form. Such form as ideology, I suggest, likely reminded its audiences of another time and place, another form of social life. At a time when distinct cultural modes of production—agrarian precapitalist and emergent capitalism—overlapped and came into conflict, the content of the corrido spoke directly and critically to the present at two levels of social critique, but its form provided an implicit model of a perceived better past, an anchoring point in a new storm rising.

The formal ideological relationship of the corrido to the revolutionary crises in Mexico's interior was not that altogether different. For during the Porfiriato most of Mexico was experiencing some level of Anglicization compounded by bourgeois French influence. As Cockcroft tells us, and it is worth quoting him at length, in 1890, a member of the ruling Mexican elite

> expressed his satisfaction to the Chamber of Deputies, "on seeing foreigners as owners of high finance, of credit institutions, of the electrical power plants, of the telegraphs, of the railroads, and of all those things which signify culture and the progress of Mexico." Education, which was for the elite (by 1911 illiteracy still plagues 84 per cent of the population), included teaching of English because, in the words of educator Ezequiel Chávez, "it was believed necessary . . . given the growing union between the Anglo-American people and our people." Justo Sierra, minister of public education, encouraged the "saxonization" of Mexico—including more immigration—to develop the nation's culture and economy. A national normal school was created in 1887, and from then until 1919 almost all Mexican textbooks became the private business of Appleton

Publishing Company of New York, and were written by U.S. authors.
(1983:88)

The pervasive influence of bourgeois French culture on the Mexican
elite of this period is only too well known. With regard to the fate of
the corrido, however, it is worth noting the internalization of European
modernism, articulated through Paris, by Mexican poets such as Amado
Nervo. While ostensibly a revolt against nineteenth-century bourgeois
culture, modernism contained its own contradictions: "modernists . . .
turned their backs on political, economic, and social problems as they
sought refuge in the world of the imagination"; elitist in its continuous
innovations and refinements of language, modernist poetry "was de-
signed for the upper class" (Meyer and Sherman 1979:475–76).[6]
In this context, the form of the corrido—its rhymes, meter, music,
and stanzaic patterns spoke dialogically as an oppositional voice of the
"illiterate" Mexican masses. The corrido articulated a different cultural
mode of production against the Díaz-led imposition of a European and
American bourgeois ideology of form. When the corridistas at Celaya
sang in 1915, they articulated both a critical political vision of the
world at the level of content and a counteraesthetic, an equally political
ideology of form. When the corridistas of south Texas sang of Gregorio
Cortez in 1901, they too sang this political poetics, but for *these* Mexicans, their folk Spanish-language corridos also spoke critically and
formally to a world in which domination was articulated in English.

CONTRADICTION AND THE
CORRIDO: THE REPRESSION OF
WOMAN'S VOICE

At a critical historical moment, then, the epic heroic corrido offered
an oppositional voice to external domination, a voice registered at various levels of discourse. Yet as a representation of patriarchy, which it
most assuredly is, the corrido necessarily carries within it a large element
of internal domination and repression, a repression of the gender Other.
    Maria Herrera-Sobek has argued recently for a fivefold archetypal
representation of women in the Mexican corrido (1990). However, she
defines the corrido tradition rather broadly to include what I would
more comfortably call quasi-corridos, including what Américo Paredes
has called "movie corridos," ersatz ballads produced in Mexico City

by the mass media to accompany a series of B movies. Both corridos and films nostalgically create a historically dubious "charro" ranching world dominated by hard-drinking, womanizing, boastful men. Paredes associates this exaggerated movie-made machismo with Mexico's desire to sense its own strength after a historical experience of international inferiority (Paredes 1967). I amplify on Paredes only by noting that this rural "manly" nostalgia also masks the failure of the ruling party, the PRI, to redistribute land to the peasants.

But in speaking of the definitive epic heroic corrido—definitive as a source of powerful poetic influence—Herrera-Sobek observes that "in its epic character the *corrido* is similar to the *canción de gesta*. Both forms extol the exploits of protagonists, who are usually male. Women generally play secondary roles in the narratives" (1990:xiii), and she identifies "the treacherous woman" and the "good mother," in secular and Virginal roles, as the dominant "secondary" images in this particular corpus (1990:67–72; 4–8). Be that as it may, women simply do not appear that often at all in this corpus, even in these secondary imagistic roles. Whatever the merit of Herrera-Sobek's observations with regard to the entire corrido corpus, women make few appearances in the epic heroic folk corrido. It cannot be the general case, as she wants to imply, that "*corridos* depicting the heroic exploits of Mexican fighting men *need* such a negative figure ... to precipitate the hero's descent" (1990:72; emphasis mine) if this female traitor is absent from many of the greater Mexican corridos. For example, there are no such female figures in the more representative folk corridos about Celaya, the seditionists, or Gregorio Cortez.

A treacherous female figure does appear in the folk epic corrido "Valentín Mancera," which Herrera-Sobek analyzes. However, because her Jungian typological approach focuses on identifying the distinct archetypes, she does not explore the dialectical relationship between this image of treachery and that of another kind of woman—the good mother, which she reserves for an earlier chapter (1990:68–71). Shortly before the hero Valentín Mancera is betrayed by a treacherous woman and killed, he has this encounter with his mother.

> Su madre, triste, decía:
> —¡Válgame Dios, Valentín!
> ¿Hasta cuándo te reduces?
> ¿Cuál será tu último fin?
>
> Valentín le contestó:
> —No llore, madre adorada

vale más morir peleando
que correr de la Acordada
—Echeme su bendición
que ya me voy pa' Galvanes
                    (Mendoza 1954:177)

His mother, sadly, did say
—Dear God, Valentín!
When will you calm down?
Where will you finally end?

Valentín answered her:
—Don't cry, adored mother,
It is better to die fighting
than to run from the authorities

—Give me your blessing
For I am going to Galvanes

Against the forces of social domination that are aided by a treacherous woman, Mancera finds support in the maternal. And although this maternal theme, this affirming presence of woman, is itself not characteristic of corridos, it is a theme that seems to appear more often than the treacherous woman.[7]

Of far greater importance than these limited negative and positive female images is the corrido's larger gender politics and poetics of exclusion and repression. Woman is almost wholly excluded or repressed in the male world of the corrido, in the ballad's predominant imagery and subject and equally so in its principally male-defined performative context. (And a case could be made that the corrido's form—its rigid, repetitive quatrains, its linear, hard-driving narrative style, its sharply bounded universe with its formal openings and closings—is male-engendered.)

Yet, like all repressions, this one cannot be forever contained. In "Valentín Mancera" the hero acknowledges and defers to the maternal as a source of strength. Compared to the image of an activist treacherous woman, this maternal emergence represents a potentially far more radical challenge to the patriarchal ethos of the corrido. Though articulated in what some might see as a "submissive" maternal imagery, the figure of the mother stands as an active counteralternative to the hegemonic world of the father—real and poetic—in the influential construction of his sons. Moreover, in Tinker's description of hearing his first corrido at Celaya, we encounter the concept of the *active* maternal and familial, of the woman who struggles wholly on behalf of her community, occasionally killing in its defense. As the three corridistas sang of Celaya, the audience included not only Villa's ragged soldiers but also "their *soldaderas*—those amazing Amazons who cooked for their men and, with pots and pans, and often a baby on their backs, kept up with the regiments on gruelling marches; or when need arose, snatched a rifle from a corpse and fought as fiercely as any male" (Tinker 1961:7).

This image of women's participation is amplified by Meyer and Sherman's portrait of the women who accompanied the soldiers:

> The soldaderas were more than camp followers. They provided feminine companionship, to be sure, but because neither the federal army nor the rebel armies provided commissary service, they foraged for food, cooked, washed, and, in the absence of more competent medical service, nursed the wounded and buried the dead. Both sides were dependent upon them, and in 1912 a federal battalion actually threatened mutiny when the secretary of war ordered that the women could not be taken along on a certain maneuver. The order was rescinded. Not infrequently, the soldaderas actually served in the ranks, sometimes with a baby slung in a *rebozo* or a young child clinging at their skirts. Women holding officer ranks were not uncommon in the rebel armies.
>
> The soldadera endured the hardships of the campaign without special consideration. While the men were generally mounted, the women most often walked, carrying bedding, pots and pans, food, firearms, ammunition, and children. Often the men would gallop on ahead, engage the enemy in battle, and then rest. By the time the women caught up, they were ready to move again, and the soldadera would simply trudge on. Losing her special "Juan" in battle, she would wait an appropriately decent period and then take on another, to prepare his favorite meal and share his bed. (1979:556–57)

These women were not primarily *soldadas* (soldiers), but they were responsible for military logistics—the heart of any campaign, according to military analysts. The active, nurturing social reproduction and defense of community through "women's work" was crucially important at this moment in history. This is the image of the maternal that informs the poetry we will examine, an active maternal that serves as a creative resource for the most radical revisionary strategy toward the world of the father and his poetry and toward society. The gender basis for this radical revisionary subversion already lies within this patriarchal culture. It too is part—a necessary part—of any son's anxiety of influence and, progressively revised, can also play a larger oppositional role in a transformed corrido as it looks out to a continuing external domination.

THE RISE AND FALL OF THE
GREATER MEXICAN EPIC CORRIDO:
FROM RESIDUAL TO EMERGENT

Yet even with this latent gender contradiction, the corrido had a larger oppositional mission in society, although it did not last, at least not at the full performative strength it acquired between 1848 and 1930. According to Américo Paredes, by the 1930s "when Mexico's Tin Pan Alley took over the corrido, its decay was inevitable." Paredes explains: "At first radio and the movies employed folk singers and composers, and Mexican popular music had a brief golden age. But soon the demand for more and more new songs wore the folk material thin" (1958a:102). It is as if, Paredes seems to be suggesting, the demand for corridos produced a new body of songs that were "thin" in their articulation of the traditional aesthetics and social vision.

This is a judgment confirmed by Dickey (1978) with respect to corridos, and comparatively collaborated by Patterson (1975) with respect to the political transformation of American folk song into "country western" at about this same period of time and through these same processes. Patterson traces this transformative process to the commodification of a Southern oppositional folk song culture in response to two demands posed by a new advanced capitalism: The first was a demand for a noncontroversial music appropriate for a general audience and suitably edited for radio play. The second entailed the transformation not so much of the music itself, but rather of its social base.

Like greater Mexican campesino society, both the black and white agrarian base of Southern folk song was disrupted by an advanced capitalism that "between the late 30s and the early 50s" succeeded in "driving them out of the rural South and into southern, northern, and western cities and into industrial and service occupations" (Patterson 1975:283–84). These urban migrants managed to retain some of their musical culture in these new settings for a time, through radio and recordings, but the lack of a sustaining organic community base soon meant a "thinning" of the erstwhile oppositional musical culture.

Similarly, in an analysis focused on Mexicans in Texas but, as Paredes suggests, applicable to greater Mexico, Dickey reports:

This "golden" age of recording and radio, where the technology was new and the folk material was rich, was not to last, however. The social fabric of the Tejano (Texas-Mexican) communities was changing, the people were becoming more urbanized and influenced by American ways; as a result there was a demand for new ... *corridos* more than for the old songs. With increased professionalization, commercialization and the blending of traditions and innovations in Tejano music by the late 1930s and the 1940s, new trends were emerging in the music. (1978:17)

Neither Paredes nor Dickey specifies the social forces, but they undoubtedly resemble those social forces that Patterson identifies as the sources for the diminishment of folk song as an oppositional form.

This constellation of new forces—advanced capitalism—meant that very few, if any, new corridos of epic heroic quality continued to be played after the 1930s. The earlier heroic corridos, like those of Celaya and Cortez, continued to be sung, and were sometimes recorded and even played on the radio, but not as frequently as other kinds (Dickey 1978:19; Peña 1982:39). These other kinds of corridos concerned more everyday themes and issues of interest to the community, including natural disasters, betrayed love affairs, contraband, murders, and immigration. Despite their subject matter being rooted in the everyday experience of the greater Mexican people, these corridos tended to be increasingly the products of professional composers who, though closely related to the community, nonetheless had an ear out for the commercially conditioned demands of radio stations and recording companies. These demands tended to produce corridos more attuned to the sensationalistic (drug-dealing murders, etc.), and poetically constrained both by recording and radio play time and what appears to be, over time, a less than rigorous poetic aesthetic. It is within this commercial world that we also find Paredes's "movie corridos" of extreme machismo.

As such, the corridos composed in the period between 1930 and 1960 rarely, if ever, spoke directly to social conflict. To the extent that social conflict was addressed, it was to depict and protest the victimization of Mexicans, at least in the U.S., through discrimination (Peña 1982). Rarely did there appear within this period the carefully crafted heroic world of a man confronting another defending his right, and often that of his community, with his pistol, real or metaphorical, in his hand. Yet the heroic corrido did not altogether disappear. While now decidedly historical, the heroic corridos of conflict from the Border and the Mexican Revolution continued to be heard or read in a variety of forums. One might hear them in cantinas, or in open-air plazas. Some recordings were available, and people played them at home (as my father played them for me) or occasionally heard them played on the radio. For a more intellectual public, Vicente Mendoza's important collection appeared in 1954. Shortly thereafter, Américo Paredes's *With His Pistol in His Hand* was published.

To clarify the corrido's relationship to its past, present, and future, we may conceptualize this historical relationship by using the fluid, subtle, and historically sensitive Marxist cultural theory of Raymond Williams. Williams's great contribution is to allow us to see how subordinate groups are dialectically related to domination in cultural terms and how this relationship can be transformed over time.

The epic corrido of greater Mexico never became fully archaic, in Williams's terms; that is, it was never wholly restricted to one definite historical period. Rather, the corrido took on the status and quality of a residual culture that "by definition has been effectively formed in the past, but it is still active in the cultural process, not only and often not at all as an element of the past, but as an effective element of the present" (Williams 1977:122). If, in its "pure" state, such a residual form once played an active role in contesting the hegemony of domination, as did the epic corrido, seemingly, it is at even greater risk of being transformed, as happened to the epic corrido after 1930. This is so because "at certain points the dominant culture cannot allow too much residual experience and practice outside itself, at least without risk" (p. 122). Domination attempts to work its cultural hegemony by continually producing a "selective tradition"—by admitting only those discourses that verify and legitimize its own power, and "it is in the incorporation of the actively residual—by reinterpretation, dilution, projection, discriminating inclusion and exclusion—that that work of the selective tradition is especially evident" (p. 122).

Nonetheless, the active residual may maintain its counterhegemonic stance at least in part because "certain experiences, meanings, and values which cannot be expressed or substantially verified in terms of the dominant culture, are nevertheless lived and practiced on the basis of the residue—cultural as well as social—of some previous social and cultural institution or formation" (p. 123).

What Williams does not, and does not have to, specify in his general treatise is precisely how the residual remains effective in the present. As regards our case at hand, it is clear that the dominant culture—the binational bourgeois culture of the Border—does limit the corrido, even as some aspects of the corrido (the less-than-epic recorded corridos mentioned earlier, for example) continue to express "certain experiences, meanings, and values . . . lived and practiced on the basis of the residue." Residual traditions are one resource for subordinate groups in their ideological struggle against domination; but in contesting cultural and, ultimately, social hegemony, subordinate groups can also turn to "new meanings and values, new practices, new relationships and kinds of relationship" that "are continually being created." As Williams recognizes, defining this emergent culture is very problematic. For one, "it is exceptionally difficult to distinguish between those which are really elements of some new phase of dominant culture . . . and those which are substantially alternative or oppositional to it. . . . the social location of the residual is always easier to understand" (p. 123). Williams is likely right on this point, but the distinctions might be more helpful were he not to insist on such a sharp sense of the emergent as wholly "new," since the seemingly "new" more often consists of new transformations of older, that is to say, residual, forms.[8] Perhaps only the residual forms keep the emergent forms at some distance from the dominant culture, while only the "pure" new practice allows the emergent to be an "effective element of the present" and to work as a counterhegemonic practice. If this is at least sometimes the case—and I do not wish to generalize here—then we may ask how the new and the residual work together to respond effectively to domination and its hegemonic assault.

It is from this perspective that I want to approach the poetic texts I have chosen. As a fully active contestative practice in its own right, the epic corrido waned from the 1930s to the 1960s, but as an active residual practice in new transformed poetic emergences, the epic corrido continued to carry its powerful poetic and counterhegemonic influence into a new period.[9] These transformations played a role in a new social struggle against domination, even as the poetic emergent and residual carried on their own "internal" struggle of poetic influence. This internal struggle in the service of the social requires that the later poets possess a full knowledge of the precursor. The key figure in the transmission of such knowledge is Américo Paredes, the corrido's foremost scholar and foremost poetic son.

His face is turned toward the past. Where we perceive a chain of events, he sees one single catastrophe which keeps piling wreckage upon wreckage and hurls it in front of his feet. The angel would like to stay, awaken the dead, and make whole what has been smashed. But a storm is blowing from Paradise; it has got caught in his wings with such violence that the angel can no longer close them. This storm irresistibly propels him into the future to which his back is turned, while the pile of debris before him grows skyward. This storm is what we call progress.

Walter Benjamin, Illuminations

It's a wise child that knows its own father.
The Odyssey,
trans. Robert Fitzgerald

2

Américo Paredes, Tradition, and the
First Ephebe

A Poetic Meditation on the Epic Corrido

"In 1915, oh but the days were hot! So says the *corrido*, 'Los Sediciosos' commemorating the Texas-Mexican uprising of 1915." And so comments Américo Paredes, who was born along the Lower Border that same year, even as "bands of Border men under the leadership of Aniceto Pizaña and Luis de la Rosa raided as far north as the King Ranch, burning ranches, derailing trains, killing American civilians, and attacking U.S. army detachments" (1976:32–33).

Though widely acknowledged as the master of corrido scholarship and as the elder statesman of Chicano intellectual activists, Paredes is almost wholly unknown as a poet. Yet, as I shall argue in these next two chapters, his corrido scholarship, his politics, and his poetic efforts are, ultimately, not separate endeavors. Before he published any corrido scholarship, and at an early age, his poem "Guitarreros" (Guitarists) revealed his strong poetic interest in the corrido and was shaped by its influence. Later in his life, as I discuss in the next chapter, his scholarship itself is poetically endowed by the epic heroic corrido, thereby becoming an example of what Lukács, after Schlegel, calls "intellectual poems" ([1910] 1974:18) and what C. Wright Mills calls "sociological poems" (Miller 1986).

In this chapter, I want to concentrate almost exclusively on "Guitarreros," which I believe is Paredes's best poetic effort to date. This evaluation is supported, at least implicitly, by the poet himself, who in 1964 selected this one poem for publication in the *Southwest Review*. The poem's success to me seems to derive in large part from an intense engagement with its most psychoculturally available precursor, the epic heroic corrido.

"GUITARREROS": A FORMALIST
PERSPECTIVE

"Guitarreros" represents an effort to incorporate the influence of the corrido in the interests of producing a quite different and strong poem, an effort that ends in a kind of fruitful poetic and political defeat. Here is the poem as it was written in 1935 and almost in the form in which it was published in the *Southwest Review* in 1964. (I have reinserted the epigraph that was accidentally omitted from the 1964 printing. The epigraph means, "They brought down the black bull never before brought down.")

> Bajaron un toro prieto
> que nunca lo habían bajado.

Guitarreros

Black against twisted black
The old mesquite
Rears up against the stars
Branch bridle hanging,
While the bull comes down from the mountain
Driven along by your fingers,
Twenty nimble stallions prancing up and down the *redil* of the guitars.

One leaning on the trunk, one facing—
Now the song:
Not cleanly flanked, not pacing,
But in a stubborn yielding that unshapes
And shapes itself again,
Hard-mouthed, zigzagged, thrusting,
Thrown not sung
One to the other.

The old man listens in his cloud
Of white tobacco smoke.
"It was so," he says,
"In the old days it was so."

In consummate and powerfully detailed imagery, our poet is imagining a musical performance scene, although this is not wholly clear until lines 6–8, when guitar playing first becomes evident. "Now the song," and now, also, the import of the epigraph and lines 1–5 becomes clearer. Two musicians are under an old mesquite tree whose dark trunks have grown intertwined (as they often do in south Texas) "black against twisted black," and the two likely sit "one leaning on the trunk, one facing." But the mesquite branches are also horses on the run rearing up, "black against twisted black." The imagery of horses is then smoothly shifted to the guitarists as their combined twenty fingers become like "twenty nimble stallions prancing up and down the *redil*"— the strings and necks of their guitars. This "ranching" metaphor is then nicely interlocked with another, for it is these music-making stallions that drive down a bull from the mountain—the image introduced in the epigraph.

To understand fully the image of the bull, one must trace the epigraph to its source, "El Hijo Desobediente" (The Disobedient Son), Paredes's favorite corrido,[1] and one that Simmons has called among the best (1957:41). Here is the version Paredes gives as the one he learned as a young man from the corridistas of the Lower Border; another version is provided by Mendoza (1954:266–68). The translation is my own.

El Hijo Desobediente

Un domingo estando herrando
se encontraron dos mancebos,
echando mano a los fieros
como queriendo pelear;
cuando se estaban peleando
pues llegó su padre de uno:
—Hijo de mi corazón,
ya no pelees con ninguno.—

—Quítese de aquí mi padre
que estoy más bravo que un león
no vaya a sacar la espada
y la parta el corazón.—
—Hijo de mi corazón,
por lo que acabas de hablar
antes de que raye el sol
la vida te han de quitar.—

—Lo que le pido a mi padre
que no me entierre en sagrado,
que me entierre en tierra bruta
donde me trille el ganado,
con una mano de fuera
y un papel sobre-dorado,
con un letrero que diga,
"Felipe fue desdichado."

—La vaquilla colorada,
hace un año que nació.

ahi se la dejo a mi padre
por la crianza que me dió;
los tres caballos que tengo,
ahi se los dejo a los pobres
para que digan en vida,
"Felipe, Dios te perdone."—

Bajaron el toro prieto,
que nunca lo habían bajado,
pero ora si ya bajó
revuelto con el ganado;
ya con ésta me despido
por la estrella del oriente,
y aquí se acaba el corrido
de El Hijo Desobediente.

The Disobedient Son

On a Sunday during branding
Two young cowboys did meet,
Each going for his steel
Each looking to fight;
As they were fighting
The father of one arrived:
—My beloved son
Do not fight with anyone.—

—Get away from here, my father
I feel more fierce than a lion,
For I may draw my knife
To split your heart in two.—
—My beloved son,
Because of what you have said
Before the next sunrise
Your life will be taken away.—

—I only ask of my father
Do not bury me in sacred ground,
Bury me in brute earth
Where the stock may trample me
With one hand out of the grave
And a gilded paper,
With an epitaph that reads
"Felipe was an ill-fated man."

The red yearling
Born a year ago,
I leave to my father
My upbringing to him I owe;
My three stallions

> I leave to the poor
> So that they may say
> "May God forgive you, Felipe."
> They brought the black bull down,
> Never before brought down,
> But now the bull has come down
> With the rest of the stock;
> Now with this I say farewell
> Guided by the eastern star
> This ends the ballad
> Of the disobedient son.

The epigraph of "Guitarreros" and the bull coming down from the mountain in line 5 give us sufficient textual authority to propose that Paredes's poem is about the imagined singing of this particular corrido. The ballad now comes to be represented in the poem by the black bull, and it is "El Hijo Desobediente" that the guitarists are "bringing down" from their consciousness and driving along with their nimble fingers. But like a strong bull and unlike a stallion, the song, or, to be more precise, its performance, is

> Not cleanly flanked, not pacing,
> But in a stubborn yielding that unshapes
> And shapes itself again,
> Hard-mouthed, zigzagged, thrusting,
> Thrown . . .

The poem concludes with an old man listening to this powerful corrido in a cloud of white smoke, an old man who simply comments " 'It was so . . . In the old days it was so.' " What was so? First, one might say that what the old man means—perhaps the "meaning" of the poem—is that the moral world of "El Hijo Desobediente" sung by the two guitarists *was so*, a world in which men acted in defense of their honor and also felt a deep sense of obligation and fealty toward their elders. Second, it is also likely that as the old man listens, he is thinking that this powerful style of singing *was so*. Thus "it was so" refers to the passing of an older world, to an entire moral and aesthetic universe that *was so* but no longer is.

POETIC VICTORY AND DEFEAT

We have already poetically historicized "Guitarreros" in discussing its epigraph and Paredes's allusion to his favorite corrido. Clearly, corrido singing is the "subject" of his poem; but this obvious point may be understood in a deeper, richer sense.

If poetry is about the crafting of poetry, as Harold Bloom, following the lead of Wallace Stevens, hypothesizes, then let me propose that "Guitarreros" is not so much about corrido singing as about how strong poems should be made. In Bloom's terms, strong poems are not simply made about poems, they are made *against* antecedent strong poems. The poem that has come before has great potency and influence for the later poet. Yet, in this theory, no strong poetic latecomer is wholly accepting of his strong fatherly precursor, and the ephebe engages the father in a creative struggle through any combination of six defensive strategies cast as poetic tropes. The result, of course, is the ephebe's own poetic achievement even if, by Bloom's terms, this necessarily falls short of complete victory. These six rhetorical strategies or "revisionary ratios" tend to appear in matched pairs. Bloom chooses to call them *clinamen* and *tessera*, *kenosis* and *daemonization*, and *askesis* and *apophrades* and finds them operating in whole or in part in the strong poetry of Anglo-American culture. In part, they structure the poet's reception of tradition and poetically manifest what Bloom calls the poet's anxiety of influence.[2]

I propose that "Guitarreros" is a relatively strong poem and is structured in large part by a dialectical movement of these rhetorical strategies, responding to the influence of its strong precursor, the corrido of greater Mexico, exemplified by "El Hijo Desobediente." Let us chart some of these strategies using Bloom's categories, even while purposefully misreading those categories to derive less individualistic and more collective terms of discourse.

We have already seen that from the very beginning, the strong corrido precursor is present in the young poet's consciousness. Here we may avail ourselves of more biography than Bloom is likely to use and revise him by using his theory more historically. In the 1930s Paredes did not have a printed text of the ballad before him as we do; rather, he had been continual witness to corrido performances in his native border country of south Texas. His poem is fashioned in response not to what he read, but to what he heard and felt in the presence of folk poets. The world of the corrido is immediately evoked by the poem's epigraph and title, both rendered in Spanish.

Having invoked his poetic precursor, Paredes opens his poem with an introductory section of eight lines that execute a *clinamen*, which

I shall call Swerve (as Bloom also does). In *The Anxiety of Influence*, Bloom tells us that a *clinamen* appears as a corrective move in the ephebe's own poem "which implies that the precursor poem went accurately up to a certain point, but then should have swerved, precisely in the direction that the new poem moves" (1973:14). In a later statement, Bloom amplifies this point: A poem's opening swerve

> is marked by dialectical images of absence and presence, images that rhetorically are conveyed by the trope of simple irony ... and that as psychic defense assume the shape of what Freud called reaction-formation.... Just as rhetorical irony ... says one thing and means another, even the opposite thing, so a reaction-formation opposes itself to a repressed desire by manifesting the opposite of the desire. (1975a:97)

Implied error and asserted correction. Absence and presence. Irony and the literal. Desire and repression. These are the dialectical meanings conveyed by the imagistic and formal composition of the first eight lines. The manifest content, however, may be only a secondary key to this understanding; we must also be attentive to the role of form in the poetic relationship (a concern that receives relatively little of Bloom's attention).

Even as the corrido's presence is established in the epigraph, the corrido's form is immediately abandoned: The corrido's Spanish gives way to the English of the ephebe's poem; the oral corrido's regular meter and rhyme yield to a written poem with varying meter and little rhyme. Most importantly, the conventional diction of folk song is replaced by a constellation of modernist imagery—"black against twisted black"; a mesquite like a stallion; fingers also like stallions, which drive along a bull like a song. These formal choices are the essence of this ephebe's Swerve, and they implicitly and initially "say" that his poem is a wholly different, and perhaps better, way to craft. We have therefore also a formally articulated ironic moment, for in its very form this new poem has also culturally swerved toward a very different kind of audience.

Yet this new poetic form is necessarily caught in a moment of further irony conditioned paradoxically by the appearance of tradition. For even as we have a kind of poetic "correction" to implied traditional error, this seemingly formal declaration of poetic independence quickly begins to be thematically dominated by the corrido. What appears to be a formally autonomous poem in lines 1–5 begins to reacknowledge tradition as two folksingers begin slowly to emerge:

While the bull comes down from the mountain
Driven along by your fingers,
Twenty nimble stallions prancing up and down the *redil* of the guitars.

Our young poet is directly addressing his fellow precursory poets—"your fingers"—as it becomes increasingly clear that they are playing their guitars and singing the ballad alluded to in the epigraph.

In explicitly recognizing his precursors and their poetic crafting, the ephebe is beginning to engage in the revisionary movement that Bloom calls the *tessera*, and which I shall call Accommodation. In this movement, the initial formal Swerve begins to falter, or at least it readjusts to the emerging presence of tradition in the imagistic content of the poem. Accommodation is an expression of a momentary truce between poet and precursor. The young poet talks to and talks only about his fellow poets as they begin to craft their poem, and his complimentary imagery, fingers like "twenty nimble stallions," reveals his admiration for them. In one sense, the precursor is exerting his control over the younger poet, yet guitarreros are at the same time within the control of our poet, for their singing can be "heard" only through his poetic skill. Only, the later poet seems to say, through his more "modern" verse can one make sense of this precursory power, and its presence in his poem is both dominating and dominated. In the movement of *tessera*, Bloom tells us,

> the later poet provides what his imagination tells him would complete the otherwise "truncated" precursor poem or poet. . . . In this sense of a completing link, the *tessera* represents any later poet's attempt to persuade himself (and us) that the precursor's Word would be worn out if not redeemed as a newly fulfilled and enlarged Word of the ephebe. (1973:66–67)

No longer swerving, or at least not as much, the young poet is in imagistic awe of his precursors' power. Nevertheless, while making this concession, he also extends a generosity to them, for their power would remain historically truncated were he not willing to acknowledge tradition and re-present it to us in his art. The poet has returned to his precursor, but on his own terms or at least in a momentary Accommodation.

However, having made this initial temporary adjustment—this compromise—between self and tradition, the ephebe completes the poem by wholly acknowledging the force of the poetic fathers and seemingly negating his own poetic presence. This later negotiation with the precursor is the movement of *kenosis*, or what I shall call Withdrawal. In this poetic stance, the ephebe appears wholly to humble himself before the authority of tradition, although he continues to exact a price from the precursor. Although "apparently emptying himself of his own afflatus, his imaginative godhood," the later poet "seems to humble himself as though he were ceasing to be a poet, but this ebbing is so performed . . . that the precursor is emptied out also, and so the later poem of deflation is not as absolute as it seems" (Bloom 1973:14–15).

This Withdrawal, this humbling and poetic emptying out, begins with the line "Now the song," as our ephebe engages in a direct evaluatory encounter with the strong precursory poem. What does he think of it and, by implication, how does it compare to his own "song" before us? His awed description betrays too much, for clearly our young poet is overwhelmed and his poem is emptied of all sense of poetic self. Now his poem is suffused by this seemingly absolutely powerful poem from the past, which like a good strong bull or cow pony (the metaphor is slightly but perhaps profitably confused here), is

> Not cleanly flanked, not pacing,
> But in a stubborn yielding that unshapes
> And shapes itself again,
> Hard-mouthed, zigzagged, thrusting,
> Thrown not sung
> One to the other.

The lines clearly suggest the full awe and admiration of the ephebe for his precursor song, but their other necessary effect is to vitiate the ephebe's own poetic effort. Yet, of course, the young poet still has some degree of poetic control as the truce of Accommodation lingers, but it is now a quite shaky truce as the precursor appears in full power and poetic majesty and quite literally takes over the ephebe and his poem.

Here, the content of the particular corrido the guitarreros are singing—a ballad about sons, fathers, disobedience, and dire consequences—exerts its force. A miscreant son violates the moral hierarchy and rules of his society and meets his fate in a world where "the representative of God on earth was the father" and his "curse was thought to be the most terrible thing on earth" (Paredes 1958b:11). Symbolically, moral order is restored at two levels in the corrido. First, even as the young vaquero manfully and calmly accepts his fate, he acknowl-

edges his social being and affirms the natural order of things by dis-
tributing his goods, especially his stock, and by asking to be buried in
a secular natural setting. Second, the corrido ends with the other vaqueros establishing control over the renegade bull. Like the miscreant
vaquero, the black bull is strong but potentially dangerous, perhaps
even evil, and he must be brought down, brought under social and
moral control. This moral universe *was so* but is no longer possible
and, with the ephebe, we stand morally empty before it, knowing that
we have to construct our moral existence without it. For all its moral
power, the normative impact of the past has been blunted by time and
change, and only the moral desire of the young poet cast into poetry
can give us limited imaginative access to it.

Both the moral and artistic dimensions of the corrido world are
finely captured through the single powerful metaphor of the guitarreros
controlling and driving the song, like the vaqueros control and drive
the black bull. The guitarreros and the vaqueros, of course, must also
exercise an intermediary control over their "livestock," one group literally, and the others through the art of their fingers to produce a tightly
and finely crafted artistic whole. This is a world in which unbridled,
undisciplined moral and artistic disorder must be controlled by artful,
moral human beings, lest they suffer the degradation of their kind.

We cannot but sense our poet's admiration for the artistic and moral
world of the corrido. Even as the form of his poem violates the folk
tradition, it is his generosity to folk tradition in his art which brings
that world to us, and he ultimately affirms its values with the better
part of himself. Yet while lending final assent to this dominant influence,
he nevertheless implicitly and explicitly demonstrates its historicity and
thus, in Bloom's terms, "the precursor is emptied out also" in relation
to the ephebe even as he is being overwhelmed by the precursor. The
ephebe fully accomplishes the twin tasks by the ingenious introduction
of the old man in the last four lines of the poem:

> The old man listens in his cloud
> Of white tobacco smoke.
> "It was so," he says,
> "In the old days it was so."

Most literally, the old man is an elder, that is, an old man with authority;
as Paredes described greater Mexican culture of early south Texas, "de-
cisions were made, arguments were settled, and sanctions were decided

upon by the old men of the group, with the leader usually being the patriarch" (1958b:12). In effect, the elder in this poem settles this poetic struggle between the poet and tradition, but does so through a Withdrawal. That is, although in one obvious sense he represents tradition, he is also the young poet's speaker and in his twin role as traditional image and poetic voice, he limits both tradition and the ephebe, "emptying" them out in relation to each other.

This dual movement of limitation is primarily carried by the old man's "It was so." But, again, what is it that "was so"? At one level, the old man is commenting upon the guitarists' powerful singing performance, which is now essentially a historical artistic performance. Today we are left with a different style of "singing," which is not singing at all, namely the ephebe's poem. If it is stylistically and performatively less impressive than the "hard-mouthed, zigzagged, thrusting" song, then we are the poorer for it; yet, at the same time, folk tradition has also reached its performative limits. It can no longer speak to us directly; the precursor's voice is muted in time, and only the ephebe's poem *is so*, for all its poetic weakness relative to the powerful song of the past. Both past and present have their artistic limitations: the past is powerful, but the present is alive.

A final way to grasp this paradoxical relationship of influence is to note the parallel journeys of the two ephebes, Felipe, the young hero of the corrido, and our young poet. Both depart from traditional norms (Swerve), readjust and acknowledge their swerving (Accommodation), and finally affirm tradition to the point of self-negation (Withdrawal), but do so in a way that takes a toll on their fathers. Both ephebes must die—Felipe literally, our poet figuratively—under the influence of the powerful order that is their inheritance. That order lives on in our consciousness only because of the ephebe's effort to challenge it, but here he finally acknowledges the superiority of the father, even as the father must acknowledge his own kind of debt to the son.

In principle, the poem need not end here. With more time, experience, learning and self-confidence, the ephebe may mount a new challenge, following the dialectical, antithetical completion of Accommodation in a next movement, which Bloom calls *daemonization*, and I shall call Rebellion. Here the ephebe would begin "a movement towards a personalized Counter-Sublime, in reaction to the precursor's Sublime" as the "later poet opens himself to what he believes to be a power in the parent-poem that does not belong to the parent proper, but to a range of being just beyond that precursor" (1973:15). The ephebe seeks his own autonomous voice and, "Turning against the precursor's Sublime, the newly strong poet undergoes *daemonization*, a Counter-Sublime whose function suggests *the precursor's relative weakness*" (1973:100).

But our ephebe's poem ends short of Rebellion. There is no strong counterassertion, no attempt to articulate a new, distinctive poem that implicitly denies the adequacy of the precursor. In this poem, at least, our ephebe cannot find—perhaps chooses not to find—his own distinctive voice. Indeed, Paredes's unresolved relationship to the precursor is resolved only in 1958, with the publication of *With His Pistol in His Hand*, as we shall see in chapter 3.

"GUITARREROS": INFLUENCE, THE SOCIAL, AND THE DISCOURSES OF DOMINATION

Paredes's "Guitarreros" is suffused with the power of the precursory tradition of the corrido. That strength, however, turns out to be also a limitation, leaving the poem to end in the past tense with no word of the present or future. In this sense, Paredes's poem-as-poem is produced in a struggle with a strong precursory poem-as-poem, a losing though creative struggle for the latecomer.

But the corrido is a genre of strong folk poem deeply implicated in social history—in politics, conflict, and social change—and later poems that would rival it must also address these concerns in their present historical moment. The latecoming rival cannot simply write another corrido, but rather must fully and maturely internalize and use the poetic and political energy of the corrido in order to write a new poem wholly relevant to his time, even as he creatively draws on the past. This, our ephebe is unable to do: unable to come to full poetic terms with the precursor, he cannot move beyond his admiring contemplation of the past to gradually and creatively transform it into a poetic and politically critical meditation on the present. In these terms, the truncated achievement of "Guitarreros" relative to the precursory tradition also limits its capacity to address the poet's contemporary world of political discourse.

However fine a poem "Guitarreros" is, unlike a corrido, it offers no particulars of its historical moment and no ideologemes or statements about disenfranchisement, economic exploitation, social deprivation, or racism in south Texas in the 1930s. Indeed, the poem is notable for its total negation and repression of any statement about the cultural discourses of domination, including "Americanization," that were accepted by an emerging, though still small, petty bourgeois Mexican-American class. Institutionally this outlook is best represented by the League of United Latin American Citizens, a men's social service club founded in urban San Antonio and Corpus Christi in the late 1920s. Expressing at times a disdain for proletarian life and the traditional Mexican rural past, league members saw Americanization as the best guarantee for upward mobility. This meant not only the learning of English but, more significantly, less emphasis on the retention of Spanish and great emphasis on the rapid acquisition of an American civic political culture. The league and similar groups did struggle against racial discrimination, although they seemed far more reluctant to articulate a politics of class consciousness. Other groups tried to combine the latter together with a stronger sense of ethnic nationalism—one thinks of the fiery Emma Tenayuca, who organized several violent strikes among the Mexican-American cigar, government, and pecan-shelling workers in San Antonio in the 1930s—but in the world of public discourse, it was the petty bourgeois who were gradually hegemonic, validated, as always, by those who dominated, even as a culture of resistance maintained largely among the working classes continued as a substratum (Montejano 1987:156–254; García 1991).

Regarding this south Texas of conflict, struggle, and dominating discourses, Paredes's poem is silent. The total domination of the corrido, the latecomer's inability to move beyond the revisionary ratio of Withdrawal in the face of the precursor, render the poem strangely impotent, politically as well as poetically at this level. Yet we sense here neither ignorance of nor escape from the social context, but rather repression, a repression captured, once again, in the evocative closing line, "It was so." It is as if the poem understands but refuses to say *why* the moral and aesthetic world it so admires *isn't so* anymore. How did it come to an end? This is a question for later revisionary ratios, steps "Guitarreros" does not take, steps that might poetically address the question of politics, which Paredes did broach in "Flute Song," a less repressed, though poetically less satisfying, poem of that same year:

> Why was I ever born
> Heir to a people's sorrow,
> Wishing this day were done
> And yet fearful for the morrow.

Useful for its glimpse of the poet's social sorrow, his fears and wishes, this bit of verse, conventional in its meter and rhyme, abstract in its rhetoric, is uninspiring as poetry. It does not show the focused imagery, the complex poetic argument, the compelling rhythm of "Guitarreros" because, I submit, it is not experiencing the challenge of a precursor, and the result is poetic insipidity, a "weak" poem.

Here we enter into Jameson's third-level analytic, the ideology of form. And it is in the formal competence of "Guitarreros"—the formal poetic reasons that Paredes and his editors selected it for publication—that we find this ephebe's best response to his poetic precursor and, at the same time, his repressed ideological critique of present social conditions. Recall that for Jameson, it is at this level that we find the traces of overlap and conflict in History (with a capital H), now conceived as the struggle between distinct cultural modes of production.

In "Guitarreros" Paredes's formal achievement—his skillful articulation of a modernist poetics—executes the Rebellion that the poem's imagistic content does not. It is in the poem's form that we find a complete disjuncture with corrido aesthetics and, therefore, the ephebe's greatest poetic autonomy. This Rebellion necessarily carries the younger poet into the coterie of formal modernism at a historical moment when modernism is performing its own critical ideological service *contra* capitalism in a wider social sphere. At the same time, however, at the level of local politics, the modernist form isolates this poem too severely from its immediate context. In its aesthetics, and relative to the struggle immediately at hand, the poem's form too quickly anticipates the future and is closed off from the immediately contextual present. The poem therefore cannot address the present in an aesthetic form that would resonate with it even while educating it toward the future. The ephebe has not yet learned to bring his precursory political-poetic tradition into his own form so as to make it relevant to the present. In Raymond Williams's language, we might say that the residual is not residual enough. It suffocates any new emergence except in purely formal terms.

In a context of struggle, a more complex, subtle, yet explicit and public poetic engagement with the precursory tradition and the political present was required. Some twenty years later, a much more poetically and politically experienced Paredes was ready to again try to craft such a poem. But this time his poem would be in prose.

For even if we know the person represented, whose portrait we may call "like" or "unlike"—is it not an abstraction to say of an arbitrarily chosen moment or expression that *this* is that person's likeness? And even if we know thousands of such moments or expressions, what do we know of the immeasurably large part of his life when we do not see him, what do we know of the inner light which burns within this "known" person, what of the way this inner light is reflected in others? And that, you see, is more or less how I imagine the truth of the essay to be. Here too there is a struggle for truth, for the incarnation of a life which someone has seen in a man, an epoch or form; but it depends only on the intensity of the work and its vision whether the written text conveys to us this suggestion of that particular life.

The great difference, then, is this: poetry gives us the illusion of the life of the person it represents; nowhere is there a conceivable someone or something against which the created work can be measured. The hero of the essay was once alive, and so his life must be given form; but this life, too, is as much inside the work as everything else in poetry.

Georg Lukács, "On the Nature and
Form of the Essay"

> The words of a dead man
> Are modified in the guts of the living.
> W. H. Auden,
> "In Memory of W. B. Yeats"

3

With His Pistol in His Hand
The Essay as Strong Sociological Poem

Américo Paredes's classic work of corrido scholarship, *With His Pistol in His Hand: A Border Ballad and Its Hero* (1958), offers us the poetically mature and politically engaged resolution of the dialectical tensions between the precursory tradition and contemporary creativity that "Guitarreros" articulates but does not resolve. But to speak of scholarship as *poetically* mature requires that we blur genres, a tendency already evident in Georg Lukács's "On the Nature and Form of the Essay" ([1910] 1974) and requiring Clifford Geertz only to "poetically" label and conceptualize that which by 1980 was a growing, if not quite "mainstream" intellectual practice (Geertz 1980). Here, then, I want to examine the poetics of the anthropological essay *With His Pistol in His Hand*.

It is not often that an anthropological study becomes a poetic performance, if by the latter we at least imply, following Mukarovsky (1977), that a textuality partakes of "poetic designation," meaning "every use of words occurring in a text with a predominant aesthetic function" (p. 65) which renders "the sign itself the center of attention" (p. 72). However, Mukarovsky does not wish to be misconstrued on two important issues. First, poetic designation and function apply not only to formal poetry or other figurative language; rather, "this function participates, at least potentially, in every human act" (p. 69), whether poem, ritual, conversation, or anthropology. Second, this focus on the sign "itself," while weakening the relationship to any immediate reality, "does not preclude a relation between the work and reality as a whole; on the contrary it is even beneficial to this relation" (p. 71). His summary statement is a charter for the kind of analysis I wish to undertake:

> The aesthetic function . . . is potentially present in every utterance. The specific character of poetic designation, therefore, rests solely in its more

radical exposure of the tendency inherent in every act of designation. The weakening of the immediate relation of poetic designation of reality is counterbalanced by the fact that the poetic work as a global designation enters into relation with the *total* set of the existential experiences of the subject, be he the creative or the perceiving subject. (1977:72–73)

My analysis also proposes to restore Mukarovsky's full formulation, the second half of which—the matter of social intent—is often repressed in much contemporary analysis. There is in such contemporary analyses a too singular concern with the first half of his formulation, with the text as pure sign, and a relative lack of concern with the poetically designated text "as a global designation" which "enters into relation with the *total* set of the existential experiences of . . . the creative or the perceiving subject."

In the present case, I want to take Paredes's poetically designated text beyond its obvious reference to an immediate reality—the Mexican corrido and a community of corrido specialists—to its more global designation as a political poetics that, marshaling the influence of the ballad, addresses and helps to form a generation of poets, intellectuals, and activists. Thus to understand the poetics of *With His Pistol in His Hand*, we must turn to the social experiences of those political creative and perceiving subjects involved in the textualization of this author and his work.

THE APPEARANCE OF
WITH HIS PISTOL IN HIS HAND

As we have seen in chapter 1, *With His Pistol in His Hand* is substantively a study of the heroic corrido as it appears and develops along the lower Texas-Mexico border—south Texas—since the Spanish settlement of the area in the mid-eighteenth century. More specifically, it is a study of the life, legend, and corpus of ballads generated by the activities of one individual, Gregorio Cortez. The historical facts of Cortez's life, as set out by Paredes, are as follows.

Until June 12, 1901, Cortez was a rather ordinary Mexican-American in Texas, an agricultural laborer like so many others who, from his own perspective, was witnessing the intensification of a largely Anglo-American and capitalist domination of Texas, including the predominantly Mexican-American region of south Texas. This domination of the native population, which was increasingly comprised of immigrants of Mexican descent, took the form of class and racial subordination, the latter evidenced in part in the rough-and-ready lynching "justice" often administered to Mexican-Americans accused of crimes (Limón 1986a).

Such was the fate that Cortez undoubtedly expected on June 12 in the moments after he killed Sheriff W. T. Morris in Karnes County in central Texas in an exchange of pistol fire that also left Cortez's brother, Romaldo, seriously wounded. In his last official act, Sheriff Morris, a former Texas Ranger, had come out to the farm where the Cortezes, migrants from the border, were sharecropping. The sheriff was looking for reported horse thieves. Because neither he nor his accompanying deputy spoke Spanish well, if at all, they mistakenly accused the Cortezes of the thievery, and Sheriff Morris drew his gun to arrest Cortez. Probably fearing they were about to be gunned down in cold blood, Romaldo charged the sheriff, not knowing that his brother had a gun hidden behind his back. Morris shot Romaldo, but in the next instant was himself cut down by Gregorio. As Morris's deputy ran for his life and help and the sheriff lay dead before him, Cortez knew that he faced certain Texas justice.

Entrusting his brother to his family, Gregorio began a long horseback ride south, toward the Mexican border. Along the way he evaded numerous posses, through skillful riding and help from local Mexican-Americans. He also killed a second sheriff. When he eventually learned that the authorities had incarcerated his wife and children and were carrying out reprisals against those who had helped him, he turned himself in to the authorities near Laredo, Texas, where Mexican-Americans still had some measure of political control. Nonetheless, he was returned to Karnes County where, under constant threat of lynching, he was tried and convicted. In one of those paradoxes that has always characterized Texas, Cortez was eventually pardoned by an Anglo Texas governor. The governor was not reelected.

Cortez's adventurous ride to freedom stirred the folk imagination of the Mexican-Americans of Texas, who had already experienced half a century of domination. Soon after, or perhaps even during Cortez's ride, the community's corridistas began to compose and sing the ballad of Gregorio Cortez. As Paredes says, they sang "in the *cantinas* and the country stores, in the ranches when men gather at night to talk in the cool dark, sitting in a circle, smoking and listening to the old songs and the tales of other days" (p. 33).[1] Paredes offers this English translation of one of the better short versions of the ballad as a representative text.

El Corrido de Gregorio Cortez

In the country of El Carmen
A great misfortune befell;
The Major Sheriff is dead;
Who killed him no one can tell.

At two in the afternoon,
In half an hour or less,
They knew that the man who killed him
Had been Gregorio Cortez.

And in the county of Kiansis
They cornered him after all;
Though they were more than three hundred
He leaped out of their corral.

Then the Major Sheriff said,
As if he was going to cry,
"Cortez, hand over your weapons;
We want to take you alive."

They let loose the bloodhound dogs;
They followed him from afar.
But trying to catch Cortez
Was like following a star.

All the rangers of the county
Were flying, they rode so hard;
What they wanted was to get
The thousand-dollar reward.

Then said Gregorio Cortez,
And his voice was like a bell,
"You will never get my weapons
Till you put me in a cell."

Then said Gregorio Cortez,
With his pistol in his hand,
"Ah, so many mounted Rangers
Just to take one Mexican!"

Cortez's epic counter was neither the first nor the last of such encounters with Anglo-Texan authority, nor was it the first or last to inspire corridos. Ten years earlier, Catarino Garza, journalist and guerrilla leader, had taken up organized arms against the Texas Rangers and inspired a balladry. And fourteen years later new corridos could be heard along the border about *los sediciosos* (the seditionists), bands of

Mexicans who rose up in armed rebellion in 1915–16 against Anglo-Texan authority. In reprisal the Texas Rangers carried out massive killings of combatants and civilians alike, a practice that even an eminent champion of the Rangers, historian Walter Prescott Webb, felt obligated to criticize as an "orgy of bloodshed" (1935:263).

When it appeared in 1958, *With His Pistol in His Hand* received its principal attention from the communities of folklorists and scholars of the Southwest and certain elements of the Anglo lay public in Texas. As such, the book might have remained another circumscribed scholarly text for specialists. However, in the 1960s the book found a wider audience when the first significant groups of largely working-class Mexican-American youth attended colleges and universities in the Southwest and joined with other youth in movements of political protest and cultural rebellion. (As we will see in chapter 4, this activity among Mexican-American college youth evolved into the Chicano movement, which, in addition to its practical politics, also generated a great deal of intellectual and artistic work within the Mexican-American community.) Published on the eve of this political, intellectual, and artistic florescence, Paredes's scholarly anthropological study became a powerful influence on a new generation of Chicano writers, intellectuals, and activists as they produced a new critical social discourse. It was able to exert such an influence precisely because Paredes had by this time worked out a subtle and complex relationship of content and form to the epic corrido. *With His Pistol in His Hand* is, in effect, a new kind of corrido, one whose complex relationship to the past enabled it to speak to the present. Let us first appreciate the balladlike form of *With His Pistol in His Hand*.

THE RETURN OF THE MEXICAN
BALLAD: A FORMAL ANALYSIS

Paredes's book opens with a dedication to his father and to an older generation and their folklore:

> To the memory of my father,
> who rode a raid or two with
> Catarino Garza;
> and to all those old men
> who sat around on summer nights,
> in days where there was a chaparral,

> smoking their cornhusk cigarettes and talking
> in low, gentle voices about
> violent things;
> while I listened.

Even as the imagery of this dedication establishes the writer's special authority to recall and transform the past, his use of English language, meter, and free verse establishes his authority to speak to the new generation, to Mexican-Americans educated in a modernist and post-modernist climate.

Following the dedication, we encounter a quite brief introduction, as if the author is anxious to move quickly to the main text. Yet its precise economy—its tight form—alerts us to the traditional cultural precursors that inform this text:

> This book began as the study of a ballad; it developed into the story of a ballad hero. Thus it became two books in one. It is an account of the life of a man, of the way that songs and legends grew up about his name, and of the people who produced the songs, the legends, and the man. It is also the story of a ballad, "El Corrido de Gregorio Cortez," of its development out of actual events, and of the folk traditions from which it sprang. (p. 3)

With His Pistol in His Hand preserves its dual origins: part 1 narrates the story of Gregorio Cortez, while the formal scholarship and technical analysis of the Mexican ballad are reserved for part 2.

To more explicitly alert us to the style of his text, even as he provides useful scholarly information, Paredes offers a brief, general definition of the corrido: "*Corrido*, the Mexicans call their narrative folk songs, especially those of epic themes, taking the name from *correr*, which means "to run" or "to flow," for the *corrido* tells a story simply and swiftly, without embellishments" (p. 3). This style is precisely what we will recognize when we begin the main text, a story told "simply and swiftly, without embellishments."

Finally, he tells us that his is not a simple story about just any balladry or, for that matter, any Mexican balladry; it is a story about the balladry of borders and conflict, particularly the conflict between the Anglo and people of Mexican descent in the United States. With this rhetorical move Paredes "locates" his Chicano readers and, as a corridista would, appeals to their understanding of the social relations and historical context for his story.

On the page following the introduction, Paredes presents a partial version of a corrido printed without commentary. For Chicano readers the verses and musical notation are more than a useful example of the topic at hand; they evoke all our memories and experiences of the style of our traditional folk form and its sound. "In the country of El Carmen," we read and the entire world of the corrido opens before us. As we then begin to read the first chapter of part 1, "The Country," we sense that a new type of corrido, one in the form of scholarly prose, is developing before us. For like a corridista, Paredes quickly establishes the "scenic structure," the geographical locale and opposing social forces. Here is Paredes's own analysis of the traditional corrido's opening stylistic devices, taken from part 2:

> a scenic structure . . . is typical of the Border heroic *corrido*. The setting in motion of the action is a few swift lines, the introduction of the hero speaking out his boast in the second scene, after his first exploit, thus giving the whole narrative a middle-of-things feeling, the tendency to tell the story not in a long continuous and detailed narrative but in a series of shifting scenes and by means of action and dialogue. . . . a couple of stanzas get the story going and then the hero appears shouting out his boast or his defiance. From that moment on, the story moves swiftly to its conclusion, with point of view shifting rapidly from the hero to his adversaries and back again, and from one position in space to another if the action covers a great deal of ground. (p. 187)

Quite conscious not to use too many words, lest he lose his audience or distort the clarity of the situation, Paredes gives us twenty-six simply and elegantly written pages that provide the essentials we need to grasp the full social significance of the Cortez incident. But while a corridista could assume that his folk audience would have immediately understood the full signification of stanza 1 of the actual "The Ballad of Gregorio Cortez," where a sheriff has died, and stanza 2, where the killer is identified as Cortez, Paredes knows that his contemporary Chicano audience requires a few more words to delineate the social structure and cultural relationship that may have been obscured by the passing of time. Chicanos coming of age in the 1950s knew about segregated barbershops near the University of Texas at Austin, about Texas Rangers breaking up Mexican farmworker strikes in the Lower Rio Grande Valley, and about appalling social conditions for Mexican-Americans, but they may not have known about the violence of 1915. So Paredes recounts an interview he had with Mrs. Josefina Flores de Garza in 1954. Mrs. Garza, he explains,

> gave me some idea how it felt to be on the receiving end of the Ranger "orgy of bloodshed" of 1915. At that time Mrs. Garza was a girl of

eighteen, the eldest of a family that included two younger boys in their teens and several small children. The family lived on a ranch near Harlingen, north of Brownsville. When the Ranger "executions" began, other Mexican ranchers sought refuge in town. The elder Flores refused to abandon his ranch, telling his children, "El que nada debe nada teme" (He who is guilty of nothing fears nothing.)

The Rangers arrived one day, surrounded the place and searched the outbuildings. The family waited in the house. Then the Rangers called the elder Flores out. He stepped to the door, and they shot him down. His two boys ran to him when he fell, and they were shot down as they bent over their father. Then the Rangers came into the house and looked around. One of them saw a new pair of chaps, liked them, and took them with him. They left immediately afterwards.

From other sources I learned that the shock drove Josefina Flores temporarily insane. For two days her mother lived in the house with a brood of terrified youngsters, her deranged eldest daughter, and the corpses of her husband and her sons. . . .

The daughter recovered her sanity after some time, but it still upsets her to talk about the killings. And though forty years have passed, she still seems to be afraid that if she says something critical about the Rangers they will come and do her harm. Apparently Ranger terror did its work well, on the peaceful and inoffensive. (p. 27)

The recounting of this terrible incident is the rhetorical climax of what Paredes wants to accomplish in his first "stanza": to succinctly and graphically establish the social scene of his poem. Yet if women are usually excluded from the corrido, in these most charged lines of Paredes's opening stanza, it is women, particularly a mother with her brood, who are at the dramatic center of the narrative. In this most moving and substantial way, Paredes introduces women into his discourse, women driven to madness by state terrorism in the service of social domination.[2] This particular gendered point of oppression could not but foster deep resentment among Paredes's Chicano readers, whose patriarchal culture viewed the mistreatment of women as a particularly reprehensible thing. Though Paredes's new corrido continues to be a patriarchal tale, its composer has allowed us to glimpse that repressed dimension which also endures domination—a theme to which we shall return.

Once the scene is set, the traditional corrido usually introduces the hero in its next few stanzas, and does so in legendary proportions: Three hundred Texas Rangers are said to surround Cortez, yet he escapes; "But trying to catch Cortez / Was like following a star"; and later Cortez is said to directly address and taunt his pursuers. These are the fictive elements permitted to the corridista in the exercise of his poetic license. As such, they draw on a larger story of legendry with its own independent oral existence, a body of legends known to his listeners that enhances and fills out their appreciation of the sparse, sung ballad.

So, too, Paredes introduces us to the legendary Cortez in his second chapter, "The Legend." Here Paredes employs an omniscient narrator to recount the legends for readers unfamiliar with them. Amplifying on the ballad, this account tells us that Cortez was a quiet, polite, good man; both a fine horseman and a knowledgeable farmer; a superb rifle and pistol shot. He had been living a quiet life along the predominantly Mexican border country when his brother, who "was just like the young men of today, loud mouthed and discontented," persuaded him to "move away from the river and go up above, where there was much money to be made" (p. 36). Again, Paredes needs a few more lines to accomplish for his audience what a traditional singer in 1901 could assume about his; namely, that the legend of Cortez was already taking hold in the community's consciousness, and that this consciousness would inform their appreciation of his ballad. Paredes's Chicano audience, however, needed a direct and elaborated, albeit economical and fictive, rendition of this legendry.

Like much folklore, however, the corrido is not simply a narrative of totally mythic fictions. It is at the same time, a historical account that, within a mythos and an ideological perspective, nonetheless permits its audience to discover a remarkable range of social reality. Whatever the fictive dimensions of this particular ballad, its audience would at the same time learn that, in fact, Cortez had killed a sheriff in a place called Karnes County and afterward had claimed his right to do so in defense of his life and that of his brother. They would also learn certain factual details of the southward flight, of which the most general and important is that Cortez did outride and outshoot the vaunted Texas Rangers, that they "captured" him only when he turned himself in after learning about the reprisals taken against his family and community.

Adapting the corrido's narrative conventions, Paredes presents his primary research on the historical facts of the case in chapter 3, "The Man." Here we learn, interestingly enough, how remarkably close the legendary aspects of the ballad correspond to the emergent historical narrative as Paredes discovered and constructed it. In presenting his historical reconstruction, Paredes is also attentive to another corrido convention, to tell the story "with point of view shifting rapidly from the hero to his adversaries and back again." Unlike the Anglo historical reconstructions of Texas society, in which the Mexicans are presented as stereotypes, Paredes's narrative tells a great deal about both sides and, like the corrido, brings both sides to life. What we discover to some extent in the original corrido and to a larger extent in Paredes's new corrido is that Anglos are *people:* they are capable of fear, doubt, anxiety, anger, fairness, meanness, pettiness, and generosity, although the negative qualities predominate in their treatment of Mexicans.

In the fourth and final chapter of part 1, "The Hero's Progress," Paredes reviews the fact and fancy, the variants and versions, of the Cortez legendry and balladry and demonstrates their intertwined relationship. As a postnarrative review, this chapter is a prose equivalent of the conversations that men may have after a corrido performance, as they evaluate the corrido, its hero and his circumstances, and try to get at the truth.[3]

WITH HIS PISTOL IN HIS HAND:
THE RETURN OF THE DEAD

Paredes's close integration of corrido aesthetics with the shaping of his prose poem represents a final coming to terms with the precursor. The expressive potency that so suffused the relatively young poem "Guitarreros" has now been fully integrated into this much later, extended, and mature poem. We may read *With His Pistol in His Hand* as an extended exercise in the final revisionary ratios that Bloom calls *askesis* and *apophrades.*

In "Guitarreros," we observed, Paredes stopped short of a full Rebellion save for that of form. In the short dedicatory poem that appears at the beginning of *With His Pistol in His Hand* he chooses not to dwell on that Rebellion, but instead to represent a more mature relationship in which he reacts to the precursor's influence by a seemingly almost total acceptance of his dominance.[4] Not to be confused with the earlier stage of Withdrawal, this acceptance reflects the ephebe's positive presence and control, even as he appears wholly generous to the precursor. This is the phase Bloom calls *askesis*, or what I shall call Perspective. For Bloom there is an equivalence between *askesis* and the Freudian psychic defense of sublimation, in which desire—sexual or aggressive—is transformed into the opposite, that is, into a controlled selflessness and a studied acceptance. The trope that corresponds to sublimation, in Bloom's scheme, is metaphor, poetic images that speak of one thing but refer to something else.

Paredes's dedicatory poem is about his father's generation, those who rode "a raid or two" with Catarino Garza and sat around the campfire talking about "violent things," but it is also an extended metaphor for the precursor himself, as in a sense was "Guitarreros." There are two critical differences here. First, the formal character of the dedication—its metrics, diction, and tone—is "modernist" and yet is also a more subtle approximation to the character of the corrido than "Guitarreros." It is as if to say, "I do not need to rebel in my form; I can come perilously close to your influence without being swallowed up whole as a formal poet." Second, the dedicatory poem quietly substitutes the poetic son for the old man of "Guitarreros." Now it is the poetic son, not the old man, who listens, and he listens not as a passive audience to the discourse of the precursors, but as a young ambitious poet actively gathering and synthesizing in preparation for his own strong poem. Though he sits passively, his active prediscursive reflection is itself the poetically rendered taking of Perspective.

Seemingly cast as a dedication to the father and the precursor generation's political poetics, this short poem is an important coming to terms with them. The poetic son is no longer Swerving, no longer in Withdrawal, nor in open Rebellion, but is in mature comprehension of their presence as preparation for his own distinctive yet even more fundamentally indebted poetic discourse. In the intellectual prose poem that follows, Paredes then carries us beyond Perspective into the later revisionary move that constitutes a yet more mature and final encounter with the precursor. This is how Bloom describes this most mature of revisions of the precursor's power, the *apophrades*, or Return of the Dead: "The wholly mature strong poet is peculiarly vulnerable to this last phase of his revisionary relationship to the dead. This vulnerability is most evident in poems that quest for a final clarity, that seek to be definitive statements, testaments to what is uniquely the strong poet's gift (or what he wishes us to remember as his unique gift)" (1973:139-40). *With His Pistol in His Hand* has to be thought of in just these terms—definitive statement, testament, the strong poet's gift.

In this phase of poetic struggle against the precursor, the latecomer poet achieves the nearly impossible: he fully integrates the precursor into his own poem and yet, at the same time, stands fully in control of himself. The precursor master poem appears to speak again, but only

in the words of the latecomer as the reader senses both their distinctiveness and their uncanny resemblance. The dead, says Bloom, have
returned to inhabit the house of poetry, though its construction is not
their own. Bloom believes that the latecomer poet achieves this effect
and this introjection of the precursor's influence through the trope of
metalepsis, the substitution of a trope for a trope, a figure of speech
for another figure of speech (Bloom 1975a:101–3). If we conceive of
the extended performance called the essay as a trope and view it as a
poetically endowed, condensed representation of a reality, as Lukács
suggests, and if a folk ballad is of the same order, then in this case one
extended trope—Paredes's essay—has been substituted for another—
"The Ballad of Gregorio Cortez." Ultimately, it seems, this metaleptic
substitution is what the *apophrades*, the Return of the Dead, is all
about in purely linguistic terms, although in psychoanalytical terms, it
also represents introjection, the nearly total absorption of the anxiety-
producing issue as a way of warding off its influence and creatively
managing our aggressiveness toward it (Bloom 1975a:102).

In poetic terms the imagistic and technical yield is that the precursor
is wholly and magically contained within the later poem, simultaneously
endowing it with its power and yet paradoxically in its control. In this
final revision, Bloom tells us, the later poet "holds his own poem so
open again to the precursor's work that at first we might believe the
wheel has come full circle, and that we are back in the later poet's
flooded apprenticeship, before his strength began to assert itself in the
revisionary ratios" (1973:15–16). That is, we may have the momentary
sensation of returning to the phase of *kenosis*, or Withdrawal, where
the later poet appears wholly dominated by the precursor. But in the
much more mature phase of *apophrades*, "the poem is now *held* open
to the precursor, where once it *was* open, and the uncanny effect is
that the new poem's achievement makes it seem to us, not as though
the precursor were writing it, but as though the later poet himself had
written the precursor's characteristic work" (1973:16).

By the end of Paredes's text, "The Ballad of Gregorio Cortez" has
become wholly identified with Paredes's rewriting of it, and he wholly
identified with "The Ballad of Gregorio Cortez." Or, put in terms closer
to Bloom's, one has the eerie sensation that "The Ballad of Gregorio
Cortez" could not have existed until the strong writing of *With His
Pistol in His Hand*, in the same way that the latter could not exist
without the ballad. Through Paredes's corrido in prose the Dead return

to inhabit the Living, thereby renewing the poetic life of each. But, I would add, revising Bloom, it is poetic life with social purpose as well.

THE RETURN OF THE DEAD AND
THE POLITICS OF THE LIVING

With His Pistol in His Hand is simultaneously a scholarly study of the greater Mexican corrido and a prose poem deeply influenced by the poetics of its subject. In it we see the precursory dead come alive once more in a mature, paradoxical later poem. But the Return of the Dead is also a political poetics, and here Bloom's figure of speech is quite apt, though in a way his neoformalism did not intend.

As we saw in chapter 1, literal death—flesh-ripping death—abounds everywhere in the social world of the corrido and deeply informs its thematics, and it is death as a consequence of politics. By 1958, when *With His Pistol in His Hand* appeared, Texas Rangers no longer gunned down Mexican-Americans as often. Yet in an indirect and perhaps metaphorical way, violent death continues to figure as a political issue in their lives.[5] Drawing on the poetics of the corrido, Paredes's prose poem gives aesthetic life to the precursory dead in order to reengage them in a struggle for cultural life and death.

As José Saldívar (1991) has brilliantly noted, one specific site of such a struggle is to be found in the way that Paredes's book contests the authoritative depiction of the Texas Rangers as law-abiding, fearless, virtuous warriors of the plains, a portrait whose principal source is the writings of the eminent historian Walter Prescott Webb. At issue is the historical exculpation of the Texas Rangers for the cold-blooded killing of hundreds, if not thousands, of border Mexicans. Paredes brings back the Dead to haunt those, like Webb, who would shelter history's murderers.

But there is another kind of murder that Webb's version of history commits, and that is to ideologically erase the culture of its victims by casting them as social and cultural inferiors, cowardly mixed-blood bandits wholly deserving of their deaths and their culture's extinction. As such, Webb's book is but one example of a field of dominating discourses chiefly, but not exclusively, historical and social scientific that prevailed in the post–World War II period. The net ideological effect of this discourse is to continuously delegitimize Mexican-American culture and to present it as a wholly *internally* generated and shaped constellation of socially dysfunctional values (Romano 1968; Vaca 1970).

Later in his career Paredes offered his own explicit assessment of this body of literature (1978), but his study of Gregorio Cortez constitutes a poetically constructed critique of these hegemonic discourses at a critical historical moment. Taking its poetic influence from a socially influential folk poem, Paredes's own poem also works its own social influence.

In this particular struggle against the discourses of domination, Jameson's first level of political history—"of punctual event and a chroniclelike sequence of happenings in time"—has a greater analytical importance than Jameson seems to give it (1981:75). That is, for many Mexican-Americans, at that historical moment, any record of the events of their history was of great political significance. For those who had been told that Mexican-Americans had no history or, worse still, a history of social deviance, the mere knowledge of a heroic figure like Cortez and of the formal complexity of the corrido could have a decisive counterhegemonic effect. Departing from this initial, literal kind of political awareness, Paredes's book then places these cultural performances in a context of class power relations. Using what Rosaldo (1985:410) calls a fine nonreductive sense of the relationship between culture and power, Paredes's prose poem offered the Mexican-American intelligentsia a level of analysis in which class and social domination became the principal lenses for reading. Both Cortez and the Texas Rangers become ideologemes for class, as does Paredes's prose corrido itself; as a text, it represents a continuing race and class struggle by Mexican-Americans against domination. The potency of the book's ideology did not escape the University of Texas Press, which, according to Paredes, at first refused to publish the book unless he deleted all critical references to Walter Prescott Webb and the Texas Rangers. He refused, the Press eventually relented, and the book appeared.

However, Paredes's book accomplishes its first two political missions because it fundamentally relies on its ideology of form, Jameson's third level of reading. As we have seen, *With His Pistol in His Hand* is, to a considerable extent, like its precursor, a story told "simply and swiftly, without embellishments." Yet *With His Pistol in His Hand* also offers an early example of what is now called the "experimental moment" in anthropological writing (Clifford and Marcus 1986; Marcus and Fischer 1986).[6] Arguing the need for a critically reflexive postmodern ethnography, Fischer, for example, recommends the practice of "intertextuality, inter-reference, and the interlinguistic modalities of post-modernist knowledge," the use of "multiple voices and perspectives, the highlighting of humorous inversions and dialectical juxtaposition of identities/traditions/cultures, and the critique of hegemonic discourses," creative techniques that can "contribute to a reinvigorated ethnographic literature, one that can again fulfill the anthropological promise of cultural criticism" (1986:202).

By "intertextuality" Fischer refers partially to the tendency in some ethnic autobiography to shape the present text as an often transforming repetition of "behavior patterns previously established toward some prior significant other," often a father figure. This is the psychoanalytical concept of transference, "the return of the repressed in new forms" (p. 206), which results in the generation of the ethnic text as the "conquest of an anxiety . . . that cannot be articulated in rational language but can only be acted out" (p. 204)—relations, Fischer notes, that are the subject of Bloom's work on the poetics of influence.

As a multiple-voiced performance, *With His Pistol in His Hand* is just such a polyphonic ethnography, a dialectical juxtaposition of identities, traditions, and cultures. In addition to the obvious contrast between Anglo and Mexican, Paredes shows us the varying identities within the Mexican-descent community itself. A few examples. In chapter 2, "The Legend," a fictional traditional figure recalls the singing of "El Corrido de Gregorio Cortez" and says,

> "That was good singing, and a good song; give the man a drink. Not like these *pachucos* nowadays, mumbling damn-foolishness into a microphone; it is not done that way. Men should sing with their heads thrown back, with their mouths wide open and their eyes shut. Fill your lungs, so they can hear you at the pasture's end." (p. 34)

And, we discover that our mythic hero also has several identities, including some not so heroic, which speak to gender and domination and which Paredes critiques with a kind of humorous inversion. For when Cortez is finally captured and brought to jail, *several* women show up to claim him as theirs, even while his poor wife also waits in jail.

Humor, irony, and inversion, however, best serve Paredes in attacking hegemonic Anglo racist discourses about Mexicans in Texas, and here too he borrows from the corrido tradition, which often makes fun of Anglos. Paredes quotes Webb: " 'Without disparagement, it may be said that there is a cruel streak in the Mexican nature, or so the history of Texas would lead one to believe. This cruelty may be a heritage from the Spanish of the Inquisition; it may, and doubtless should, be attributed partly to the Indian blood.' " Nonetheless, despite this cruel streak, Webb describes " 'the Mexican warrior' " as inferior: " 'The whine of the leaden slugs stirred in him an irresistible impulse to travel with rather than against the music.' " To all this, Paredes wryly comments: "Professor Webb does not mean to be disparaging. One wonders what his opinion might have been when he was in a less scholarly mood and not looking at the Mexican from the objective point of view of the historian" (p. 17). Later, in his discussion of the shoot-out between Cortez and Sheriff Morris, Paredes ironically appropriates and juxtaposes Webb's observations in a new context. After Morris is shot, his deputy runs, according to Paredes, preferring to "travel with rather than against the music" made by "the whine of leaden slugs" (p. 63).

Multiple voices, inversions, humor and irony, and the dialectical juxtaposition of identities, traditions, and cultures: these are, for Fischer, the techniques that can be of service to the writing of a new kind of ethnography. And in some incipient anticipatory way, Paredes's book involves just such practices, including also the blurring of genres between ethnic autobiography and historical ethnography, between folk poetic forms and "the poetics and politics of ethnography" (Clifford and Marcus 1986). The text's blurring of forms as such constitutes a critique by way of an alternative model to the linear, hierarchical discourses in the service of advanced capitalism.

Yet, these anticipatory formal messages of a new kind of cultural production do not constitute the formal totality of Paredes's book. It is not a postmodernist tract, not vulnerable to the suspect collusion between postmodernism and the later stages of advanced capitalism (Jameson 1984). This tendency toward a politically problematic "future" mode of cultural production is checked precisely by the corrido's influence on *With His Pistol in His Hand*. Suspended as it were between a style of the future and an older precursory expressive mode—a definition of modernism I will elaborate in my concluding chapter—Paredes's ideology of form is perfectly positioned—unlike "Guitarreros"—to speak its political unconscious to a new generation, itself modernist in character.

Through its very form *With His Pistol in His Hand* became an important rhetorical vehicle for reaching a particular audience in the late fifties and sixties. It is an ideological statement in which the writing of a culture partakes of the culture itself rather than objectifying, reifying, or distancing it. In Williams's terms, we may say that it is able to be superbly effective in the present as a counterhegemonic discourse. It is precisely so because it so wholly incorporates the now residual form of the corrido into the crafting of a therefore more potent emergent cultural practice that already anticipates the future. But this process of incorporation requires the poet's own internal axis of confrontation with his strong precursors, even as he confronts the political present. The potent Dead return to shape Paredes's late poem, but also to speak once again politically against a continuing domination of the Mexican-descent community in the United States. Yet, while this complex representation of a powerful residual tradition worked against domination, in large part it did so by speaking its mediated message to a specific and new audience—a new generation of Mexican-American intellectual literary activists.

PART TWO

SOCIAL CONFLICT, EMERGENT POETRY, AND THE NEW EPHEBES

But, if we are to grasp the long-term significance of the ethnic revival, and not reduce it to the limited issue of the current upsurge of ethnicity in the West, which has provoked so much comment, then we have to take a much broader historical perspective and shift our emphasis away from immediate technological or economic issues to a consideration of the slower rhythms of political formation and cultural change.

Anthony D. Smith,
The Ethnic Revival

Cultures are slow to die; when they do, they bequeath large deposits of custom and value to their successors; and sometimes they survive long after their more self-conscious members suppose them to have vanished.

Irving Howe, *World of Our Fathers*

4

Chicano Poetry and Politics
The Later Recognition of the Precursor

It was a little difficult to read the rough, hand-lettered collapsing sign that once had been firmly tied to one of the oak trees on the West Mall of the University of Texas at Austin. In the early fall of 1966, a steady drizzle had done its slow destructive work, but most of the writing was legible enough to attract my attention. Scrawled on one of the several pieces of the sign, the word "Mexican," like a powerful magnet, arrested my fast walk to the library and pulled me toward the oak. I went up to the tree and visually reassembled the blurred words—"American," "students," "farmworkers," "support," "meeting," and the time and place of the latter. Another piece of the sign, already sliding close to the ground, bore some poetry—a Mexican folk proverb—"Una mano no se lava sola" (A single hand cannot wash itself). That night at the meeting, I joined what would later be called the Chicano movement— *el movimiento*—and lent my hand to its development.

The mixture of politics and poetry that had brought me to this first meeting continued there. As arriving students crowded into the room at the Texas Union and milled around, someone played records of corridos on a small record player. Sounds and titles from my childhood and teenage years—"Arnulfo Gonzalez," "Valentín de la Sierra," "Jacinto Treviño"—that I had forgotten in the last few years at the university gradually became familiar once again. This time, however, it was in an academic context where such "Mexican" folk songs did not belong. Or did they?

Over the years since, I was to ask myself this question in different ways and with different answers. This book is one partial answer. First, however, like a traditional corrido singer, I ask my audience's permission to continue with my narrative and set out a more extended political and poetic context for my inquiry.

I was very much like the fifty or so other students who attended that first meeting and the formation of the Mexican-American Student Organization, later the Mexican-American Youth Organization. Shortly thereafter we would discover that we were also very much like many other Mexican-American students holding similar meetings on campuses throughout the nation, particularly in the Southwest. Of Mexican-American descent and from a lower-working-class background, born and raised in a predominantly Mexican-American south Texas—the country's poorest region—I was slightly different from the others perhaps only in being a little older and a first-year graduate student in English in what then appeared to be a roomful of undergraduate sociology majors. Whether students of sociology or English, at Texas or UCLA, we had other things in common. Almost without exception, we were the first in our families to attend college, not to mention a major university; indeed, many were the first in their families to graduate from high school. We were scholarship boys and girls, the first in our families to experience the full culture of a higher education in all its negative and positive dimensions. And, while we are on the subject of boys and girls, it is essential to note what was commonplace and taken for granted in 1966: As I listened to the corridos in that Texas Union room, I started going around the room meeting *men* students, encountering women only when I made my way to be served at a food and drink table, food and drink they had prepared.

For most of us, attending a major university meant encountering regions, institutions, student bodies, and faculties at some social and cultural distance from our ethnic, working-class life experience. Our lives thus far had been fundamentally shaped by a sharp antagonistic relationship with precisely those sectors of Anglo-American society that predominated in our new academic milieu. Fraternity boys, our present and future rulers, riding by in expensive cars might yell, "Go home, grease balls!" We were used to that. But it was a new, more difficult, and far more unsettling experience to hear a distinguished anthropologist at Texas lecturing on the "fatalism" of Mexican-Americans and their cultural disinterest in education. (This, after I had been the beneficiary of a Mexican-American *jamaica*—a community church bazaar in my parish—to raise funds so that I could buy books when I left for college.)

In this moment of some ambivalence and considerable alienation, this college generation was eventually led to political and cultural action by the most deprived sector of the Mexican-American community—the agricultural workers. In the early 1960s, and on their own initiative, farm laborers in California, south Texas, and everywhere else that Mexican-American agricultural workers were to be found began, once more, a period of intense labor unionization and a struggle for a better life.[1] Led principally by Cesar Chavez, this farmworkers' movement proved to be a cultural catalyst for Mexican-American students, providing us with a central symbol in which to ground our political and cultural sentiments and our new education. As the least acculturated and most economically exploited members of Mexican-American society, the farmworkers were an ideal resolving symbol. Their heroic struggle both authenticated native Mexican-American culture and furnished a focal point for needed social analysis and action. It may well be said that the Mexican-American student movement started in the mid-sixties initially as a series of farmworker support committees on campuses in the Southwest and across the country. This campus committee work provided financial and material assistance to the farmworkers, usually by way of food drives, personnel to walk picket lines in the fields, and the organization and direction of boycotts of nonunionized farm products in the cities where the campuses were located.

But without ever abandoning this focal concern with the agricultural sector, the Mexican-American student movement soon embraced other political and cultural concerns, beginning with its own autonomous definition as a student movement and the formation of campus organizations such as the Mexican-American Youth Organization (MAYO) in Texas and El Movimiento Estudiantil de Chicanos en Aztlán (MECHA) almost everywhere else. Indeed, before long, the growing sense of autonomous cultural politics led to the articulation of a new name for this movement and its members: Chicano.[2]

Next to standards of living in the agricultural sector, education—or lack of it—was, and continues to be, the most pressing social issue for the Mexican-American community. The high school dropout rate for Mexican-Americans was alarmingly high. Because of the problem's saliency and their own site of struggle in educational institutions, education became the paramount issue for students in the Chicano movement, and they addressed this concern in three broad ways. First, they assisted community-level groups in attacking local public school districts for their failure to properly educate young Mexican-Americans. Second, Chicano students pressured the colleges and universities they were attending to increase the admission and retention of Chicano students. Finally, and perhaps of longest-lasting consequence, the Chicano movement sought to change the cultural and intellectual climate of the university to reflect the cultural and intellectual presence of Mexican-Americans. To this end, they argued for the creation of new curriculums, new research units, and the hiring of faculty specialists. They also emphasized the need for support and sponsorship, both within the university and in the society at large, of Mexican-American culture and the arts, particularly the literary arts (Gómez-Quiñones 1979; Acuña 1981:355–65).[3] Given the central interests of this study, we need to say more about these literary developments.

THE CHICANO LITERARY CONTEXT

In chapter 1, I strongly implied the impossibility of imagining the turn-of-the-century greater Mexican revolutionary period without corridos. Similarly, it is equally impossible to conceive of the Chicano movement from 1965 to 1972 without its artistic literature, particularly its poetry. Though this moment of literary history still awaits an extended treatment, Tomás Ybarra-Frausto offers us a fine survey of the key features—sociological and poetic—of the period:

> In the decade of the 60s, a generation of Chicano poets propelled by a new sense of identity and a profound awareness of their cultural heritage achieved prominence as their poetry questioned the limitations and presumptions of the dominant literary establishment. Seeking new forms and a new vocabulary, they created alternative outlets for publication and established the poetry reading as an integral part of the mass mobilization of the period. The creation of a mass audience through the establishment of a Chicano underground press, collective readings and sponsorship of *festivales de flor y canto* was an attempt at removing poetry from the market and commodity system and establishing it as a central concern of daily life. If the prevailing mood in the literature of the dominant culture was one of skepticism and anguish, Chicano poetry of the 1960s presented a positive alternative as it projected itself with human dimensions and human concerns. Poetry was made accessible, optimistic and reflective of a manifest struggle against cultural and human despoliation. (1978:104–5)

Four themes in Ybarra-Frausto's assessment bear directly on my general argument: the poetry's awareness of its cultural heritage; its intimate connection with a militant politics; the collective social circulation of this art, especially the oral transmission of the poetry at readings and at the annual Chicano *flor y canto* (flower and song) literary festivals; and the poetry's sense of optimism and humanity against the dominant culture's skepticism and anguish concerning the human condition—though toward the end of the period, there was a strain, never dominant, of a modernist "skepticism and anguish." In all these respects, we can already sense an affinity with and a transforming continuation of the cultural poetics of the corrido.

One cannot emphasize too strongly the constant copresence of poetry and politics during this period. Moreover, it was a time when Chicano poetry was almost exclusively the province of male poets: José Montoya, Rodolfo "Corky" Gonzales, Juan Gómez-Quiñones, Tomás Rivera, Ricardo Sánchez, Alurista, Sergio Elizando, Rolando Hinojosa, Abelardo Delgado, Rudolfo Anaya, Miguel Mendez, Tino Villanueva, and Raul Salinas, among others. Bruce-Novoa's study of fourteen Chicano authors includes only two women, Bernice Zamora and Estela Portillo, and his authoritative book on Chicano poetry includes only one woman, Zamora, among thirteen poets (Bruce-Novoa 1980, 1982).

A decisive shift toward a female-dominated poetry in the seventies and into the eighties was inaugurated by Estela Portillo's editorship in 1973 of the first major collection of Chicana writing (Portillo 1973). Marta Sánchez does not fully historicize but clearly acknowledges this interesting gender shift in her more recent study of Chicana poetry (1985), a shift sharply coincident with the historically specific emergence of other forms of Chicana feminist discourse in the mid-seventies (García 1989). However, in the sixties and very early seventies both Chicano politics and Chicano poetry were dominated by charismatic men. Rodolfo Acuña, one of the most active participants in, and better observers of, the Chicano movement has offered this telling insight:

> The entire Chicano leadership pattern, in face, closely resembled the pattern of the Mexican Revolution, where revolutionary juntas and local leaders emerged. These leaders took care of their home bases and were supported by their own followers . . . all adhered to this basic pattern, inspiring intense loyalty among their followers. (1981:360)

Indeed, Acuña himself is a strong example of his own description of this male legacy of leadership, with its conjunctive relationship to the influential trajectory of the earlier revolutionary, also male-dominated, corrido period.

THE CORRIDO AS MEDIATED
PRECURSOR

The general influence of the corrido on Chicano poetry in the 1960s has not escaped critical notice. For all of its residual character, the corrido still had a live, direct presence in the consciousness of those involved in the movement, either from our immediate working-class background or as part of the emergent political culture. New and old corridos were sung at farmworker and other political rallies as well as at literary festivals like *flor y canto*. The influence of the corrido, however, was also absorbed in a mediated fashion through the widespread reading of Paredes's *With His Pistol in His Hand* and the gradual emergence of its author's charismatic social persona. Together they also provided the continuing mediated poetics of the precursor, a poetics never separate from politics.

We can substantiate this particular relationship with extended testimony from one of the leading Mexican-American literary intellectuals of this generation, Tomás Rivera. At the time he is describing, Rivera was a graduate student at Southwest Texas State University in San Marcos, Texas.

Back in 1958, we thought writing should be a money-making proposition. To make money there had to be a gimmick, we thought, so we went to the people who were making it at the time, Mickey Spillane and people like that. We actually tried to imitate Spillane. We thought people would notice, that it would bring us fame and glory. We sent off the manuscripts *y pues nada* [and nothing]. *Los chicanos que metíamos allí* [The Chicanos we stuck in there] were cooks and prostitutes, very stereotyped characters, as were the Anglo ones. I don't demean cooks or prostitutes, just the fact that we would stereotype them without benefit of dignity.

Then, one day I was wandering through the library and I came across *With a Pistol in His Hand* by Américo Paredes, and I was fascinated. I didn't even know Paredes existed, though we were only thirty miles away, *pero no había comunicación alguna porque no había Movimiento ni nada de eso. Saqué el libro ese. Lo que me atrajo fue el apellido Paredes* [but there was no communication at all, because there wasn't a Movement or anything like that. I checked out that book. What attracted me was the name *Paredes*]. I was hungry to find something by a Chicano or Mexican-American. It fascinated me because, one, it proved it was possible for a Chicano to publish; two, it was about a Chicano, Gregorio Cortez, *y sus azañas* [and his deeds]. (*Y los corridos, también* [And the ballads, too], I grew up with the *corridos de Texas*.) That book indicated to me that it was possible to talk about a Chicano as a complete figure. I went back to the old newspapers and checked the accounts for how they handled Gregorio Cortez and found the grotesque exaggeration, as Américo says. Then I would go back to Américo's book and wonder which one was right. Was Américo lying too? Was he overdoing it *también*

[also]? More importantly, *With a Pistol in His Hand* indicated to me a whole imaginative possibility for us to explore. Now that, also, was in 1958, and it was then I began to think, write, and reflect a hell of a lot more on those people I had known in 1945 to '55.

That's the personal trajectory of the evolution of my role as documenter. I guess that sense of it came from feeling that Américo had documented one person *para siempre* [forever]. It was very important. I felt that I had to document the migrant worker *para siempre* [forever], *para que no se olvidara ese espíritu tan fuerte de resistir y continuar* under the worst of conditions [so that their very strong spirit of endurance and the will to go on under the worst of conditions should not be forgotten], because they were worse than slaves. *El esclavo es una inversión* [A slave is an investment], so you protect him to keep him working. A migrant worker? You owe him nothing. If he came to you, you gave him work and then just told him to leave. No investment. If he got sick, you got rid of him; you didn't have to take care of him. It was bad, labor camps and all that. (1980:150–51)

Rivera's statement is key in several respects.[4] For one, it clearly reveals the effects of cultural hegemony on young Mexican-Americans, a hegemony that fostered an ambivalence toward their native culture and led them to internalize and reproduce negative stereotyping discourses; for Rivera, "cooks and prostitutes." But for a Mexican-American intelligentsia, particularly those with a strong desire to write, there seemed to be no alternative discourse, no useful models from which to speak, to resolve that lingering ambivalence, until "one day wandering through the library," as Rivera says, or perhaps at a bookstore, they came across *With His Pistol in His Hand* and then passed it around like a Holy Writ.

To find Paredes's book was to discover at least three things not at all evident to young Mexican-Americans in the early 1960s. First, young Chicanos discovered the probability that the received conventional history of the Mexican experience in the Southwest was distorted and falsified. Mexicans were not bandits; they were, or could be, like Cortez, men of honor, integrity, and courage. Equally important in this regard was the converse proposition, namely that Anglos had not always acted as paragons of virtue and civic obligation, nor was their authority legitimate. Second, young Chicanos recognized what Rivera calls "the imaginative possibility" of Paredes's book, the fascinating discovery that, contrary to dominant stereotypes, Mexican-Americans could write creatively in a modernist style. The name *Paredes* on the book's cover "proved it was possible for a Chicano to publish." Rivera's reading of

Paredes's book articulates, once again, Jameson's first and third levels of the political unconscious. But, in the 1960s Paredes's prose corrido also evoked an explicitly conscious sense of race and class relations, a sense evident in Rivera's reading also. For Rivera absorbs Paredes's corrido influence and uses it to focus our attention on the still continuing social plight of Mexican-Americans. He speaks of a world of politically produced social deprivation, of racial stigma, of disempowerment most visibly evident in farmworker society but by no means confined to it.

Yet even as the text of *With His Pistol in His Hand* provided the powerfully mediated influence of the precursory corrido to a new generation, the author of the text did so as well. When people in the Chicano movement gathered and the conversation turned to the subject of Américo Paredes, one could often detect the gradual emergence of an unsung proto-ballad of Américo Paredes. It is as if such conversations—a kind of Chicano movement oral tradition—constructed the known life and career of this man into a folklore narrative combining ballad and legend. Like all narratives, this narrative varied from group to group and performance to performance. Certain motifs were sometimes stated, sometimes implied, but the overall narrative structure that emerged recalled the traditional ballad's and legendry's thematic structure.

As with the traditional ballad, these conversations first established a setting and implied a social context for the appearance of the hero and the central narrative action. In our conversations, the story sometimes began with a confrontation between our hero and the Anglo authorities: An Anglo teacher tells the young Paredes that college is not for boys "like him"; has he considered attending vocational school? Or an assimilationist middle-class Mexican-American publisher in San Antonio refuses to publish Paredes's early stridently ethnic nationalist poems. Or, perhaps most dramatic of all, in the late 1950s the chief editor of the University of Texas Press refuses to publish *With His Pistol in His Hand* unless Paredes deletes all critical references to Walter Prescott Webb, J. Frank Dobie, and the Texas Rangers. Paredes refuses to do so, and the editor finally relents. When the book does appear, a former Texas Ranger tries to get Paredes's address from the Press so that he can "pistol whip the sonofabitch who wrote that book."

This conversational proto-narrative then fills in the hero's background in a way that is almost absolutely factual and yet has the aura of legendry. Our hero was born in the auspicious year of 1915, during the height of the Texas Rangers' killing of Mexican-Americans in south

Texas. He is said to be a good and simple man, but also already a bit extraordinary, highly gifted intellectually and a bit of the bohemian. He is exceptionally attractive to women and highly respected by men, a well-known popular singer on radio programs, a prize-winning poet and a journalist, a man who could and did defend his family's honor. The narrative continues. Paredes marries and divorces a well-known, equally bohemian local popular singer. Restless and curious about life beyond south Texas, he leaves the border and eventually winds up in central Texas, near Karnes County, at the University of Texas at Austin—but not before spending a few years as a correspondent in Japan and China after World War II. "Did you know that Don Américo covered the Chinese Revolution?" says someone.

When he does arrive at the University of Texas to study English literature and creative writing—his central career goal—he faces another racially motivated confrontation: the U.S. government initially refuses a visa to his wife because she is half Japanese. For a moment Paredes thinks of living in Mexico, but the government relents. Now in his mid-thirties and a married man with children, Paredes had already completed two years of community college coursework. He completes his bachelor's degree with highest honors in one year, a master's in two, and then a doctorate in three more, while teaching several sections of freshman English to support his family. During this period, he also publishes a few scholarly articles, short stories, and poems and wins two writing prizes. He reworks his dissertation on the balladry and life of Gregorio Cortez into *With His Pistol in His Hand*, teaches for one year in El Paso, and is invited to rejoin the Department of English at Texas as a faculty member.

As a faculty member from 1958 to 1966, Paredes engages in an intellectual politics that continually attacks the dominant society's disparaging view of Mexican-Americans. His chief weapon is his careful creative scholarship on Mexican-American history. He also tries to promote social activism among the university's Mexican-American students, but the assimilationist perspective is still too prevalent among them at that time, and they do not respond to his efforts. Like Gregorio Cortez, Paredes finds himself engaging the opposition largely alone, although he does find a Romaldo-like "brother" in George I. Sanchez, a progressive professor.

While Cortez had aroused the consciousness of his community by riding and shooting his way toward them and soliciting their help,

Paredes's ideological and cultural community began to come to him in the mid-sixties. The hero and the nascent Chicano student movement in Texas and throughout the Southwest joined in struggle and mutual support on issues such as the farmworkers, the need for courses in Mexican-American studies, and increased political representation. (The hero's legend continues to develop to the present day: "I thought he was *real* tall!" says a Chicano at the University of California at Santa Barbara when he first meets Paredes.) Together, then, this author and his book provided one model for the development of the Chicano movement, and that model was itself wholly indebted to the precursory master poem—the corrido.

In this way, the corrido was historically repositioned by the Chicano movement to permit the genre to have a continuing influence on the development of contemporary Chicano literature. As Erlinda Gonzales-Berry observes, "many of today's poets were undoubtedly nourished on *corridos* and popular verse forms which abound in oral tradition" (1980:45). This judgment is supported by Sergio Elizondo, who notes the corrido's influence on Chicano poets, with "Alurista, Albelardo and Ricardo Sánchez, among the best known" (1980:73). More specifically, for my purposes, José Saldívar, in a fine "precis," as he calls it, offers a succinct analysis of the corrido and its influence, and argues for the significance of Jameson's theoretical work for a new Chicano literary criticism. On the corrido's centrality to Chicano poetry, Saldívar writes: "A study of Chicano literature must . . . begin with an attempt to define at least one of the cultural paradigms which emerge from the historical experience of the Chicano Border frontier life" and "I am suggesting that the *corrido* is the central sociopoetic Chicano paradigm" (1986:13).

Curiously, however, Saldívar then seems not to see how widespread the influence of the corrido is: "Given the strength of the *corrido* paradigm in the Chicano experience, it is bewildering that subsequent contemporary Chicano poets have not looked to it consciously or unconsciously for structuration and content" (1986:13). As we have already seen, the maleness of Chicano poetry from 1965 to 1972, its close identification with a charismatic male politics, its direct and mediated indebtedness to the corrido are defining characteristics of this poetic period. I would add still another: the saliency of the long poem, or what Ortega calls "narrative or saga poetry, relating a Chicano world vision" (1977:35).[5] Formally, this saliency might be explained by the political necessity to undertake a sustained dialectical engagement with the full scope of past and present history, a motivation perhaps, for all epic engagements. But is not such an overweening, aggressive poetic ambition also clearly related to the maleness of the period? Moreover, I propose, the Chicano long poem of the period is also generated by the continuing powerful influence of the only other long poem in the greater Mexican experience—the epic heroic corrido—and the necessity for young, aggressive Chicano males to come to grips with its daunting political and patriarchal poetics.

THE EPIC HEROIC CORRIDO AND THREE POETIC CULTURAL REVISIONS

In the chapters that follow I chart, intertextually, the corrido's precursory poetic influence on three major Chicano poets: José Montoya, Rodolfo "Corky" Gonzales, and Juan Gómez-Quiñones—each a charismatic figure in the Chicano movement of 1965–1972 who has continued to have a significant presence. Each of the three has authored a long poem in which there is a clear and sustained recognition of the precursor. Yet while the precursor's presence is obvious, the nature of his influence is not—that is my task in these pages. These three also represent different activist emphases within the movement—Montoya in the arts, Gonzales in public politics, and Gómez-Quiñones in intellectual life—which is not to say that they do not share these emphases as well; Gonzales, for example, continues to be active in alternative education and Gómez-Quiñones is a key figure in California politics, while Montoya is also a college professor.

For readers who wonder why I have not included Alurista, Sergio Elizondo, Raul Salinas, and Ricardo Sánchez—all authors of long poems and recognized figures in the Chicano movement—I can at first plead the worst of authorial defenses—time and space considerations—but also offer other, better reasons as well.[6] First, notwithstanding Elizondo's observation that one can detect the corrido's influence on Alurista and Sánchez, I am not persuaded that this influence is as clearly marked and poetically negotiated as it is with the poets I have chosen. Rather, Alurista and Sánchez are engaged with a collage of influences, none really master precursors, from pre-Hispanic, indigenous poetics to the "beat" poetry of the fifties, to African American culture. The result is an interesting but rhetorically overextended and incoherent poetry in search of a sustaining tradition. Something of this same argument applies to Raul Salinas's engaging "Trip Through the Mind Jail" (its very title and dedication to Eldridge Cleaver already partial evidence), though I find it a more successful poem, one more conscious of a sustaining tradition. But Salinas's primary precursor is not the corrido so much as, perhaps, the most famous of greater Mexican legends, *la llorona* (the Wailing Woman), although I am as yet not clear on this. (For my discussion of *la llorona*, see Limón 1986a.)

In contrast, Elizondo's own *Perros y Anti-Perros* (Dogs and Anti-Dogs) makes for a better case in terms of the influence of the corrido, at least on the formal grounds of structure and meter. Yet there is some question as to whether Elizondo meant his work to be an "epic" as its subtitle, an editorial appendage, suggests (Bruce-Novoa 1982:96), rather than what it most manifestly is, a collection of distinct, though related, poems.

Finally, there is the more vexing case of Rolando Hinojosa's "Korean Love Songs." Neither the poet nor his work were an organic part of the sixties political culture, though Ramón Saldívar (1984) has analyzed the poem in terms quite consistent with those employed here.

In the three long poems I have chosen, on the other hand, the influence of the corrido is most salient. Moreover, these three poems seem to me to embody and express three particular sociocultural attitudes toward history and society within the Chicano movement of those years. For the Chicano community, these poems became what anthropologist Sherry Ortner (1973) calls redressive key symbols, texts that articulate poetically discursive, narrative cultural modes of viewing and addressing one's world.

All of us who participated in the movement can recall a moment, in 1965 or 1966, of initial confusion and groping as we sought to define and then come to terms with our estranged sociocultural condition, both with respect to our present and our past. It is this initial condition of Alienation that José Montoya well exemplifies in "El Sol y los de Abajo." This alienated condition seemed to resolve itself in the late sixties, as a new mood of Assertion in conjunction with a strident and dominating cultural nationalism appeared. No one will dispute that Rodolfo "Corky" Gonzales's "I Am Joaquín" is the exemplary assertive statement, poetic or otherwise, of this period. Finally, the years 1970 to 1972 marked the movement's simultaneous diminishment and recognition of the need for more sophisticated, complex understandings

capable of taking us into the next decade. This new introspective attitude of Reflection is exemplified by the work of Juan Gómez-
Quiñones.

At each of these moments, the long influential hand of the fatherly
precursor—the epic heroic corrido and its political culture—mediated
by Américo Paredes, shaped and was shaped by the new ephebes. But
these new ephebes were also children of women and of modernism,
and it is through these poetic and political resources that the struggle
with society and the precursor were to be waged.

We lived in Oakland during the war so everyone in the family could work in the defense plant; my *jefita* [mother], my dad, my two sisters, and a brother. I spent my time in the streets of East Oakland. Those were the good times. In early 1950, my *jefito* [father] split out to New Mexico, but we stayed.

José Montoya, "Interview"

We are alone. Solitude, the source of anxiety, begins on the day we are deprived of maternal protection and fall into a strange and hostile world.

Octavio Paz,
The Labyrinth of Solitude

5

My Old Man's Ballad
José Montoya and the Power Beyond

No Mexican-American intellectual coming to political and cultural awareness in the mid-1960s could have missed the enormous significance of the appearance of *El Grito: A Journal of Contemporary Mexican-American Thought*, published in Berkeley in 1967. Edited by Octavio Romano and Nick Vaca in its initial phase, *El Grito* was the first major publication of the Chicano movement, and its effect on the emergent political and cultural consciousness of young Chicanos cannot be overestimated. The first political analyses of race and class domination, the first trenchant critiques of the social sciences, and the first contemporary creative writing by Chicanos appeared in that exciting journal. Two years later Romano published *El Espejo* (The Mirror), an important collection of writings from *El Grito* as well as new contributions.

In greater Mexican culture, a *grito* means a yell or cry in an everyday sense. In a more socially marked sense, however, it refers to a battle cry or a cry for political action such as that by Father Hidalgo for Mexican independence from Spain in 1810. It can also refer to a celebratory cry that men, usually, may make when they particularly like a cultural performance, a song such as a corrido. In all its denotations, a *grito* is usually a male-gendered performance, and the journal's title was well suited to the muscular critical character of the texts, almost exclusively by male authors, that its editors chose to print. For these reasons, José Montoya's "La Jefita," a female-centered poem, stood out among these early writings. (*Jefita*, "little chief," is a slang honorific for "mother.") The poem begins

> When I remember the camps
>   And the nights and the sounds
> Of those nights in tents or
> Carts I remember my *jefita*'s
>   Rolling pin
>   Clik-clok; clik-clak-clok

And her small cough.
(I swear she never slept!)
(Montoya 1969a)[1]

A painter and art teacher by profession, José Montoya has been and continues to be one of the premiere political cultural activists in the Chicano movement. Originally from New Mexico, now active in the Bay Area, he has worked in rural and urban community organizing, and with Chicano prisoners, has founded Chicano poetry and art groups and taught Chicano studies at California State University at Sacramento—all with a deep concern and love for his people and with a sense of barely muted outrage at their social mistreatment (Bruce-Novoa 1980:115–36).

A widely anthologized author and a prolific and engaging reader of his poetry in public settings, Montoya can be said to have launched his poetic career with the publication of "La Jefita," a depiction in verse of a documented Mexican-American farmworker's existence. At the center of this charming, well-wrought poem is a tender, sensitive rendering of the speaker's mother. She is at the heart and hearth of this dominated universe, mitigating its corrosive effects with her nurturing familial love. In contrast, the speaker's father occupies a "demanding and distant" role (Hernandez 1991:78) in this poetic world:

But by then it was time to get Up!
My old man had a little whistle
That initiated the world to
Wakefulness.
    Wheeeeeeeet! Wheeeeeeeet!
Get up, you damn lazy kids!
(Montoya 1969a)

Here, social domination is countered principally by the critical transcendence of maternal self-sacrifice, and, as Guillermo Hernandez observes, "The poetic voice conveys a feeling of rebellion toward the father, a figure whose role the narrator-son is condemned to imitate in life" (1991:78).

We also note that "La Jefita," in its muted rebellion and pro-maternal stance, comes to us in a modernist idiom. Here, I refer to Montoya's acknowledged admiration for the poetry of Dylan Thomas (Montoya 1980b:50). For is there not in "La Jefita" a trace of the Welshman's rhythms and his rhetoric of remembrance of youthful innocence in the face of change? (I think of Thomas's "Lament," "Fern Hill," "I see the boys of summer," and "Once it was the colour of saying," in particular.)

In "La Jefita" Montoya is a long way from the epic heroic world of the corrido and, for that matter, from any poetically, politically aggressive public stance. Yet it is important to begin here, with this modernist female-centered poem, because it is this sort of poetic world that suggests Montoya had available one possible alternative—one kind of counterpoetics—when he did encounter the power of the precursor. Yet rather than elaborate this alternative poetic world, rather than refuse the traditional male-centered terms of struggle posed by the precursor, Montoya accepts the latter, and ultimately loses poetically, in his long work of 1972, "El Sol y los de Abajo" (The Sun and the Downtrodden). This poetic loss also limits the poem's public political capacities, although at the moment of its writing, circa 1965 (Hernandez 1991:53), it captures well all of our alienation and incapacities.

THE ARGUMENT OF
"EL SOL Y LOS DE ABAJO"

"El Sol y los de Abajo" opens with little to recommend it as a poem, at least in the first thirteen lines. What Montoya has to say is just that, *said*, with little poetic mediation. Prosaic language is arranged in the quadrangle shapes of a seeming poem to quite literally tell us that were it not for racism and class oppression, Mexicans might have made it as *hacendados* like one Don Ramon Hidalgo Salazar. Instead, we are, like the speaker's father, descendants of the underdogs who never reached our sun. Like him, we

> compounded the grief by
> abandoning his land for another
> so foreign and at once so akin
> as to be painful.
>   (Montoya 1972b)[2]

In the third stanza things improve somewhat with the poet's better sense of prosody. He seems to allude to Yeats's "A Dialogue of Self and Soul" to tell us that, like his father, "I have dragged"

> Myself and soul in some
> Unconscious, instinctive

Search for the splendor
De los templos del sol.

This stanza also alerts us to the poetic-political direction that the poem eventually takes. However, the poet suffers an immediate relapse as the fourth stanza returns us to an unimaginative catalogue mode of presentation. Those who did not reach the "temples of the sun," *los de abajo*—are to be found in the gutters, battlefields, cotton rows, and barrios, and the listing continues into the next stanza.

Nevertheless, this prosaic listing is poetically relieved in two places. Between stanzas four and five, we find the interesting though undeveloped image of a man caught inside a societal telescope; more importantly, toward the end of stanza six, the speaker compares his memories of tradition to Goya etchings. The unmediated memories of oppression dominate here, but we soon learn that the speaker also has other memories—memories of "Times that were *tiempos finos*" (fine times). The recollection of these better times brings forth better art.

The next nine to ten stanzas are indeed far better poetry. They are an artistic delineation of these "fine times" and emerge as a poetic and moral counterweight to the earlier poetically unrelieved catalogue of oppression. At the heart of these better, middle stanzas is a Mexican folkloric world of *curanderas* (female folk healers) such as the poetically well-wrought Doña Chole "la ruquilla" (little old woman):

with the ugly
Hump on her back—
La curandera, bruja, life-giving
Jorobada que curó a Don Cheno
Del dolor de umbligo y la
Calentura en la cintura.

The same *jorobada* (bent-over) healing *bruja* (witch) who cured Don Cheno of his umbilical pain and his stomach fever can also dispense potions for lovers who prayed

to a remarkably reasonable
God that their wives and husbands
Wouldn't find out . . .

I question whether the poem as a whole is a satire, as Hernandez (1991) seems to suggest; these fine stanzas, however, certainly do employ satire. These are engaging people who, with folk wisdom, try to outwit the Virgin Mary in contests of logic: "cause if my husband / Finds out, he will kill me and you / Wouldn't want him in heaven then, / Como asesino" (as a murderer). Contrary to the usual flat stereotypes, folk Mexicans treat the spiritual world, not with unrelieved reverence, but with a living, healthy, satirical skepticism, and this world is kept at a distance, "Until times of need, death/grief, / Despair y los otros tiempos pesados" (the other bad times). It is a folk-theological relationship of contradiction and paradox paralleling what Abraham Kaplan has called "the Jewish argument with God" (1980). Satirical contradiction and paradox also characterize these people's relationships to the more institutional and secular spheres of life. Here too we find a display of folk wit and wisdom, as in Montoya's stanza of reported folk speech where the mother takes ironical note of Father Kelly, whose wandering hands can also bless an escapulary.

The children eat and go out to play kick-the-can until this folkloric world of care, pain, and love is interrupted by *them*—the Americans—the social worker, probation officer, school counselor, and academic who come "to crucify me with germ-bearing / Labels more infectious than rusty / Nails . . .". We are no longer in the satirical mode. However, as if the reappearance of oppression threatens once again to overwhelm the poetic itself, our poet momentarily relapses into the prosaic, albeit the angry prosaic. But he soon recalls once again that his "dismal world was so / much brighter!" and begins to breathe new, creative rhythmic life into his poem by returning to the folk world, to

> the old barn across the canal
> that housed a lechusa that
> screeched at night scaring
> the children porque era la
> anima de la comadre de mi grama.

¡*Oigan!* (Listen!), his *abuelita*—his "grama"—tells the children. Listen to the screeching owl, which in her Mexican folk perception is the soul of her children's godmother Chonita. The dreary world of oppression is socially negated as the children are taken into a realm of mystery and magic that both fascinates and causes fear, but fear of a different order.

This poem now returns to the father, as the children run to him in fear. Here, the poet exploits the opportunity to remind us of *his* father with his "field-scarred limbs," "también arrastrado"—also a victim of oppression. But, like the women, the father also possesses the folk resources to negate the oppressiveness. "At least," the poet tells us, "his noble deeds / Are enriched in ballads," and with these words we enter the final stanzas of the poem:

> Pursued by dogs,
> The horseman
> Rode through the hills
> Well armed.

> A warrior for his cause,
> Noble were his deeds.
> Nor for glory nor for verse
> You rode to fight for your people.
>   (my translation)

Turning exclusively to a formal Spanish and a formal prosodic style, the poet renders a poetic homage to his father. The father is no longer the "field-scarred" victim but rather a "jinete" (a horseman) riding through the mountains pursued by *los perros*—literally "dogs," but metaphorically all institutional oppressors. Our horseman is well armed, however, and he is, like so many other Mexican ballad heroes, a fighter for a cause, and he defends his cause and his *raza* (his people) neither for personal glory nor for the poetic immortality of the ballads but because it is right. The son then attempts to transfer this formal poetic form and its social function to his own situation. He finds himself in the same situations, but under different conditions. But he interrupts his attempted self-comparison to the ballad world with an emphatic "*¡Chale!*" (a folk speech form meaning *no!*) And, why not? The poet returns still one more time to the prosaic, not with anger but with sadness and despair, and he tells us quite literally,

> My actions are not yet worthy
> of the ballads . . . me faltan
> los huevos de mi jefe and
> the ability to throw off
> the gava's llugo de
> confución . . .

His actions are "not yet worthy of the ballads"; lacking his father's *huevos* (balls), he is unable to throw off the Anglo's (*gava's*) yoke of confusion.

His confusion, however, is not total. He abruptly turns to Mayan prophecy. In the poet's time, "Chilam Balam's prophetic / Chant has been realized—and the / Dust that darkened the air begins / To clear y se empiesa a ver el Sol" (One can begin to see the sun). Evoking the famous prophecy of the ancient Mayan priest—that one day the Spaniards would disappear and the sun would reappear—the poet ends on a note of hope, but a hope not yet fully realized: "I am learning to see the sun."

Having explicated the poem's argument, I should now like to bring to bear on it a theoretical perspective that will elucidate the relationship between this poem and traditional Mexican folklore.

"EL SOL Y LOS DE ABAJO": GENDER, FOLKLORE, AND INFLUENCE

In "El Sol y los de Abajo," Montoya draws on two formative, yet contradictory, traditions. One is the raw, hegemonic social experience of racism and class domination, which at times threatens to extend its hegemony to the poem itself. That is, his experience of domination so overpowers his poetic sensibility as to become the almost wholly artistically and politically unmediated subject matter of the poem. The poem itself tends to become a reactive and ill-formed cry of *los de abajo*, a raw cry untransformed by a creative, critical, intelligent poetics. For a moment, this poem reminds us of what Montoya himself has said about so much early *movimiento* poetry, namely, that it was "really terrible" (1980a:134).

Yet there are moments when this poem does achieve a critical emergent cultural artistry. It does so when, in the manner of "La Jefita," Montoya draws on folkloric elements of his residual Mexican culture to strengthen his art. Yet this return to the residual itself does not yield even poetic profit. Montoya is far more poetically successful when he turns to the domain of female folklore than when he chooses to encounter and draw on the precursory power of the Mexican corrido. That the precursor's influence proves too great, as it did for Paredes in "Guitarreros," results in an unsuccessful public political poem. Such strength as it has—inward-facing and private though it is—results from the poet's temporary turn not to the powerful father influence, but rather to the maternal succor of greater Mexican culture.

I also read this poem as the creative rendering of a partial series of Bloom's poetic defensive strategies, or revisions. These are presented by our young poet—our ephebe—as defenses against the dominating influence of folk tradition, particularly the strong poetry of the Mexican ballad, which, of course, appears quite literally at the end of the poem, but whose influence, I maintain, is present throughout, including, paradoxically, in its very absence.

The poem opens with an explicit reference to the father, and just as the father is quite literally present in the poet's consciousness, the father's poem, the corrido, is also quite present in the poet's unconscious, to become manifest to consciousness later. But as a work of art, the poem in its first six stanzas is a near failure, almost no work of art at all, merely a prosaic catalogue, save for the "ocular tube" image. Clearly this is an artistically unrelieved catalogue of social domination, but its lack of poetic art is also the result of a too-felt paternal poetic domination. Only social domination and the father-figure appear prominently in these six stanzas in which the poem as compelling art has yet to begin. That is, we find no evidence—no poetic evidence—that this poet is yet an ephebe, a true poetic son engaged in a serious creative poetic struggle with his announced master. The father is too much.

Only in the final lines of stanza seven, in which the speaker carries his life experiences engraved "like the etching de Goya" do we begin to edge into a palpable poetry set off by remembrance, "I remember those times . . . / Times that were tiempos finos," which in this stanza occasion a fine sensibility to the folklore of Mexican women and a fine poetry, or at least, a better poetry. Had the poet wholly persisted in the poetic elaboration of this female-centered world, as he indeed does for some nine stanzas, we would have, perhaps, a fine companion piece to "La Jefita," this time written about *curanderas, comadres,* and *abuelitas* in resistance to *los americanos.*

But the father of the first stanza lingers, and he reappears strongly in the final stanzas—a patriarchal framing that forces us to view the intervening "female poetic" stanzas as a salient deviation. Following the paternally focused stanzas of domination, this maternally centered section is not merely an extended occasion for learning more about the poet-speaker's sociocultural life, a general opportunity for, in Cordelia Candelaria's reading, "a total immersion in that life through flashbacks to scenes from the speaker/poet's past" after stanzas that she benignly misreads as an "introduction" (1986:15). Rather, it is the poet's matriarchally focused poetic reaction and attempted early subversion of his original poetical patriarchal beginning.

Lending thus a gendered implication to Bloom's theory, I read this intervening matriarchal section as a *clinamen*, or Swerve, wholly away from the father. This move, we may recall once more, is a revision

> marked by dialectical images of absence and presence, images that are rhetorically conveyed by the trope of simple irony ... and that as psychic defense assume the shape of what Freud called reaction-formation.... Just as rhetorical irony says one thing and means another, even the opposite thing, so a reaction-formation opposes itself to a repressed desire by manifesting the opposite of the desire. (1975a:97)

Stanzas eight through sixteen constitute just such a Swerve from the father poem's influence in another direction, one marked by irony, by images of absence and presence. And, although Bloom does not explicitly say so, the *clinamen* is a likely province for satire, as Hernandez (1991:72) notes of this section of the poem.

Part of what is wholly absent here is not so much images *of* absence as *absent images* that might have reasonably flowed from the first seven stanzas of oppressed men in society: images of active male heroic resistance, that is, the poet's acknowledgment and rewriting of the corrido. What is wholly present, instead, are rich images of women's everyday conversational life, replete with "contradictions and paradoxes," the essence of irony, an irony almost wholly absent from the world of the corrido, where the trope of high romance prevails (White 1973:1–42; 1978:1–23).

For the corrido is a world of unambiguous right and wrong, of heroism and cowardice, of men who issue challenges in laconic boasts, who confront each other, pistols in hand, across a clear moral-political space. In the corridos the encounter is articulated in the race/class ideologemes of "Mexicanos" versus "Americanos." In Montoya's female-centered world of the middle poem, this encounter is less clear, cross-cut by internal contradiction and articulated in a welter of ironies and concrete dialogical images, that, while also ideologemes of race and class relations, are so indirectly; more truly, perhaps, they are examples of Jameson's political unconscious at its second level.

We learn of Father Kelly, who is supposed to minister to the spiritual needs of the Catholic community but cannot keep his hands off its female members. Families—to be more precise, women and young girls—quickly clean up their houses because the social worker is coming (or the school counselor, or census taker, or probation officer), and the social condition of such families becomes the stuff of a master's thesis by some "long haired / Lost lamb maric chick." A *curandera*, herself physically deformed, sustains life in this community—no doubt in dire need of medical resources—even as she provides customers with love potions for illicit love affairs. With more than a bit of ironic wit, she then prays to the Virgin Mary that her customers' husbands and wives not find out and that her own husband not discover the truth and kill her because the Virgin wouldn't want a murderer in heaven. And, with another brand of paradoxical logic, a mother refuses to open an official envelope because "it may be / from the war saying Toti is dead!"

This section swerves from the corrido's influence in other ways as well. Absent are the ballad's largely monological, third-person narrative style and the central male hero. While we do hear the speaker-poet's narrative voice throughout, it participates in a Bakhtinian dialogic narration in which the principal and more vibrantly active other voice is that of the mother, who, as in "La Jefita," conversationally addresses her family continuously, thereby weaving a sociolinguistic fabric of some security against the intrusion of the outside (Bakhtin 1981). Unlike the corridista or the corrido hero, she wields no pistol or boasting words to defend her family, only her woman-centered language of advice, exhortation, and counsel. And if she is unlike the men of the corrido in sociolinguistic style, the two other central female protagonists in this section are also an imagistic swerve from the corrido's world. The old hump-backed *curandera*, Doña Chole, and the grandmother "with wrinkled hands" and "gnarled finger" have almost nothing in common with the relatively youthful, virile male hero of the corrido, except that their control of the community's magical folklore—healing and folk beliefs concerning owls—represents a power nearly as potent as a pistol.

I say "nearly as potent" because this Swerve, this particular poetic rewriting of women's culture, while admirable and vibrant, does not become a fully developed contribution to a strong political poetics of resistance. It does not, in well-wrought powerful verse, rearticulate this women's culture into active cultural resistance, into a well-crafted, overtly counterhegemonic emergent cultural poetics based on the residual of women's folklore, of women's voices. As Montoya has rewritten this culture, it speaks to class and race relations but not in a deeply explored, inwardly contestative manner in which the subjects draw on this folklore to politically deconstruct the authority of the hegemonic culture. As poetically rendered here, the women's culture is more an engaging form of passive resistance. Montoya's is a culturalist rather than a political poetics, a poetics that demonstrates the "values of the dispossessed" and offers only "an implicit commendation" of those who oppress it (Hernandez 1991:53). It is not a sufficiently deep or extended female-centered response to the corrido, or to domination, but it is a beginning.

That such a rendering of women's culture as passive resistance has its critical uses is not in question. But it marks only the beginning of a more active, deeper poetic transformation of a residual culture into a more clearly counterhegemonic construct, one articulated on principles wholly different from those of the patriarchal corrido.[3] This poem stops short of such a move, however, as the poet oscillates too quickly between both gender worlds, like a child running back and forth between two parents. Indeed, this is precisely what the child in this poem does, as the poet swerves from the father toward the maternal but then returns to the precursory father. This return begins in stanza sixteen, when the speaker and his playmates flee from the grandmother's world of scary owls and "run unashamedly / and hug our Jefito's field- / scarred limbs." As he comes to his father, the speaker asks, "¿ . . . y mi Jefito?" (. . . and my daddy?). Posed almost as a kind of afterthought, this question, together with the father's socially diminished "field-scarred" status, initiates a brief movement of *tessera*, or Accommodation, which is carried over into the next stanza.

Unlike the Swerve, Accommodation is not a move of negation, but one of acceptance *and* limitation, or in Bloom's words: "the *tessera* represents any later poet's attempt to persuade himself (and us) that the precursor's Word would be worn out if not redeemed as a newly fulfilled and enlarged Word of the ephebe" (1973:67). As Montoya attempts to forge this precise relationship of limitation and enlargement, he reminds us of the father's diminished, "worn out" status but then quickly tells us that "at least his noble deeds are enriched in ballads." To make the latter point, he provides us with four lines of such a "ballad," beginning with "A caballo iba el jinete." However, as Hernandez (1991:74) correctly notes, this is, of course, not a traditional ballad but rather a literary rendition, or what Bloom calls "a newly fulfilled and enlarged Word of the ephebe."

But the truly creative poetic son cannot rest here. He cannot merely renew the precursor's Word, even as his own "newly fulfilled and enlarged Word." If he is to mature poetically, he must fully escape the precursor's influence and sustain the wonderful illusion that he is fashioning his own truly independent poem. This movement, however, also requires that he begin to unconsciously fully negate the corrido's power and right to speak for him at all, even as he appears to continue to acknowledge it. We then enter the revisionary ratio of the *kenosis*, or Withdrawal, when the younger poet *seems* to accept the precursor's poetics as the only way to speak, even as he wholly denies it and himself. In this movement the ephebe "seems to humble himself as though he were ceasing to be a poet, but this ebbing is so performed . . . that the precursor is emptied out also, and so the later poem of deflation is not as absolute as it seems" (1973:14-15). That is, in the Accommodation, the full strength of the precursory poem is wholly acknowledged, as Montoya does when he pays a formal homage to his father as hero and to his father's poetry. But then, in Withdrawal, the ephebe humbles himself by negating his own comparable poetic possibilities. Again, Montoya is wholly literal: "*¡Chale!* / My actions are not yet worthy / of the ballads," also implying that he, as a poet, is not worthy of the ballad form. But there is yet a further implication: Is the ballad form worthy at all in our time?

To more fully understand Montoya's use of this revisionary ratio, we need to momentarily turn to two other, though weaker, examples of his struggle with his strong precursor: "Los Vatos" (The Guys), published in 1969, and "El Louie," Montoya's most famous poem, published in 1972.[4] Both poems are concerned with the world of the *pachucos*—the Mexican-American urban youth street society and culture of the 1940s and 50s and its association with gang violence. Both also represent extended examples of the revisionary ratio of *kenosis*, poems written wholly in Withdrawal.

José David Saldívar (1986) describes "Los Vatos" as a quite conscious transformation of the corrido, formally and thematically, into a new poem for its own time. He is certainly correct to note the corrido's omnipresence in Montoya's poetic consciousness: "Chicano and Border history are announced in the very rhythms and structure of his running lines—namely, in the *corrido*-like form he employs." But the corrido's influence is even more thorough, as Saldívar notes:

> "Los Vatos" in this light is an exemplar unalien Chicano paradigm. It is realist and observationist in its rhetoric, as though the singer-poet were telling us what he had seen and experienced during the pachuco epoch, guitar and pen in hand . . . an observer of concrete actualities of Fresno,

Fowler, Sanger, and Sacramento, California . . . [Montoya] conducts not
only a reading of the pachuco consciousness and its effects on a Chicano
family, but he also investigates and transforms the model of narration
implicit in the *corrido*. (1986:11)

Much the same could be said of Montoya's other corrido-like poem
"El Louie," although the protagonist, Louie Rodriguez, is not as engaged with his family as is Benny.

One of my two general interpretive differences with Saldívar is that
in a way he is only too right about the powerful presence of the corrido
in this ephebe's consciousness and in "Los Vatos." Indeed, so powerful
is that presence that both "Los Vatos" and "El Louie" are not strong
poems relative to their precursor, are, paradoxically, too close to actually
being corridos. At first glance, both poems almost seem to be wholly
in the revision of Accommodation, where the precursor's form is redeemed fully in the words of the ephebe and the corrido in its full
majesty is omnipresent, if contained. But, on further reflection, both
poems seem examples of Withdrawal, where both poetic son and precursor are emptied out, reduced in what they might mean or say to us,
as if the precursory form had come to end and its continuation were
in serious doubt. In saying this, I broach my second area of disagreement
with Saldívar.

Saldívar seems to want "Los Vatos" to be as politically and socially
affirmative as the Border corrido, a poem as aware of and critically
responsive to the politically dominant Other as, let us say, "The Ballad
of Gregorio Cortez." "Los Vatos," he explains,

> through its *corrido*-like form recapitulates the pachuco experience in its
> relation to a racist society and reduces both experience and vision to a
> paradigm. That is, Montoya's self-conscious reference to the *corrido* as
> a social and historical form evokes in Chicano readers the sense of Border
> and Southwest life-struggle inherent in the *corrido* and all but compels
> belief in the sociopoetic vision of reality implicit in it. . . . It draws on
> an historically and ideologically specific Chicano Border form and on the
> content of individual and collective experience, structures it and develops
> from it imperatives for social resistance. (1986:12)

My position is quite the opposite: that both "Los Vatos" and "El Louie"
are diminished as sociopolitical statements in comparison to their precursor, and that in this diminishment Montoya is signaling an end to,
or at least a severe reduction in, the corrido's ability to be transformed
for our time, at least in his hands. For little is said or even implied in
either poem about a political "life-struggle" against a racist society; nor

do I hear any "imperatives for social resistance." Rather, the poems depict a world of intracommunity violence, which, while socially conditioned, is nonetheless also self-generated and certainly self-inflicted. Nor is it even a cathartic violence, of the kind that takes place when two mature Mexican men stand face-to-face, pistols in hand, on a matter of honor. Instead, we are witness to the mindless violence of a gang of adolescents, first cutting Benny across the belly and then stabbing him, again and again, in the back ("here?" Benny says before he dies); or we see Louis Rodriguez dying in a cheap hotel room "from too much booze."[5]

"My actions are not yet worthy of the ballads," the ephebe concludes in "El Sol y los de Abajo," as in recognition that in "Los Vatos" and "El Louie" he used and diminished the corrido form to demonstrate to us unworthy actions. His "not yet" hints of future worthy actions to which a creatively transformed ballad might speak. For the moment, however, the ephebe is conscious only of his failure and that of the ballad to speak for his time. He and his precursor are both empty.

In Withdrawal, the poetic son fully acknowledges the power of the precursor even while emptying out that power by denying it any continuing force in the contemporary world. It is to say, "yes, you *were* my strong father, but you are old and weary and mortal." Unlike Accommodation, the grudging acceptance of tradition, Withdrawal comprises both full acknowledgment and full rejection. Montoya says *¡Chale!* to himself as poet but also to the continuing poetic viability of his father's ballad.

The paradoxical result is a self-created sense of freedom—illusory though it may be—as the influence of the precursor is bracketed and negated, even if it means a sense of fragmentation and loss for the ephebe. We can quite clearly see this relationship if we compare the formal rigid strength of the composition before *¡Chale!* to the lines that follow, where the poet suffers the fragmenting effects of the *gava*'s—the Anglo's—yoke of confusion. The *gava* is not entirely to blame; this poet is also suffering the dizzying fragmented feeling of freedom, the freedom from the precursor.

For Bloom, the negative freedom of the *kenosis* dialectically sets up the next movement. *Kenosis* prepares "the ruined way for the over-restituting movement of *daemonization*, the repression or hyperbole that becomes a belated or counter-Sublime" (1975a:99). In this movement "the later poet opens himself to what he believes to be a power in the parent poem that does not belong to the parent proper, but to a range of being just beyond the precursor" (1973:15). By locating this expressive resource, this range of power, the ephebe believes he can override the precursor and go directly to the Muse and thereby craft an original and more powerful poem. "Turning against the precursor's Sublime," Bloom tells us, "the newly strong poet undergoes *daemonization*, a Counter-Sublime whose function suggests *the precursor's relative weakness*" (1973:100).

"El Sol y los de Abajo" ends short of this revision. In the final stanza the ancient Mayan prophecy becomes this power just beyond the range of the precursor as well. At the opening of the poem the father failed to find the sun; now, with the knowledge of ancient wisdom, our young ephebe thinks that he has found the original source of power that will enable him to see the Sun—to learn the source of ultimate poetic and political power. What is missing is the actualization of this newfound power—the production of a new poem of the Counter-Sublime, a poem to match or exceed the formal thematic strength of his father's deeds and ballads. In this trial of influence, the precursor's poem remains supreme, impulsing but at the same time overwhelming our young poet's ability to craft a poem worthy of both the precursor's model and his own political moment. At this poetic juncture—*¡Chale!*—wearied and exasperated by his struggle with a too strong father, the ephebe cannot continue. He is "learning to see the Sun," but he cannot fully appropriate and begin to render poetically this power beyond.[6]

POETICS, POLITICS, AND OTHER PRECURSORS: THE PARADOXICAL POWER BEYOND

This promise of a stronger political poetics as a result of "learning to see the Sun" would be more assuring were it not already a hint that the ephebe is about to travel the wrong road to reach his goal. If we take him seriously, as Hernandez suggests we must, this poem closes with the possibility of a turn to a pre-Conquest indigenous poetics as a source of strength for a new poetry.

Fortunately this is a promise that Montoya does not keep. Other poets, however, principally Alurista, have followed this pre-Conquest indigenous path, defining for themselves different precursors. The result, in my opinion, has been a dense, richly allusive, but ultimately opaque and politically limited poetics keyed not on social engagement, but on inwardness, indigenous purity, and metaphysical transcendence (Bruce-Novoa 1982:69–95). All these spiritualist stances are, paradoxically, based on two indigenous societies—Aztec and Mayan—that practiced no small amount of social domination. This particular set of alternative "precursors," if precursors they really are, has not well served Chicano movement poetry in its struggles with past and present.

There are better traditions on which to draw in these struggles, powers "beyond" the precursory corrido. Here I am thinking of a woman-centered poetics and its close relation, the Anglo-American modernist poetic tradition, and how both may be integrated with the influence of the precursor and rendered political. It is relative absence of any tradition beyond the corrido that renders "El Sol y los de Abajo" weak before society and its strong precursor. Let us consider this case within the Marxist cultural theoretical framework set out earlier.

First, while "El Sol y los de Abajo" may be read as an artistic structure of ideologemes speaking *of* class and race relations, the poem does not fully and adequately speak *to* these relations. In a sense we appeal here to Marx's distinction between *a class in itself* and *a class for itself*. It is the former, rather than the latter, that dominates Montoya's poem. In the first six stanzas we have an almost totally passive, markedly unpoetic recording of such relations, surpassed, in the poem's middle section, by a better poetics and a politics of resistance, if somewhat turned inward. However, we do not hear an active, contestative voice and stance in the poem against the day-to-day social domination that is so much a part of the poem's record, its "political history" in Jameson's first-level analytical terms.

Toward the end of the poem, our poet-speaker begins such an effort, immediately inspired by his precursor. Yet, his voice falters in Withdrawal, and he is unable to offer a political poetics that is contestative to his time *and* toward his precursor. At best, he can only feebly imitate the precursor and reproduce him in the present, in the movement of Accommodation, but he cannot go beyond him to construct his own poem of *active* class and race ideologemes. In large part, this limitation flows from another in this poem: In the final section, the strong presence of the corrido—associated with an early-capitalist, agriculturally keyed mode of production—mires the poem's ideology of form in the now too-static reproduction of the past. In Williams's terms, the poem remains too wholly residual. If this poem is to be politically vital for its moment, it must join to a corrido aesthetic other sources of counterinfluence.

Earlier we noted Montoya's comparatively greater success in writing the poetics of women's culture, but also his failure to fully explore this poetic direction and his patriarchally destined return to the father-precursor. Like "La Jefita," the woman-centered section of "El Sol y los de Abajo" *is* a poetic achievement remarkable, perhaps, for a man. Had Montoya's patriarchally dominant Muse not pulled him back toward the male precursor, here, in this world of women, he might have found and exploited an additional voice on which to build a better poem. Such a poem would not have abandoned the oppositional poetic mission of the corrido but would have added to it the repressed, excluded voice of woman. Such an addition, however, can occur only in a far better-integrated, more subtle text than Montoya achieves in his overly gender-bifurcated poem.[7]

Here the poet might have listened to himself, to the scene of instruction in poetry and politics that he offers in "Los Vatos." As Benny leaves his family's home to face those who would kill him, he passes his mother:

> He walked past her without seeing her and in his thoughts
> Illusive like a moth, the incredible notion
> To crawl into her and the chance to be born again
> Passed before him.

There is yet a second potential source of counterinfluence. The ephebe could establish some degree of control over this precursory form by joining it to a new modernist aesthetic form so that the poem might more adequately speak to the present. Elsewhere Montoya demonstrates a firm knowledge of such sources of emergent poetic authority—with Whitman in "Pobre Viejo Walt Whitman" (Poor Old Walt Whitman), with e.e. cummings in "In a Pink Bubble Gum World," with Dylan Thomas, again, in "Resonant Valley," and with Yeats in "El Sol y los de Abajo." In a later interview, Montoya describes his discovery of Anglo-American modernist poetics:

I also got exposed to the poets that were being read at the colleges at that time. The only poetry I had remembered before that time were those horrible, long Longfellow-type things *que nos hacían leer* in high school [that they made us read in high school]. So I was turned off. But . . . one *vato* [guy] that I read was doing something that was exciting to me because

he seemed to do it with a facility that I could relate to somehow ...
that was Walt Whitman. *Me caiba su poesía* [I dug his poetry] so I went
with his trip for a long time. By then I was also starting to read T. S.
Eliot, Ezra Pound and the Welshman Dylan Thomas. *Y me fui prendiendo
con esos vatos* [and I got attached to those guys]. And the other *vato*
that I really dug a lot around that same time was William Carlos Williams.
I also thought *he* was getting away with something. And I thought all
these guys were getting away with something I was being told not to do.
Por eso los veía como rebels *a ellos.* [That's why I saw them as rebels.]
How could they get away with it and I get put down for trying it.
(1980b:50)

Perhaps because of the overwhelming demand of a Chicano cultural
nationalism in the political moment in which he is writing, Montoya
seems not to draw fully on this Anglo-American modernist tradition in
his long poem as he had done in "La Jefita." Yet here would seem to
lie a better source of counterinfluence, itself critically revised, to draw
upon in the poetically and politically effective transformation of the
precursor for the contemporary Chicano intelligentsia. Indeed, Montoya himself has urged young Chicanos to read these modernists
(1980b:49).

Ultimately, the failure to overcome a continuing gender contradiction
and the failure to write a distinctively modernist poem become one
issue. Together they make "El Sol y los de Abajo" an inadequate response to its present moment; they render it incapable of acting as a
poetic charter to guide us through this moment in which all manner
of social contradictions need to be overcome. As a poetic document,
as a moment in political history, however, "El Sol y los de Abajo"
speaks richly to our collective yoke of confusion in the early days of
the Chicano movement.

The child has to make a choice between love of self and love of the other . . . the boy's self-love or narcissism turns him away from his mother. But the self so loved is fraudulent: self-love replaces parental love, but . . . only at the cost of splitting the ego into parent and child. . . . man finally succeeds in becoming father of himself, but at the cost of becoming his own child and keeping his ego infantile.

Norman O. Brown,
Life Against Death

Much like a new resemblance of the sun,
Down-pouring, up-springing and inevitable,
A larger poem for a larger audience
Wallace Stevens, "An Ordinary
Evening in New Haven"

The Daemonizing Epic

Rodolfo "Corky" Gonzales and the Poetics of Chicano Rebellion

With José Montoya we were instructed in the ways that too close an adherence to the precursor can vitiate a contemporary political poetics. We have a radically different case with Rodolfo "Corky" Gonzales's "I Am Joaquín: An Epic Poem," a more ambitious poem that, after a long review of the history of greater Mexico, asserts the right of Mexican-Americans to national self-determination and the creation of a mestizo nation.

In this poem, as we shall see, the dominant revisionary strategy is *daemonization*, which I call Rebellion, a movement that entails the poetic fiction of a radical break with the precursory poetic father. After an initial revisionary strategy of evasion and deferral and a less-than-potent poetics, this new poetic son does begin to fashion his own strong poem but, paradoxically, not before recognizing and initially partaking of an enabling nurturance from the image of Woman. In the final analysis, however, Gonzales also prefers to struggle strictly within the realm of patriarchy.

"I AM JOAQUÍN": CHICANO TEXT
AND PRECURSORY ORIGINS

Rodolfo "Corky" Gonzales may well have been the best-known activist in the Chicano movement. The author's blurb to the 1972 edition of "I Am Joaquín" describes the breadth of his activism:

Rodolfo "Corky" Gonzales was born in Denver in 1928, the son of a migrant worker. He has been a National A.A.U. boxing champion, professional boxer, packing house worker, lumberjack, farm worker, and businessman. Long involved in the civil and human rights struggle for the Mexican American, he is currently director of the Crusade for Justice, a

Denver-based Chicano civil rights organization with activities throughout the West. He is also founder and president of Escuela Tlatelolco, the first all-Chicano school in America (preschool to college). He is the publisher of El Gallo newspaper, a playwright (*The Revolutionist, A Cross for Maclovio*) and poet (*Sol, Lágrimas, Sangre*). "I Am Joaquín" was first published in 1967.

Cordelia Candelaria has rightly labeled "I Am Joaquín" as "the most famous of all Chicano poems" and mentions its extensive distribution, including its production as a film (1986:42). In explaining the poem's immense popularity, Bruce-Novoa points to its style: "The writing is simple, free of complicated poetic tropes; the language easily accessible, communicating a readily memorable impression" (1982:48). He also notes the poem's "uncritical utilization of standard Mexican nationalistic imagery, its appeal to the clichés of Mexican populism, perpetuating stereotypical imagery, while using it to establish a Chicano heritage" (1982:56). Stylistically and in other ways, Bruce-Novoa comments, "I Am Joaquín" resembles "the simplification process of oral tradition" (1982:56); more specifically, "The poem . . . defines itself as the *corrido*, thus inscribing itself within its self-established code of values. This explains its use of cliché, of repetition, of simple language, of few but key images" (1982:64). Unfortunately, here Bruce-Novoa repeats a common mistake—that oral tradition "simplifies"—and he limits the familial resemblances between Gonzales's self-styled epic poem and the precursory corrido tradition to superficial stylistic similarities. Further, his reading is constrained by a neoformalist focus on the temporally bounded text open to prior texts such as the corrido only through resemblances and allusions.

My argument is quite another. Beneath the surface stock imagery of Gonzales's long poem is a more dynamic anxiety of influence in which a struggle with the precursor shapes the poem at every step and conditions its political efficacy. Candelaria comes closer to my mark in her understanding that Gonzales "modifies the epic heroic model" in which the epic corrido participates, and, more specifically, that Gonzales is "modeling his epic hero after a particular legend" and, we add, a particular corrido hero, Joaquín Murrieta of California, though Gonzales is responding to the wider epic corrido tradition as well.

About Joaquín Murrieta there is no historical consensus that separates folklore from social reality; there is even the possibility that Murrieta never existed at all. But according to legendary history, Joaquín

Murrieta was an honest Mexican miner in northern California in the early 1850s, just as Anglo-Americans were coming into newly acquired California to exploit its recently discovered gold. Murrieta turned to social banditry against the Americans, because, again, according to legend, "he had been oppressed, robbed and persecuted by the Americans . . . had been driven from a piece of land—had been insulted and grossly maltreated without justice—had been flogged—and he was determined to be avenged for his wrongs four-fold. He had robbed many—killed many, and more should suffer in the same way."[1] Murrieta was eventually caught and killed by the California equivalent of the Texas Rangers.

Murrieta's exploits in defense of his right and honor passed into legendry and balladry. We have only incomplete versions of the latter, and they are technically not true ballads but rather descriptive songs such as this one (Acosta 1951:64; my translation):

> I have ridden through California
> In the year of 1850;
> I have ridden through California,
> In the year of 1850,
> With my saddle inlaid with silver
> and with my pistol full;
> I am the Mexican
> Named Joaquín Murrieta.
> I am not an American,
> But I understand English;
> I am not an American
> But I understand English;
> I learned it from my brother
> Backwards and forward;
> I can make any American
> Tremble at my feet.
> I am he who can vanquish
> Even African lions,
> I am he who can vanquish
> Even African lions,
> I am going to cross this road
> To kill the Americans.

The origins of this song are unknown.[2] In meter, rhyme, and verse patterns, it is not a corrido, yet it does present the traditional heroic figure, pistol in hand, opposing the forces of oppression, the *americanos*. The text also presents the manly boasting associated with the corrido, but, unlike the corrido, this song is one continuous first-person boast. Whereas the corridista inserts occasional lines of boasting dialogue within a larger narrative of events, this song is spoken entirely by the figure of Joaquín Murrieta. I stress this point because this self-centered poetics also characterizes "I Am Joaquín." In his daemonizing break with the traditional epic corrido, it is as if Gonzales had just such a quasi-corrido model in mind as the basis for his poetic moment of Rebellion.

"I AM JOAQUÍN":
FROM CORRIDO TO "EPIC"

Though the poem's title evokes the presence of the Mexican ballad hero and the subtitle announces "an epic poem," the four opening stanzas constitute a Swerve from this identification of a prior poetic presence. In these stanzas the poem deviates from the epic heroic ballad tradition in its use of English, its highly irregular meter and rhyme, and its setting in "the whirl of a gringo society."

More significantly, the opening line—"I am Joaquín"—announces an immediate contrast with the traditional corridista, who never sings about himself in the first person and rarely mentions himself at all, except to ask permission from the audience to begin his song. Gonzales's introductory statement to the poem is revealing here. " 'I Am Joaquín,' " he says, "was written as a revelation of myself and of all Chicanos who are Joaquín" (1972:1). Yet even as the narrator of this poem speaks on behalf of all Chicanos, he nonetheless does so forcefully in the first person and soon he gradually emerges as this corrido's hero as well. In contrast, the traditional corridista is an omniscient narrator who sings about others, not about himself.

Moreover, the traditional corrido hero is always introduced in classically heroic terms: honorable, strong, fearless, aggressive. But Gonzales's hero introduces himself as a postmodern "anti-hero" who, like his generation, is initially "lost," "confused," and "destroyed." If this poem is to be an epic or a corrido, then it must be so in the trope of irony—that which is not what it appears to be—which Bloom identifies as the primary trope of the revisionary ratio that I call the Swerve.

Once the poetic son has taken this initial evasive action, it is as if he begins to sense that, nonetheless, he cannot complete his poem without the precursor's help. Like a young man turning, reluctantly perhaps, to his father for help in a moment of crisis, our poet slowly begins to acknowledge and deal directly with the master poem while still insisting on his autonomy. Through the poetic revision of Accommodation he acknowledges the master poem, even as he implicitly points to its limitations and audaciously "suggests" how it might be "improved."

The entire long section from "I am Cuauhtémoc" (line 38) through "by deception and hypocrisy" (line 261) is such a compromised return to a sustaining tradition, made most immediately evident in the linking lines 35-37, "I withdraw to the safety within the / circle of life— / MY OWN PEOPLE." What follows is a return that, as a poetic narrative account of his people, implicitly acknowledges the corrido. But it is, at the same time, the poetic son's "attempt to persuade us" that the precursory form can (and should) be "newly fulfilled and enlarged" in the hands of the new young poet (Bloom 1973:67). How does Gonzales accomplish this in this section?

If a typical Mexican corrido focuses on a single, specific historical event in a circumscribed temporal moment—the killing of an Anglo sheriff, a victory on a revolutionary battlefield—this Chicano epic has far greater narrative ambition. Like the corrido, this epic narrates history, but its poet has taken a further completing and enlarging step, namely a presumed narration of the *whole* of Mexican history. Further, while corridos speak to limited social conflict, this epic thematically addresses a much larger domain of conflict both within Mexican society and with a dominant Anglo culture. Included in this enlarged domain are women: the Virgin of Guadalupe (line 96), the "black-shawled / faithful women" (lines 216-18) followed by the Virgin of Guadalupe and the Indian goddess Tonantzin (lines 225-27), and the black-shawled woman who enters in line 416.

Finally, if the initiating Swerve was uttered in unconscious irony, as a corrido that is not a corrido, this supernarrative takes the predictable trope (in Bloom's terms) of synecdoche. The narrative as a whole is intended to stand for a form that is only local and partial—the corrido—just as the macrocosmic narrative of conflict writ large is a representation of the speaker's own internal conflicts and efforts to find his identity.

With line 262, "I stand here looking back," the poet inaugurates the revision of *kenosis*, or Withdrawal, which is

> a more ambivalent movement than *clinamen* or *tessera*, and necessarily brings poems more deeply into the realms of antithetical meanings. For, in *kenosis*, the artist's battle against art has been lost, and the poet falls or ebbs into a space and time that confine him, even as he undoes the

precursor's pattern by a deliberate, willed loss in continuity. His stance *appears* to be that of his precursor ... but the meaning of the stance is undone; the stance is *emptied* of its priority, which is a kind of godhood, and the poet holding it becomes more isolated, not only from his fellows, but from the continuity of his own self. (Bloom 1973:89–90)

The speaker-poet begins his account of loss and undoing, of falling and ebbing as he realizes the extent of his oppression. But in poetic terms, he has also lost his battle against art, the art of the corrido, because he is at this point unable to write a "corrido" for his own time. Yet even as he admits defeat, he extends his Withdrawal by writing a lengthy account of his political and poetical regression. This account breaks with the preceding heroic narrative, and now *defeat* predominates. Unable to narrate heroically, the poet, in Bloom's terms, "undoes the precursor's pattern by a deliberate willed loss in continuity. His stance *appears* to be that of the precursor ... but the meaning of the stance is undone."

Such a concurrent emptying out of tradition and diminishing of the present self either leads to total poetic and social negation, as in Paredes's "Guitarreros," and in Montoya's poems, or prepares the ground for the poetic strategy that Bloom calls *daemonization*, or the Counter-Sublime. In this movement there is a seeming total abandonment, actually a full repression, of the precursor, in favor of a new beginning.

In *daemonization* the precursor, who was consciously limited in the *kenosis*, seems to disappear altogether as the new poet attempts a seemingly new poetic vision to replace that of the precursor. Believing that he has vanquished the precursor, the ephebe consciously thinks himself free and poetically engages in what Bloom calls "the over-restituting movement of *daemonization*." Now the ephebe's imagery and tone partake of hyperbole: "the trope of excess or of the over-throw and like repression finds its images in height and depth, in the Sublime and the Grotesque" (1975a:99). For Bloom "the glory of repression, poetically speaking, is that memory and desire, driven down, have no place to go *in language* except up onto the heights of sublimity, the ego's exultation in its own operations" (1975a:100). Hence, I call this movement Rebellion.

Gonzales's move to Rebellion begins with line 387, as the poet concludes his litany of oppression and despair, which he has cast as an undone "corrido" of defeat that negates himself *and* his precursor. He ends his own undoing by recognizing that "they," having taken and dominated everything else, have overlooked his people's art. He offers three examples of the latter: first, "the art of our great señores," the great Mexican muralists, and then "Mariachi music, the / heart and soul / of the people of the earth." Both these examples are named in clauses, but the third art form is rendered in a full sentence:

> The *corridos* tell the tales
> of life and death,
>   of tradition,
> legends old and new,
> of joy
>   of passion and sorrow
> of the people—who I am.

Here we at last explicitly meet the master poem, semiconsciously present throughout, and it is fitting that the corrido appears by name just as the poet is about to fully enter the ratio of Rebellion. For Rebellion can have its greatest glory only when, like two corrido heroes, pistols in hands, the ephebe and the master poem fully confront each other *mano a mano.* Yet, strangely enough in this hand-to-hand poetics, full *daemonization* does not follow immediately after this identification. Woman, who has been a minor visitor in this poem twice, now reappears to fill the moment between confrontation and Rebellion, like a mother appealing to a confrontational father and son. She appears, moreover, in what are the least abstract, most imagistically detailed, vibrant, and rhythmic—all of which is to say, the best—lines in this poem.

> I am in the eyes of woman,
>   sheltered beneath
> her shawl of black,
>   deep and sorrowful
>   eyes
> that bear the pain of sons long buried
>   or dying,
>   dead
> on the battlefield or on the barbed wire
>   of social strife.
>
> Her rosary she prays and fingers
> endlessly
>   like the family

> working down a row of beets
>   to turn around
>   and work
>   and work.
> There is no end.
> Her eyes a mirror of all the warmth
>   and all the love for me,

"And," the poet continues in a crucial identification, "I am her / and she is me."

> We face life together in sorrow,
> anger, joy, faith and wishful
> thoughts.

Then, in a deliberate confusion of gender identity:

> I shed the tears of anguish
> as I see my children disappear
> behind the shroud of mediocrity,
> never to look back to remember me.

Here this poetically strong turn to the maternal ends, and Gonzales immediately takes up the rhetoric of *daemonization* with its attendant hyperbole, its wildly oscillating poetics of low:

> I have existed
> in the barrios of the city
> in the suburbs of bigotry
> in the mines of social snobbery
> in the prisons of dejection
> in the muck of exploitation
> and
> in the fierce heat of racial hatred.

and high:

> my faith unbreakable,
> my blood is pure.
> I am Aztec prince and Christian Christ.
> I SHALL ENDURE!
> I WILL ENDURE!

This is the Counter-Sublime in full view; the moment when the poetic son thinks himself wholly independent of the precursor. The latter, nonetheless, is always *there*, if repressed, still powerfully conditioning and acting as the base for the younger one's mad flight into his "own" sublime. Joaquín is starting to write of his own deeds, of the creation of the student-farmworker movement and its heroes, always in confrontation with the precursor. Joaquín's actions are now, in Montoya's terms, "worthy of the ballads." Yet at the time this poem was written, in 1966, these were actions in progress, accomplishments largely to come. What we are witnessing here is the hyperbole of a fresh *beginning* rather than an accomplished poetics and politics. Nonetheless, as social poetry, the climax of this full *daemonization* constitutes the high poetic and political moment for the nationalist aspirations of the Chicano movement in 1967–1969:

> And now the trumpet sounds,
> the music of the people stirs the
> revolution

Finally, we were writing our own corridos, and Gonzales and the Chicano youth community were both heroes and corridistas. But history and the dialogue with tradition and the poem also end here. No continuing confrontation with the past follows, for this ephebe and his compatriots think they have forged a new movement that will endure, a movement indebted to history on the surface and in the depths of the unconscious, but one which at a middle level chooses to break with the past.

"I AM JOAQUÍN": POETIC
NATIONALISM AND THE SOCIAL

Tracing the relationship of "I Am Joaquín" to its strong precursor within Bloom's framework historicizes the poem with reference to its literary tradition, but not with reference to its present historical moment. Clearly, the poem is an extended exercise in the political and cultural nationalist affirmation of the Chicano movement and of the Mexican people in the United States. In Candelaria's reading, the poem moves from the self-abnegation of its historical sections to present-day affirmation: "The poet thus lays out the specific dramatic conflict as a polarity—the noble, formidable raza past pitted against the hostile dominant society's perception of *raza* as ignoble and without value. . . . Adopting a reflective, quiet tone, Gonzales suggests resolution of this conflict (in literary terms, the falling action) by becoming increasingly lyrical" (1986:47). But Candelaria somewhat oversimplifies the historical dimensions of the text: "we apprehend the nature of the poet's response to the heritage that produced him, a response that does not allow the centuries of subjection and agony to overcome the human will to act as an agent of self-determination." This resolution to overcome is climactically evident in the final stanzas, in which

> we rebel against the dominant culture's negation of Mexican America, and we reclaim the source of our future power which lies in the legitimation of our identity. With Joaquín "we refuse to be absorbed" by the larger society because our "spirit is strong" and our "faith unbreakable." (1986:47–48)

In a generally similar vein, although with strong religious overtones inherited from the informing work of Mircea Eliade, Bruce-Novoa reads the poem as a series of withdrawals and assertions in and out of history whose net effect is to render the poem a "rescue" from an "enveloping chaos":

> The poem's main thrust is to rescue Chicanos from an enveloping chaos due to the loss of their land. The poem begins from the situation of contemporary Chicanos living in the Other's space, in Eliade's terms; within that chaotic space, Chicanos must define—cosmicize—their own area. To do so they must recall the paradigmatic process that defined the culture and renew it; they must discover the primordial hierophany. For this reason, the Chicano Everyman, Joaquín, retreats first into his people, and then into history to seek the essential knowledge. When it is found, the people can move forward in orderly fashion toward a common goal. (1982:49)

While there is truth in both Candelaria's and Bruce-Novoa's observations, neither fully explores the poem's diachronic similarities to and, more crucially, deviations from its literary predecessors, most obviously the corrido. Regarding the poem's social context or history conceived as the temporal present, both these critics focus on the poem's ethnic nationalist rhetoric. Their readings derive from what Jameson calls "political history . . . in the narrow sense of punctual event and a chronicle-like sequence of happenings in time" (1981:75). But "I Am Joaquín" does not record so much events as the rhetoric of a certain time. Within the poem's ethnic, nationalist, culturally affirming rhetoric is a historical chronicle, again not so much of events in an ordinary sense, but of "great" events, or, as Bruce-Novoa says, the clichés of greater Mexican history. More importantly, this is a poem largely in flight, in abstract historical counterexistence to the corrido with its penchant for historical particularity. Under its rhetoric, the poem, in its nationalist abstractive language, frees itself from a compelling poetic imagistic rendering of class relations, from an artistic articulation of the ideologemes of such relations. It is, of course, the poem's very lack of historical particularity that makes this second articulation impossible. One cannot poetically craft a poem of class relations if those symbolic units that signify class are poorly developed or altogether absent. For all its rhetoric, and precisely because it wants to be a poem of *daemonization* against the corrido, this most appreciated of poems (by ethnic nationalists) largely and paradoxically fails to poetically address the *lived* experience of social domination of the greater Mexican people.

Only in one place is "I Am Joaquín" redeemed in these terms, and, once again, we are reminded of Montoya's "El Sol y los de Abajo," for Gonzales also creates an opportunity and fails to fully exploit it. Recall the particularistic, imagistically well-developed rendering of the woman/mother, her eyes "sheltered beneath / her shawl of black, / deep and sorrowful / eyes / that bear the pain of sons long buried / or dying."

Here, I come to my most fundamental disagreement with Candelaria and Bruce-Novoa. For me, these lines are a fine poetic etching of woman that any cultural citizen of greater Mexico would recognize and appreciate. Candelaria, however, does not discuss these particular lines at all, yet by her tally the poem is unfair to women:

> out of the poem's approximately 475 lines, under forty acknowledge the presence of women within the Mexican-American heritage and contemporary experience. Moreover, these lines, unlike the numerous others referring to specific men in history, make, with one exception, only anonymous references to *la mujer* [woman]. (1986:43)

Bruce-Novoa seems of two minds about women in the poem. "The passive, stereotypical role to which the woman is relegated is lamentable, but, once again, the poem traffics in Mexican clichés. . . . The poet ignores the active role women took in history preferring to limit them to the passive mother image" (1982:58). Yet he edges close to a more complex reading of this imagery when he comments on the specific passage:

> The woman's passivity continues, as does her role as a bridge to Chicano heroism. As the storehouse of tradition, she is a cultural mirror in which Joaquín studies his reflection. Simultaneously, she watches him, activating

the mirror into a judgmental instrument armed with the totality of history. Significantly, Joaquín's declaration of purpose springs from seeing himself reflected in another's eyes, which at the same time place him in historical perspective, lovingly. (1982:64)

In other words, this woman is "passive" only in the way that a seemingly calm sea is passive. Bruce-Novoa clearly senses something here but, like the poet, does not pursue it.[3]

The appearance of the black-shawled woman, as we noted, immediately precedes the poet's leap into *daemonization*. Woman emerges here when the poet, in flight from the precursor, generates a psychologically predictable source for a counterpoetics. In a struggle between two political poems, however, this search for a counterpoetics necessarily has a social significance, one more profound and important than the assertion of nationalist rhetoric.

For as the poet finds a new source of imagery—woman—for a counterpoetics against the father, he is simultaneously locating a social ground and meaning for a new political poem. Like the corrido—that is, in more concrete *and* poetically compelling ideologemes of race and class than any set of nationalist clichés—such a poem would articulate his people's lived experience with and daily struggle against domination even while overcoming the ballad's gender contradiction. If the entire passage on the black-shawled woman is an example of this better counterpoetics, a poetics that strongly responds to the precursor and to society, then these lines within it may be its very best section. Her presence enunciates lived domination and religious-familial resistance:

> Her rosary she prays and fingers
> endlessly
>   like the family
> working down a row of beets
>   to turn around
>   and work
>   and work.
> There is no end.

With these lines, which he does not sustain, the poet is at his momentary best relative to the precursor and to society; that is, here we see a well-done dual poetic critique. Facing backward toward the precursor, this ephebe has the opportunity to develop a new corrido, a ballad that will take up the genre's sense of socially meaningful historical particularity even as it extends its range beyond the purely patriarchal.

At the same time, an extended, well-etched rendering of woman would have enabled the poet to move beyond his conscious and *rhetorical* political poetics to express a deeply compelling, poetically and politically effective, figuration of the unconscious of race and class domination. Had he done so, the poem would present a strong face outward to society as well as backward to the precursor. Had he done so, the poem might have been a corrido for our times, a text partaking of, but not subsumed by, the traditional epic heroic ballad. Like the latter, such a poem would be sensitive, as these lines are sensitive, to a concrete rendering of the ideologemes of class relations even as it evolved a new hero and form for our times.

We may also note that this poetic recognition of women and a more socially engaged politics is coincident with a seeming, likely accidental, recognition of modernism. As I read and reread these lines, I knew I had read lines "like" these before, a poem with this tonality and thematic, though not with close or sharp echoes or affinities. It took me awhile, but I finally found the tonality and thematic I was sensing in T. S. Eliot's "Ash Wednesday." Yet I do not believe that this ephebe knows his Eliot, though he well may. Rather, we seem to have two independent poets, one highly canonical, one not, making roughly parallel poetic moves.

But writing an extended poem about women, no matter how well-crafted, would itself not be enough. It would not be the strongest poem that could be written against the precursor or society. No son comes to terms with his father by retreating wholly toward his mother. This, we have seen, is Montoya's poetic dilemma. No dominated people can effectively engage their oppressors with one of the gender pair—male or female; both are needed to mount the most effective response to political or cultural repression.

Having momentarily fully recognized repressed Woman, this ephebe is on the verge of crafting such a unified poem of critical androgyny. That such a poem is possible for this male poet is intriguingly suggested by the lines immediately following this female section, when the speaker identifies himself with Woman: "and I am her / and she is me." But the aggressive nationalist poet does not pursue this androgynous identification and too soon returns to the self-assertive rhetoric of masculine *daemonization*. In lines that ostensibly speak to the social present we find a telling statement of the poet-speaker's relationship to his strong fatherly precursor and his desire to be a strong replacement.

    I am Joaquín
    I must fight
        and win this struggle
        for my sons, and they
        must know from me
        who I am.

As it comes to a close, this poem is too anxious to be its own master, too eager to articulate its own presumed autonomy. In its anxiety, it generates a self-inflated, hyperbolic, male-centered nationalist rhetoric that stands at a great rebellious distance from its precursor and from an engaged social critique.

INFLUENCE, EPICS, AND THE
IDEOLOGY OF FORM

As a rebellious self-styled "epic," "I Am Joaquín" makes a strong, if unconscious, claim to replace that which came before it. Despite the litany of historical allusions, at a deeper level the poet is claiming a total break with and negation of the precursory tradition. If Montoya lacked confidence, Gonzales has more than enough. With greater maturity and development, this ephebe might come to a recognition of life's inevitable limits and return to the precursor for sustenance—poetic and political—to develop a poetic critique at once in mature revision of the precursor and in sustained engagement with society.

    But that moment never comes for this poet, and his poem stands as it is, alone in Rebellion both against society and tradition. The corrido exists as a negative influence, and this ephebe will not allow it to assist him in the construction of a truly mature strong poem. Nor is he willing to turn elsewhere, neither to a prolonged engagement with a poetics of woman nor to modernism.

    And yet, since "originality" in any human creation is probably our most impulsing creative fiction, where are we to locate this poet's informing counterinfluence to his mighty precursor? At its greatest distance from the precursor, this self-styled epic may be seen as a participant in the formulaic poetic hyperbolic so characteristic of the youth culture of the mid to late 1960s with its often exaggerated male-centered ethos. As such, it also becomes representative of a social genre of Chicano poetry whose other ephebes include Ricardo Sánchez, Abelardo Delgado, and at times Alurista. Indeed, it may well be that every

Chicano male poet—indeed every Chicano male—has spent time in this sort of Rebellion, although the poets just mentioned have made their homes there. Such is certainly the case for "I Am Joaquín."

The ideological implication of this formal affiliation is, paradoxically, that such a Rebellion is less a critique of established Anglo society than it is a protest against tradition of any kind. In these terms, indeed, "I Am Joaquín" is the most "Anglo" of poems, not in the sense of exemplifying the spirit of Anglo-American critical modernism, but in partaking of the Anglo youth culture of the sixties. Retrospectively, we can now sense the socially circumscribed and at times self-indulgent character of this sixties style. Though oppositional and counterhegemonic, the style is too much an emergent creation, little sustained by any proven residual tradition and oppositional only within a limited social sphere and temporal period.

Adrift from a sustaining critical tradition (either Mexican or Anglo) and unwilling, or unable, to pursue the poetic possibilities of the more socially grounded experience represented by Woman—a turn that would have put the poem in its best posture toward the precursor—"I Am Joaquín," in its final revision of Rebellion, opts for a form that is too ideologically bracketed within a self-centered socially restricted youth culture. We can admire this ephebe's zeal, energy, and bravado and yet recognize the narrowness of his poetic victory and the thin social resonance of his poem's politics. Adolescent in its rebellious attitude toward the father, "I Am Joaquín" remains a primer for poetic and political adolescents, which we all were in 1969.

I am the poet of the woman the same as the man,
And I say it is as great to be a woman as to be a man,
And I say there is nothing greater than the mother of men.
                    Walt Whitman, "Song of Myself"

In the future our poetry, literature and art may become genderless. I do not mean sexless, or asexual: we have asexual poetry, or attempts at it, everywhere around us, and it is appealing
in the same way that the idea of a sexless life is appealing. . . .
To eliminate sexuality in language is to eliminate vitality. When
I say "genderless," then, I mean not sexless but something like
bisexual or androgynous or omnisexual, containing rather than
excluding the two (or four or six) sexes latent in writers and
readers. The greatest writers in the world are always approaching
genderlessness, because there is no nook or cranny of their
natures, their experiences, their dream lives, that does not get
swept into their art.
                                        Alicia Ostriker,
                                  Writing Like a Woman

Who is the third who walks always beside you?
When I count, there are only you and I together
But when I look ahead up the white road
There is always another one walking beside you
Gliding wrapt in a brown mantle, hooded
I do not know whether a man or a woman
—But who is that on the other side of you?
                    T. S. Eliot, *The Waste Land*

7

Juan Gómez-Quiñones
The Historian in the Poet and the Poetic Form of Androgyny

In the last two chapters I have been evoking the image of an ideal ephebe to the strong precursory poem, the corrido. Such a poetry would need be one of multivocalic and simultaneous image, form, and social engagement; a text at once in fruitful dialogue with its precursor and in a politically creative resonance with its present. Finally, in the most creatively antithetical and completing incorporation of the precursor, it would be a poetry that responds to the latter's patriarchal epic poetics by bringing to it the poetics of woman as well as a fine but critical sense of modernism. Such a poem is Juan Gómez-Quiñones's "The Ballad of Billy Rivera," published in 1973.

Those concerned with the serious understanding and political development of the greater Mexican people know and appreciate the cultural work of Juan Gómez-Quiñones as a leading activist and intellectual of the Chicano movement and postmovement years. I quote at length from a recent literary biography written by Enrique R. Lamadrid:

> His efforts have been evident on various political, ideological, and cultural fronts, from the picket lines of Delano and East Los Angeles to the reorientation of major educational institutions. Best known as a Chicano historian, his major fields of research include Chicano labor history and the Mexican Revolution. . . . He holds a B.A. in English (1964), an M.A. in Latin American Studies (1966), and a Ph.D. in History (1972), all from the University of California at Los Angeles, where he has been a professor since 1972. His community and political activities date back to his work with the United Farm Workers and the United Mexican American Students (now MECHA, Movimiento Estudiantil de Chicanos de Aztlán), and include such positions as Chairman of the East Los Angeles Poor People's March Contingent (1968), Director of Chicano Legal Defense (1968–69), Co-organizer of the Chicano Council of Higher Education (1969–70), member of the Board of Directors of the Los Angeles Urban Coalition (1970–72), Director of the UCLA Chicano Studies Center (1974–87), and member of the Board of Trustees of the California State

Universities and Colleges (1976–84). He has done important editorial work on newspapers, research journals and anthologies, and has major works on Mexican and Chicano history. . . . He also has substantial media experience with radio, television, and one film. His seminal essay on aesthetics, culture and politics is entitled "On Culture" and has been reprinted several times. (1990:5)

Yet, as Lamadrid correctly acknowledges, this important "cultural worker and ideological spokesman with roots in the struggle of his community" (1990:4) is not as well known for his poetry. Later, I will suggest reasons for the relative neglect of a poetry that, because it is wholly implicated in precursory tradition and the contemporary political cultural scene, speaks singularly and eloquently to deep cultural ideological concerns in the closing phase of the Chicano movement from 1969 to 1972.

As is most evident in his small collection *5th and Grande Vista (Poems, 1960–1973)*, Gómez-Quiñones's poetry is deeply influenced by the poet's professional and lived sense of history. A native of the northern Mexican state of Chihuahua, he moved with his family as a young boy to East Los Angeles, the large, long-standing Mexican working-class enclave of this city, and to the particular barrio at Fifth and Grande Vista. The first poem, identified as a "prologue," in *5th and Grande Vista* is "Canto al Trabajador" (I Sing to the Worker; reprinted in Appendix B). The poem is dedicated to the poet's father, Juan Gómez Duarte, a working man.

The poem's opening section is a catalogue, written in Spanish, in which the poet sings in homage to a series of workers and occupations that historically have been identified with Mexicans in the United States. At once the poem evokes two precursor traditions: that of the corridos, several of which concern occupational roles, and that of Walt Whitman, whose catalogue of workers substantially constitutes "I Hear America Singing." If we look beyond surface resemblances, however, we cannot agree with Ines Tovar that "Canto al Trabajador" and "I Hear America Singing" share an ideological outlook, namely that "the listing, like a chant, demonstrates the diversity within the oneness of the *trabajadores* (workers)" (1975:95). Rather, in *his* song Gómez-Quiñones's well-wrought ideological effect is precisely to undercut and unmask Whitman's celebratory effort in which various workers in mid-nineteenth-century America "sing" happily of their labor identities and products, "Each singing what belongs to him or her and to none else." We cannot reasonably hold Whitman responsible for knowing Marx, but even as the latter was developing his theory of labor value and the commodity form, Whitman was writing this social nonsense.

The proper relationship between these two poems is that "Canto al Trabajador" is rather a kind of radical *apophrades* to its quintessentially American precursor, a revision in which the latter has been incorporated in the service of a new socially relevant poem. Unlike Whitman's celebratory ideological falsification of American workers' brutal confrontation with an emerging capitalism, Gómez-Quiñones's poem is a proud homage that is fully sensitive to workers' lived experience under this same expanding capitalist culture. Refusing to mask this modern confrontation, the Chicano ephebe develops his counterthematic by appropriating another Anglo-American canonical figure into his own revisionary political poetics. For the Mexican workers, this poet tells us,

> Todos los meses son crueles
> > y la semilla queda aunque arranquen la mata
> todos los meses son crueles
> > para ellos de las manos esculpidas.

> All months are cruel
> > and the seed remains though they rip out the plant
> all months are cruel
> > for those with calloused hands.
> > > > > (my translation)

As Tovar explains,

> The reference to all of the months being cruel calls to mind the opening line of T. S. Eliot's *The Wasteland,* "April is the cruelest month," but, of course, in Eliot's context, April, the life-giving month, serves to cruelly irritate the sense of the bored, stupored, synthetic rich, who wonder what to do with themselves. The poet's workers, in contrast, labor all the months of the year; theirs is not the luxury to wonder what to do. (1975:95)

She might also have noted Gómez-Quiñones's continued skillful counterevocation of Eliot for his own emerging interest in community. "The seed," he tells us, "remains though they rip out the plant." Whatever the fate of Eliot's rich, these workers will persist.

Yet even as this Chicano poet incorporates two canonical Anglo-American figures, his central intertextual concern is the Mexican corrido. His song to the workers is not a narrative, to be sure, but certainly a song in honor of heroic struggle and presence. And in section II the poet offers a more focused and corrido-like homage to one worker, one hero—his father—who represents all our father-workers. As if to emphasize the poet's own generational identification, he now writes in English.

> My father's holy hand is etched
>   in holy grime.
> I remember my father's hand
>   etched in cries and sweat.
> Huddled on the corner
> I have seen
>   the men who work.

From his father's experience, this Chicano activist, intellectual, and poet has learned politics and, I would suggest, poetics.

> What I know I learned
>   from my father's worker's hand
> who is we and who are they
>   of right and wrong
>   who has built the cities
> and wherefrom came the riches.
> . . . .
> no books or street demagogues teach
> we learn from bitterness and broken bodies.
> My father's hand is etched in time
> Canto a los trabajadores.

While not fully in the presence of the primary poetic precursor, the poet has located himself as a son of a political-cultural tradition. It is a tradition motivating his own politics and, evidently, his poetry, a poetry about social conflict and, at this point, patriarchal male heroes. From this patriarchal point of departure, our ephebe begins an even more creative struggle as he attempts to write his own ballad, "The Ballad of Billy Rivera," the next poem in the collection (reprinted in Appendix C).[1]

"THE BALLAD OF BILLY RIVERA"
AND THE EMERGING KNOWLEDGE
OF THE PRECURSOR

"The Ballad of Billy Rivera" brings together five distinct, though closely interrelated, historical worlds: the pre-Conquest indigenous culture of

Mexico, the contemporary dominated condition of greater Mexican society in the United States, the Chicano movement of the sixties and early seventies, Anglo-American modernism, and the political culture of the precursory corrido. Initially in seeming conflict with each other, these worlds are ultimately reconciled and crafted by this poet into an artistic statement of community against the social fragmentation imposed by domination. Simultaneously, yet another poetic result of this well-crafted reconciliation is the most revisionary incorporation of the corrido's political poetics.

The poem opens in a way that recalls José Montoya's closing appeal, in "El Sol y los de Abajo," to the poetic-political power of Mayan mythology. But whereas Montoya there made an effort to reach beyond the precursor, the initial evocation of the pre-Conquest Indian world in "The Ballad of Billy Rivera" may be taken as a Swerve from the corrido's influence. For although he calls his poem a ballad—and as a professional scholar of modern Mexican history, Gómez-Quiñones cannot utter "ballad" without thinking of the Mexican ballad tradition— the first twelve lines of his poem adopt the poetic pose or pretense that the precursor is *not there*, that one can simply begin a new poem wholly independent of influence. I loosely translate the poem's opening, in which several lines of Nahuatl precede the Spanish:

> He who speaks with authority
> all universal and pervasive
> Quetzal
> That time which was.
>
> Before there was man
> there was the Earth
> And before all, the spirit was first
> And nature speaks, the spirit speaks
>   they-he take form
> the spirit is reborn
>   speaks and takes form
> the spirit flowers

At a far distance from any "ballad," this evanescent, allusive free verse imagistically evokes a romantic dreamlike pre-Columbian poetic culture, an evocation at great remove from the corrido's thematic and formal concretion.

Beginning in 1521, this pre-Columbian culture was destroyed by the Spanish invaders. The domination of the Mexican masses is the subject of lines 13–28, beginning with "Sabes que" (Do you know that). The people of greater Mexico became the "dispossessed," the "despised," those "who lived at the edge"; but, after enough tears, their "sentence served," from these people "came the flame." The farmworkers' strikes of the 1960s, in California and Texas, are one manifestation of this flame: "In 1965 the campesinos / struck the fields of Delano."

Nonetheless, even in the political present, our poet makes an attempt to continue his Swerve—his pre-Conquest poetics—in lines 21–28, ending with the lament "Ay Tenochtitlán, sobrevivimos" (Oh Tenochtitlán, we survive). However, I read these lines no longer as a full Swerve, but rather as an emerging recognition of the precursor in a spirit of begrudging Accommodation; that is, while maintaining some of the pre-Columbian tonal poetics of the poem's opening lines, lines 13–28 nonetheless are now a record of social conflict, struggle, and decline. In this limited sense, the poem begins to partake of the thematic and style of the corrido. While not yet fully engaging the precursor, the ephebe, nonetheless, is echoing the corrido's commitment to the recording of the everyday struggle of the people. Yet, at the same time, in a manner reminiscent of Corky Gonzales, Gómez-Quiñones is doing so using imagery more universal than concrete or local, as if to write a "larger" corrido, not of a specific time and event, but of general history itself. Here, then, in Bloom's terms, the ephebe acknowledges but tries to supersede the precursor by attempting "to persuade himself (and us) that the precursor's Word would be worn out if not redeemed as a newly fulfilled and enlarged Word of the ephebe" (1973:67).

But our ephebe's effort to write this larger, abstract corrido begins to falter. For even as he speaks of social struggle and focuses on the farmworkers, he seems to recognize, like Montoya, that he cannot yet truly write a corrido for *his* time and place. While the farmworkers are in heroic struggle, a larger sector of his political community—the urban population, particularly its youth—is failing to live up to heroic standards, and here his potential ballad falters in the face of the mighty precursor. At this moment this is a world too defeated for struggle or for heroes.

And so in lines 29–41 the young urban poet executes a Withdrawal in which he simultaneously empties out both his poetics, his community's political possibilities, and the precursor's ability to provide artistic and ideological sustenance for his world. First he tells us of a community dead to the cries of the ancient gods; then he speaks of a transformed lumpen-ersatz pop culture at far remove from the possibilities of precursory influence: "Silk and Satin, southern comfort-pepsi cops." Even the style of these lines, their hip street rhythm, empties out the corrido tradition, and at certain moments, my ear once again hears a competing precursor, the nonheroic voice of T. S. Eliot. The ephebe cannot write heroic poetry about this politically degraded state of affairs, and thus both he and his precursor are "emptied out" of their political and poetic potential. What is required is a new movement that will renew the precursor's latent presence and permit the struggle to begin anew as the ephebe attempts to speak to his time with his own "corrido."

That renewal, that beginning,

> It begins somewhere in Texas winds through to California
> Vuela, vuela Palomita
> > Madre mía de Guadalupe
> > > Por tu religión me van a matar
>
> (Fly, fly little dove
> > My mother of Guadalupe
> > > For your religion, I will be killed.)

By quoting three famous lines from the well-known corrido "Valentín de la Sierra," the poet rhetorically closes the preceding section of loss and reevokes the sustaining precursor, the corrido tradition, which begins in Texas and winds through California.

But having recognized the master poem, our ephebe nonetheless veers sharply away from it in a continuing search for his "own" voice. With sharper self-consciousness than during his initial Swerve, the ephebe gathers new strength, exults in his own poetic powers, and launches out in a new seemingly independent poetics, the poetics of Rebellion. This revisionary ratio is articulated in the idiom of a "power in the parent-poem that does not belong to the parent proper, but to a range of being just beyond that precursor" (1973:15). In this case the power, the alternative poetics for the impending Rebellion, is again the poetic power of pre-Conquest and immediate post-Conquest indigenous culture—the counterpoetics that appears at the end of Montoya's poem and at the beginning of this one. Now, however, the poet focuses on the most powerful image of indigenous cultural poetics, the Virgin of Guadalupe, the central female and maternal symbol of post-Conquest indigenous and mestizo greater Mexico. The invocation of this key maternal poetics paradoxically impels the ephebe toward a sharper contestation with the father.

The long section that follows, lines 46–105, constitutes the over-restituting movement of Rebellion. As in the analogous movement of Gonzales's "I Am Joaquín," here we again find the articulation of a radical Counter-Sublime, or hyperbolic poetic highs and lows in which the ephebe presumptuously tries to write his own political poetics in the full face of the precursor. This Rebellion against poetic authority has its political correlate as well, and lines 46–57 depict the early stage of the Chicano movement, the movement at a time when it wholly identified itself with those who took the first step toward a new political moment: the farmworkers. In Dantesque imagery that slowly shifts to the pastoral, the poet sings of this agricultural prehistory of the student movement. Here I translate from the author's Spanish:

> from that place
> Where there is found
>   the House of Torments
> where the winds
>   are forged.
> from there it returned.
> The trek began
>   by *garzas* and *carrizales*[2]
> Between rivers, silver and sown fields

This movement from the fields turns into a kind of festive politics. With a play on the word *unión,* the ephebe accelerates his daemonizing ratio into a new scene of politics and poetics symbolized by dance. Again, in my translation:

> Only in dance
>   is there union
> Only in dance
>   Are spirit, self, and soul
>   united
> That is why we love dance.
> Only in song
>   is giving possible
>   spin, Raza.
> Revenge is ours
> Goodbye dear friends
>   Goodbye false loves

Our poet begins to chart a new path leading to a new politics and a new poetics. For the moment, he has bid farewell to tradition, to the precursor, farewell to dear friends and false loves.

If the politics of the revolutionary corrido was centered on the reality and the metaphor of *tierra* (land), our new brash poet now confidently appropriates this theme for himself, an ahistorical presumption quite characteristic of the height of the Chicano student movement. As he enters full Rebellion, he speaks chiefly in English, the primary language of Mexican-Americans:

> later.
> tierra, tierra, tierra.
> There is only one relevant demand.
> freedom.
> once you get over fear
> the road is open

While clearly a statement about his present political moment in struggle against domination, it speaks just as well as a presumptuous statement about his relationship to his precursor(s). As he will discover, in both cases freedom is *not* the only relevant demand; but for the moment, he exults in it as he writes his own "corrido" (lines 76–92) about himself and his presumably autonomous politics. Here, in a formally loose, hip sixties poetic English language wholly at variance with the corrido, he finally writes his own politics and poetics:

> You never saw so many fucken pigs
>   in your whole life.
> tripping, just tripping

followed by a Spanish passage—almost obligatory as it was in the student movement (Limón 1982a)—and the line "Que vivan los mejicanos." Like Gonzales's "I Am Joaquín," this poem could end here in Rebellion, leaving a naive reader to simply conclude that a new politics and poetics had now emerged, wholly replacing the old. But, as this particular history turns out, neither politics nor poetics could be sustained, and this poet-as-historian is wise enough to know it.

Beginning with line 93, "I just want to feel high again," the poet acknowledges that the moment of demonstrations is past. We begin to sense a faltering, a waning of poetic strength whose political correlate is the waning of the Chicano student movement in the early seventies, an attenuation caused, in large part, by its difficult recognition of its internal gender contradictions (García 1989). However, in the face of this emerging issue, the ephebe can only muster a series of sentimental verses from Mexican popular commercial songs, songs usually associated with drinking and womanizing, songs that Américo Paredes caustically labels "movie corridos" (1967:29). In translation:

> I am so far from the town where I was born,
> Dear, beloved Mexico
> why not die
> For a married woman
>   crazy and in love
> I belong to the movement

Politics has become self-serving personal indulgence, and poetry the babbling of sexist sentimental nostalgia. The brief emerging power of woman articulated in the initial imagery of the Virgin of Guadalupe is now recontained in a conventional sexist outlook, as it was in the student movement. The poetic attempt at Rebellion paradoxically fails in a sexist parody of traditional corridos. It is as if a truly responsive new poem—like a new politics—cannot exist without a more progressive recognition of women.

THE NECESSARY RETURN
TO CELAYA

After his aborted attempt at Rebellion, the ephebe, as if recognizing his failure, enters the poetic movement of Perspective. Now, in a kind of exhaustion after the hyperbole of Rebellion, the ephebe pauses and turns back to the poetic father for counsel as he struggles to reorient himself. This is not to say that he is ready to surrender, to empty himself out wholly, as in Withdrawal. No—now he is even more willing to be his own poet, but now he will more fully and openly acknowledge the precursor's poetic presence, if only more carefully to use that powerful poetics in his own interest to write a truly strong poem. And he will revisit the precursor not in a spirit of Swerve, Accommodation, or Withdrawal, but in a spirit of Perspective or, in Bloom's terms, *askesis*, in which the ephebe "yields up part of his own human and imaginative endowment, so as to separate himself from others, including the precursor, and he does this in his poem by so stationing it in regard to the parent-poem as to make that poem undergo an *askesis* too; the precursor's endowment is also truncated" (1973:15).

This strategy emerges beginning with lines 106–7: "corre, corre, maquinita, / triste cantan los sinsontes" (run, run, little train / sadly the mockingbirds sing). The first of these lines is taken from the corrido concerning the battle of Celaya, which we discussed in chapter 1. Here the poet explicitly acknowledges the full presence of the precursor in its most revolutionary strength. The second line on mockingbirds, however, is not from this corrido and opens the strategy of Perspective by which the new poet both limits the corrido and yet gives up his own inflated self-concern.

That is, what follows these lines is nothing less than a truncating demythification of the epic corrido's heroic ethos as the poet records for us a likelier—which is to say, a more human—version of what happened at Celaya. It was less an occasion for heroics than for lament— "Ay Celaya," says the poet—as the *cuarteles* (troop formations) engage in battle, and "the river," more likely of blood than water, "flowed around the / hill." Rather than a corrido hero standing authoritatively in boasting confrontation, here we find a "he" who "saw the dust become the troop," and even as he yells to his side that they should take the heights on the far bank of the river, he recalls, in quite fond human fashion, their departure from the capital, when people in the streets shouted "Viva Villa." He also recalls the mayor's effort to stop them (most likely, he was a partisan for the other side) and how the town dealt with his interference. In my translation:

> The mayor ordered the machine gun unloaded,
>   since they weren't going anywhere.
> because he was innocent
>   they cut his head off as an example to the crowd

The traditional heroic corrido thematics are deflated and reduced, a move reinforced by the irregular meter and rhyme of this passage, its mixed use of English and Spanish, and the somewhat existentialist pose of the hero and his point of view. And yet, for all his reduction of the precursor, in the movement of Perspective, the poet has also yielded up part of his claim to an "original" poetic imagination for, like the traditional corridista, he too writes of Celaya and studies it poetically as a model for his writing. Having failed in his daemonizing original effort to write about Mexican-Americans—a failure correlated by the Chicano movement's political faltering—he has imaginatively returned to Celaya to learn how to write of defeat with poetic and political honor. He is seemingly on his way to a total acknowledgment of and a superior compromise with the precursor, but not before a kind of necessary relapse. As if still resisting a compromise between the residual and the emergent, the ephebe utters one more hyperbolic cry of Rebellion.

But this second Rebellion is more fitful, less certain, more ambivalent, as if the poet already senses its futility. Nonetheless, if only for the sake of nostalgic history, he must try once more, and he again turns to a sustaining power thought to lie just beyond the precursor. This time, though, he does not return to the concretion of the Virgin of Guadalupe, but to a conventional, vague emblem of pre-Conquest culture, as though entrapped once more in Montoya's chimeric closing vision. In translation:

> To the sound of ancient prayers
> the work of creation begins
> the forgotten gods have returned

From this inspiration, he surges forward once again into poetic and political hyperbole on behalf of himself and his now nostalgic, male-dominated political culture of the sixties. At the beginning and center of this second Rebellion is the key symbol, Aztlán.[3] Again, I translate:

> AZTLAN lives.
> in the fields and plains
> sown by my raza.
> —For Life—

This hyperbolic movement is sustained through lines 147–49, lines uttered in celebration of those historical predecessors of the current movement, including Joaquín Murrieta. A translation:

> Cry of Joaquín
> of the peons of Texas
> of the repatriated.

But a more sober, more subtle realization seems to descend on the poet with this cry of the repatriated—those Mexicans in the U.S. who were massively rounded up by the government and shipped in boxcars to Mexico during the Depression of the 1930s, in wholesale violation of due process. This realization closes his second and last attempt at Rebellion and opens the way for a second taking of Perspective. He repeats the theme of repatriation in lines that begin to acknowledge the limits of Rebellion yet the possibilities of a more enduring kind of victory.

> In.....................Mexicans on.....................
>   were repatriated, but they came back.
> Today the migra makes sweeps
>   through the barrio
>   arreando el mar.
>   [trying to contain the sea.]

With the ellipsis dots suggesting "any year" and "everywhere," the poet recognizes that, despite hyperbolic efforts against or for them, Mexicans have endured, have returned to lands once theirs. Despite the efforts of the migra (the U.S. Immigration and Naturalization Service), Mexicans have been as constant and pervasive as the sea. Self-inflated political and poetic *daemonization* has not spoken authentically to this greater reality, and this poetic son recognizes the futility of such self-proclamation.

He then initiates a new antithetical movement—a necessary second Perspective—that shifts his vision away from the self toward an assessment of his community's fate and faith. Returning to Spanish, he offers a variation on lines 128–30, which initiated the second Rebellion. The fields and plains, he says, are "sembrados de la Raza," that is, both sown *by* the People and sown *with* the People. But whereas in the earlier daemonizing passage, the appearance of *la raza* was followed by political movement—when the whirlwind came and lifted the People, when hope triumphed over experience, here, we find a kind of stasis: the people are not necessarily going anywhere; they simply, resistively, and eloquently just *are*. Here we find an appreciation of the People as settled, niched, persistent, enduring in fixed social spaces—in towns and neighborhoods. *They* are what is sown and grown.

Paralleling this mood shift, line 159 "—Por Vida—" (By Life) repeats line 130, except that now life consists not of political whirlwinds, but of tough, reflective, introspective experience. In my translation:

> —By Life—, we nail on walls.
> Bitter nails leave blisters of
>   hope
> What future? What past?
> You know.

This "You know" (*Sabes*) has to be understood as a quiet, implied interrogative suggesting perplexity and doubt. This "You know" also carries us into the next section, so that the poet is also asking "Do you know?"

Yesterday two weeks after the
  blowouts, 2 buildings were burnt.
Today or was it last week? or May last year, next year
In Coachella two growers signed contracts.
Ya pasó.
Sabes.

"Ya pasó" (It's over). The period of political whirlwinds—both the Revolution of 1910 and the Chicano movement—is past, an unclear, confused memory, although its vestiges remain: in the case of the Chicano movement, the growers now sign labor contracts with recognized unions, but nonviolent collective resistance has turned to sporadic violence in the schools. We have reached an end—temporary, perhaps—to poetic and political Rebellion. It is as if this poet and his political culture have exhausted their possibilities without a strong achievement in either poetry or society. The gains have been piecemeal, a reading partially anticipated by Tovar (1975:96).

In lines 150–70 the poet executes a second moment of Perspective. Following the second fit of Rebellion, the ephebe returns to the precursor and is almost wholly open to his influence but for the purpose of emptying or limiting the precursor. In the first Perspective (lines 106–26) we saw ample evidence of the precursor's influence even as the corrido was rewritten and emptied out by the ephebe. Now, however, the ephebe makes a weaker concession to the precursor. In this quite "modernist" section the precursor is not manifestly present—no references to Celaya appear, for example—but the precursor's spirit informs the ephebe's desire to narrate a poetry of defeat and loss that focuses on his community. Yet the ephebe's principal purpose in returning to the precursor is to limit or truncate its effect. To undercut the corrido's narrative of heroic confrontation, the ephebe offers modernist lines of piecemeal victory and unclear perception, a rewriting that limits the precursor but also the ephebe as well.

As the poetic son prepares for a final movement in which he will come to full terms with the precursor, he must once more limit and contain the precursor, even if this involves curtailing his own powers. Only then can the strength and critical estimate be mustered for the final reckoning in which the latecomer's poem is at its strongest. Only when the poetic son can sing his particular ballad about *his* community without evasion or slavish imitation will the precursor's full measure of influence be taken, even as the ephebe's most original contribution is felt. For the moment, as if wearied from the struggle, both poets must rest in momentary mutual defeat before their final mutually sustaining embrace. Then, in his historical intelligence, this young poet finds the alternative resources he needs to stand as a grown son, a strong poet whose strongest work is the final sections of this poem.

LIFE AND DEATH IN EAST L.A.:
MODERNISM AND THE
ANDROGYNOUS FORM

In these final sections the ephebe begins his final negotiation with the precursor's influence through *apophrades* (or Return of the Dead), the most mature poetic ratio. In this movement he calls upon the two counterpoetics that have appeared earlier in the poem: the not-fully-repressed voice of Woman and one strain of Anglo-American modernism. This final strong closing section of the poem opens with an observant and caring description of the poet's community:

> Have you ever walked the streets of
> East L.A.
> have you ever seen them shine.
> Early in the morning the air smells
> of menudo and familia, early
> in the morning, on Saturdays
> and Sundays.

Menudo, the hot (in both senses) savory beef tripe soup so favored by the working-class people of greater Mexico is both a synecdoche for this group and a ritual dish that brings *familia* (family) and friends together on Saturday or Sunday morning in kindred consumption and conversation.

The mention of Sunday morning and family gatherings prompts another vivid image: the cars of newlyweds "covered with paper roses. / rosas de papel." Then, addressing his community in Spanish, the poet extends his flower image to a more global political metaphor. In translation:

> In this too, *raza,*
> We remember the fields and the flowers.
> AZTLAN, it must be a land of roses.
> the land of a people of roses.

Returning to his central image of the paper roses, and in English, he explains:

> Sometimes, the cars are covered with
> charming paper maché
> roses.
> When *these* people get married.

Married on Sunday mornings, of course, when families eat together and talk together, and new families are created through marriage, and reproduction of another kind is set in motion. The specific imagery of East L.A. is globalized once more with the refraining "Sabes," which each time seems to sound more assured.

> Sabes.
> Have you seen the streets of East L.A.,
> Been in Denver cold in Winter
> En Tejas es donde calienta el sol.
> Roses are Rosas.

This section of the poem—this loving celebrative homage to community, family, food, roses, and marriage—constitutes the poetic son's finest hour in relation to his strong patriarchal precursor. It is the time of *apophrades,* when the Dead creatively return to inhabit the poetic houses of the Living; the time of a creative, loving coming-to-terms between poetic father and son.

Here the precursor poem is once more granted its traditional high purpose, though as revised by the ephebe. The corrido's fundamental thematic—a celebration of a cultural hero of resistance, a hero of a particular time and place—is reexpressed in the ephebe's celebration of the collective hero of history whose heroism does not consist of individual acts of violent resistance against Texas Rangers or *rurales* but of collective resistance through persistence against all odds. In the face of continuous domination in everyday lived experience, "*these* people" make life and love, bread and roses, and they do so throughout greater Mexico, in particular historical locales, in Texas, Denver, and East L.A. Here the ephebe has transformed the traditional corrido in the service of the present.

Paradoxically, this transformation occurs because this ephebe has turned to two other precursory influences to mitigate the corrido's patriarchal and premodern influence. The first is the voice of Anglo-American modernism, first, in the form of Whitman, whose "Song of

Myself" is everywhere present and incorporated in this section,[4] most evidently in the repeating lines that open and close the section: "Have you ever walked the streets of / East L.A." and "Have you seen the streets of East L.A." In his prologue poem "Canto al Trabajador," Gómez-Quiñones negated Whitman's socially naive "I Hear America Singing." But now the more utopian, socially observant and caring, truly democratic Whitman reappears in the incorporated service of the ephebe to assist him in his trial of strength with his dominant precursor as he rewrites the latter in his own terms. For it is Whitman's incorporated voice that permits Gómez-Quiñones to speak particularistically, corrido-like, of streets and people in a voice his own yet never fully his own. It is the use of the quiet Whitmanesque interrogative form that shifts the poem's tone away from the strident, rhythmically punctuated, imperative linear construction of the traditional corrido line, while still speaking of particularities.

This use of Whitman—the poet of man and woman—in the service of and against the corrido is reinforced by the ephebe's closely correlated turn to a woman's voice. The presence of woman in this section is not some haphazard poetic concession to affirmative action. Rather, her presence represents a potential voice, an alternative and fruitful resource for articulating an alternative poetics for responding to the male precursor and to society. Both Montoya and Gonzales attempted a similar Incorporation, but each evoked a female presence too conventionally defined as "woman," imagistically isolated, and structurally set apart. In this section of Gómez-Quiñones's ballad, in contrast, a strongly pervasive, influencing female Other shapes the total form and imagistic mood, the "informal tender tone" of the lines ending with "Roses are Rosas" (Tovar 1975:97).

Within the terms of his culture, yet without delimiting an "image" of "woman," this poet departs from the patriarchal, confrontational terms of conventional male heroes to articulate an entirely different heroic modality: the strength of nurturing concern, of the androgynously defined persistence of life. Honor, virtue, and strength are not epitomized solely by the man with his pistol in his hand; these heroic qualities are everywhere found in the living, persisting androgynous idiom of our *people,* articulated in androgynous symbols of food, family, marriages, and roses. The poet has appropriated the heroic thematics of the corrido, but wholly in his own terms, replacing Gregorio Cortez with a community of men and women. This is the rare, triumphant moment in the strongest of poems, when "the mighty dead return, but they return in our colors, and speaking in our voices, at least in part, at least in moments, moments that testify to our persistence, and not to their own. If they return wholly in their own strength, then the triumph is theirs" (Bloom 1973:141).

The poet, however, does not let his poem end on this note of triumph, "Roses are Rosas," for we have yet to hear about the eponymic Billy Rivera. The disturbing final section of the poem returns us to the "southern comfort-pepsi cops":

> Saturday
> and early afternoons seeping beer
> stuttering conversations of bold
> secret lives once led and never shared
> car washing, clothesbuying, body sprucing
> pepsicola-cops and paper-maché dances
> torn dresses and southern comfort breath

And Saturday yields to Sunday:

> Sunday morning mass
> tired mornings that lead to tired evenings
> and then once again.

After mass, perhaps, a piece of conversation introduces us to the seeming hero of this "corrido," Billy Rivera, a wholly belated appearance.

> Sabes que Billy o. d.
> they found him thursday dead two days

The official announcement, perhaps on the church bulletinboard or in the newspapers, provides the details:

> BILLY RIVERA'S WAKE WILL BE
> at guerra & holman mortuary
> 1724 e. florence avenue
> today 2-2-58
> from 12 p.m. to 12 a.m.
> FUNERAL WILL BE SAT. 2-3-58
> at 8:30 a.m.

What are we to make of these final lines, their quiet despair, following the engaging life-centered preceding section with its androgynous sensibility? Why does the poet abruptly reverse the chronological flow of the poem, returning us to 1958, well before Delano, the noontime demonstrations, the contracts signed in Coachella? For Enrique Lamadrid the abrupt funeral announcement has the effect of "symbolically burying the admirable but anarchic nihilism of the pachuco era of the 1950s" (Lamadrid 1990:7). Indeed, as we noted in chapter 5, the *pachuco* has assumed a mythic, balladlike signification in Chicano literature. But why does this ballad of the *pachuco* Billy Rivera, properly speaking, begin here, at the end of the poet's larger ballad about *la raza*?

Tovar notes the paradoxicality of this belated ballad: "the corridos tell the story of superhuman men who refused to submit to oppressive forces. Here, however, we have, not a Guillermo Rivera of the earlier twentieth century, but Billy Rivera, who dies on January 31, 1958 from an overdose of drugs perhaps, but also from oppression" (1975:75). More specifically, we may say that the condensed story of Billy Rivera is rhetorically placed to serve as a potent reminder to *la raza* of its past and a possible future as well as to underscore the poem's final relationship to the precursor. Keyed on an indeterminate cyclical conception of time and history, our historian-poet reminds us of the origins of the Chicano movement in social oppression and of a negative patriarchy symbolized by the *pachuco* as hero; he warns us against relapsing into this kind of political poetics now that we have achieved the possibility of the androgynous vision articulated immediately before.

This final section on the death of Billy Rivera also finalizes the relationship of Incorporation with the precursor. As if to uphold and affirm the ephebe's new "corrido" and its androgynous ethos, this final section quietly demythifies and puts to rest the exclusively male-centered world at the core of the corrido tradition. In its purely male heroic form, the corrido is no longer a viable artistic instrument for a progressive political poetics. The traditional corrido can only afford us a vision in which men live ordinary and often defeated lives, their "stuttering conversations" recalling corrido-like "bold secret lives once led and never shared" and the ragged sexuality of "torn dresses and southern comfort breath." No longer appropriate in our time, the traditional corrido hero is dead, now the lamented subject of Sunday conversations after mass—"they found him thursday dead two days"—a "hero" whose funeral is tersely announced, not sung heroically.

These closing lines cannot but remind us of Montoya's "Los Vatos" and "El Louie"; yet we also hear the pessimistic tonalities of T. S. Eliot, in a minor Incorporation. Unlike Eliot or Montoya, however, Gómez-Quiñones contains his despair. In response to the negative social character of advanced capitalist modernity, he does not opt for Eliot's transcendent poetic ritual and religion. Informed by his greater Mexican precursory tradition, this individual talent speaks of his community in valiant struggle. Following the section on roses and community, the announcement of Billy Rivera's death is not, in the final analysis, an occasion for despair. Indeed, for us in our time, it is an occasion for the celebration of this metaphorical death, by which the corrido is transformed for our time.

Our strong poet concludes "The Ballad of Billy Rivera" by enabling the ballad hero and the precursor to have returned from the Dead, wholly informing while wholly indebted to the living. As Bloom notes, the uncanny effect is that the ephebe feels like a poet who could have composed the precursory master poem had he lived in that moment and, conversely, this is how the master poem must be rewritten in our time. No longer in struggle, precursor and ephebe—father and son— have reached a poetic understanding in which other influences have also been acknowledged and embraced.

Billy Rivera's death underscores the shift to a new poetic and political sensibility, one centered on a gender-blurred social affirmation of the community's existence and living, loving persistence in a world whose new kind of hostility must be met on other terms. No longer with his pistol in his hand, the new corrido hero is armed with the equally powerful symbol of roses, and this hero is both man and woman; the new hero is the greater Mexican community.

"Roses are Rosas," and roses are an emblem of Mexican-American life in poverty-stricken south Texas, as the Chicana poet Gloria Anzaldua recalls:

> I walk out to the backyard, stare at *los rosales de mamá* [Mother's rose bushes]. She wants me to help her prune the rose bushes, dig out the carpet grass that is choking them. Mamagrande Ramona también tenía rosales. [Grandmother Ramona also had rose bushes.] Here every Mexican grows flowers. If they don't have a piece of dirt, they use car tires, jars, cans, shoe boxes. Roses are the Mexican's favorite flower. I think, how symbolic—thorns and all. (1987:90–91)

THE POLITICS OF THE MODERN
ANDROGYNOUS FORM

With these understandings of this complex poem, we may now explore the manifest and unconscious dialectical relationship between this poem's androgynous, modernistic revisionary relationship to its pre-cursor and its unconscious response to social domination in the 1970s and into our time.

In an enlargement of the corrido's socially descriptive power, this poem too offers us a political history of the greater Mexican people in a broader totality, as did Corky Gonzales's "I Am Joaquín." Enlarged beyond the traditional ballad's scope, yet more compact than Gonzales's rambling "epic," this true ballad for our time presents us with a record of history from pre-Conquest times to the Chicano movement's daily praxis to the streets of East L.A. Already here, we have a revisionary contribution to social struggle at the first of Jameson's levels, for in the future, such a record, like that of Cortez and the Texas Rangers, will motivate those who will carry on the struggle.

But this is not merely a descriptive culturalist political history telling us only what life was like in East L.A. These images are also to be read as ideologemes, as signifiers of race and class relations. To read of "the dispossessed," of "those who live at the edge," of those who live lives of "tired mornings that lead to tired evenings" is to understand poetically the effects of domination, the hidden and not so hidden injuries of class (Cobb and Sennett 1973). Within this context of the ideologemes of domination, however, we also learn that "In 1965 the campesinos / struck the fields of Delano"; that at demonstrations "you never saw so many fucken pigs"; that amid domination "Sometimes, the cars are covered with / charming paper maché / roses." This community continually resists, even if sometimes in hyperbolic terms, and the poem allows us to see the entire community in struggle, not just one single Cortez or Pancho Villa as an ideologeme of the whole.

At Jameson's third, and most fruitful, level—the ideology of form—"The Ballad of Billy Rivera," like the other poems we have analyzed, again suggests the difficulty and perhaps the pointlessness of distinguishing too sharply between "form" and "content." Through the use of the voice of Woman and a correlated use of two key poets of modernity, this ephebe has created a poem that exerts a most creative and mature counterinfluential relationship with its precursor. The potent Dead return to strengthen and sustain this poem even as this poet harnesses and shapes this energy to his own purposes through these two counteraesthetics. As before, this relationship of influence must be understood as *social* and not that of one solitary poetic ego in struggle against his precursor.

From this perspective, beyond its compelling ideologemes of class and race struggle, "The Ballad of Billy Rivera," particularly its final sections, offers a poetics of maximum formal political achievement on behalf of those who struggle in the present. This long poem continues the community-centered narrative tradition of the corrido, with its central thematic of social struggle, even as it also incorporates a modernist poetic form, a synthesis in which the positive traces of an older mode of poetic production are joined to those of a new one. Gómez-Quiñones brings modernism to bear on the corrido, thus containing its patriarchal, dominating ethos, even as he grounds this modernism in a social experience on the side of those who struggle—the continuing theme of the corrido. The politically ambivalent character of modernism, exemplified here by Whitman and Eliot, is now rewritten within the framework of the corrido tradition and its focused unambivalent concern for a people in struggle. This equally revisionary rewriting momentarily erases modernism's tormenting ambivalency and places the form of modernity on the side of those who struggle. Further, this Incorporation of modernist form, as noted before, is always intimately correlated with the Incorporation of Woman's voice to produce what I have called the poem's modernist androgynous form.

We are at some distance from the linear, strident, wholly masculine form of the corrido, a perhaps necessary form of response to nineteenth-century social domination and its own brute masculine character. For our time of advanced capitalism with its less strident but nonetheless powerful corrosive effects on community, its encouragement of internal class and gender hierarchy, its insistence on the assimilation of American culture—for this, our time, we need a social poetry whose formal quality speaks of an integrated androgynous strength. It is the poem's ideology of form—of resistive form—that is its final and most socially efficacious expression of its political unconscious. And the poem's form is efficacious and resistive because it is rooted in the formal culture of its principal audience in the early seventies. This is an experienced, educated, and critical Chicano intelligentsia to whom the corrido's patriarchal form could no longer speak directly, although the psychocultural need for a linkage with tradition remained. This is an intelligentsia for whom hyperbolic political poetics had been necessary embarrassments, although the need for politics remained. This is an intelligentsia critically suspicious of Anglo-American culture, yet reared in an Anglo-American culture of oppositional high modernism.

If I am correct in my estimation of this poem, a large measure of its success may be attributable to its author's well-established sense of history. Rather than watch a poet struggling as a poet, we see the historian in the poet, a trained historian able to appreciate the political effectiveness of the residual in culture as a resource for the present emergent political response to the hegemonic, a historian sensitive to the movement of Mexican-Americans into modernity and its contradictions.

From Raymond Williams we have taken the diachronic analytical Marxist language of "residual," "emergent," "hegemony," and "counterhegemony" to describe politically the relationship of the epic heroic corrido and Chicano poetry to their respective political moments and to each other. But we must venture to question the experimental adequacy of Williams's language, for although the cultural work of the dominated may on the whole be construed as counterhegemonic, its separation into distinct diachronic experiences may at times be our own reification and may have the unwanted ideological effect of too quickly separating past from present. If we read Bloom politically (not as he would have us read him), the unintended counterlesson to Williams's idea is that the residual is never quite residual and the emergent is never quite emergent; that, in fact, the residual can be overwhelmingly present and therefore the very term "residual" fails; that the "emergent" emerges only through the Incorporation of the residual. The Dead do return, not only to poets but also to people and, best of all, to poets of the people.

Juan Gómez-Quiñones's "The Ballad of Billy Rivera" is one of the best illustrations of a socially symbolic act as an artistically compelling site for this historical dialogue. In this ballad to a dead nonhero that really is a ballad to a heroic community, the mighty precursor continues its residual service to this community in the able hands of its best ephebe in the emergent modernist generation, a generation increasingly conscious of the compelling issue of gender. Appearing in the final days of the Chicano student movement period, this historically sensitive, formally capacious poem afforded us a symbolic charter to review this key historical moment in our lives. In the aftermath of struggle, following Alienation and Rebellion, a moment of critical Reflection was necessary to understand our past and to prepare us for our future.

Conclusion

On the basis of the foregoing analysis, I want to now address several key issues in the study of literary culture. In an interrelated sequence, these concern current debates regarding new historicist practice, especially as these broach the subject of folklore; the emerging question of minorities and modernisms; and, finally, the state of Chicano cultural criticism. Let me pose the first of these issues as the repression of folklore in literary study, a repression that always threatens to return.[1]

Whether conservative or radical, contemporary literary criticism, almost without exception, denies folklore any serious status as literature, usually by speaking of it, if at all, as "pre-literature" or "literary antecedents." At best, folklore is mined as a useful source of images and themes for serious literary writing by those whom Roger D. Abrahams calls the "lore-in-lit" critics (1972:82). The ideological effect of such a criticism is to reduce or deny the artistic worth of the verbal and primary arts of peoples already held at the margins of society.

For example, in his critique of Bloom's thin sense of history (see Appendix A), Lentricchia concludes by noting that Bloom "has not cared to see the restrictive family romance of literary language within an encompassing context of a larger cultural family of writing which would draw it into contact with the discourses of other disciplines" (1980:344). Yet Lentricchia's own recommendation is restricted to "a larger cultural family of writing," which would seem to exclude consideration of folklore.[2] Bloom, however elitist and restrictive he may be in other ways, has reminded us of "the humanistic loss we sustain if we yield up the authority of oral tradition to the partisans of *writing*, to those of Derrida and Foucault who imply for all language what Goethe erroneously asserted for Homer's language, that language by itself writes the poems and thinks" (1975a:60). Yet here we also note the repression of folklore in favor of oral tradition.

In contrast, Fredric Jameson recognizes the potential literary power of marginal groups not only through their minor writers but through their folklore, though he does not use that term:

Indeed, since by definition the cultural monuments and masterworks that have survived tend necessarily to perpetuate only a single voice in this class dialogue, the voice of a hegemonic class, they cannot be properly assigned their relational place in a dialogical system without the restoration or artificial reconstruction of the voice to which they were initially opposed, a voice for the most part stifled and reduced to silence, marginalized, its own utterances scattered to the winds, or reappropriated in their turn by the hegemonic culture. This is the framework in which the reconstruction of so-called popular cultures must properly take place—most notably, from the fragments of essentially peasant cultures: folk songs, fairy tales, popular festivals, occult or oppositional systems of belief such as magic and witchcraft. (1981:85–86)

In short, folklore—though Jameson's conception of it is flawed by what Alan Dundes (1969) has called the "devolutionary premise": the mistaken belief that folklore is in "fragments," "reduced to silence," "scattered to the winds," that is, limited to "peasants" and dying. Nonetheless, Jameson has at least cited this important creative domain from which strong influence may also spring for writers who remain in close cultural contact with it.

Folklore, though again not by name, also arises in Lentricchia's assessment of what he takes to be a now "centrist" new historicism, as exemplified by the work of Stephen Greenblatt. "A strong feature," Lentricchia tells us,

of new-historicist rhetoric and substance is on display in the typical beginnings of Greenblatt's essays, where he would violate the traditional literary sensibility with lengthy citations of bizarre, apparently off-center materials: an account, roughly contemporary with Shakespeare—thickly, arcanely detailed—of a social practice (say, exorcism) far removed from the high literary practice of the Renaissance. (1988:91)

In large measure, "folklore" could be substituted for what Lentricchia calls the new historicism's "bizarre, apparently off-center materials" and "arcanely detailed" social practices—though not all of Greenblatt's examples are folklore. For folklore comprises those expressively marked (what Lentricchia calls "bizarre") shared social practices of ordinary cultural citizens, the practices of people who are at some critical counterdistance (off-center and far removed) from both "high literary practice" and its hegemonic social context, the latter two always in their historically ambivalent relationship.

The critically read conjunction of such popular cultural practices with high literary practice appeals to Lentricchia, who hopes that "here at last is no literary business as usual" (1988:91). He is soon disappointed, however, for Greenblatt's interest in folklore or popular culture turns out to be business as usual and, by implication, so does his interest in mass democratic expressive cultures and their usually socially marginalized performers. Like most literary critics—left and right—Greenblatt values such expressions only as they contextualize "great art" by a "handful of arresting figures" (Greenblatt 1980:6).

Carolyn Porter has also noted this political difficulty in the new historicism, and she is deeply suspicious of a historicizing project that can be partially understood as the close reading of canonical texts as these are seemingly imbedded in a dense popular milieu (Porter 1988). Her analysis centers on Greenblatt's treatment (1981) of Carlo Ginzberg's rendition of the sixteenth-century Italian peasant Menocchio in *The Cheese and the Worms* (1982). In Ginzberg's historical reconstruction, Menocchio draws on his orally based peasant learning to politically deconstruct the dominant codified discourses of church law. Greenblatt's reconstruction of Ginzberg, Porter argues, erases the subversive power that Menocchio, through his oral resources, brings to bear against the discourses of domination. According to Porter, Greenblatt shifts the locus of his analysis away from these powerful peasant oral discourses—she also avoids the word *folklore*—to the internal contradictions in the dominant texts, contradictions that Menocchio, now recast as a common reader, "finds" and "uses" to politically deconstruct domination; but this identification and use presume that the elements of contradiction and subversion are located only in the dominant text. It is as if a guerrilla "finds" a weakly defended military position, and the guerrilla's subsequent victory is attributed to the weak defense rather than to the guerrilla's own psychological and material resources.

This approach, which Porter thinks symptomatic of the new historicism, rhetorically evokes the imagery of the subversive "outside" the dominant text—the historicizing move—but accords it no real power or only such power as is permitted by the centered text. With the invocation of *power*, we can add substantially to the definition of the new historicism and its limits. In Greenblatt's formulation of power and subversion, for example, an all-encompassing dominant power consistently produces, but also contains, its own subversion within the dominant text, a function of Greenblatt's overdetermined indebtedness to Foucault rather than, let us say, Gramsci. Porter asks a tough, telling question focused on the use of anecdotes—a folkloric genre—in this new historicist practice:

If anecdotes cannot historicize, then what is their function in these analyses? It seems to me that they serve as a "marginal" upon which literary
analysis itself operates ... —to appropriate the "strange things" to be
found outside the "literary," while effacing the social and historical realm
that produced them, at once plundering and erasing the discursive spaces
to which the argument appeals. This operation, in effect, retextualizes
the extraliterary as literary: it might be described as colonialist formalism.
(1988:779)

Porter's charge of "colonialist formalism" seems politically overstated,
yet much of her analysis and Lentricchia's of how the new historicist
practice tactically treats popular practice, now also defined as the powerfully subversive, seems on target. Nonetheless, Greenblatt's general
tactical appropriation of what Porter has tellingly called the "extraliterary" at least signals a recognition of the powerful domain of folklore
in a way that places it in close conjunction with written texts. It remains,
however, for the new historicism to increase its recognition of the
expressive domains "outside" the written text and critically lend them
greater political and poetic efficacy.

Here, one might follow the lead of Richard Bauman, who points to
the necessary relationship between literary criticism and folklore: "the
folklorist, no less than the scholar of written literature, confronts individual folk poets and unique works of literary creation, worthy of
critical attention as such, as artists and works of art" (1982:15). Drawing
on Mikhail Bakhtin, Bauman notes that both folklore and written literature are dialectically related to tradition and therefore to each other:

> of course, neither the artists who produce these works of oral literature
> nor the folklorists who record them are oblivious to their traditionality,
> to the relationships between these particular texts and others that pre-
> ceded them, in their own performances and those of others. So too must
> Milton have been aware of other texts of his tale of Paradise Lost, or
> Goethe of other texts of *Faust*, Joyce of *Ulysses*. But as Bakhtin has
> shown us, all texts, oral or written, within a given field of expression or
> meaning, are part of a chain or network of texts in dialogue with each
> other. To identify a particular oral text as traditional is to highlight its
> place in a web of intertextuality that, far from placing it on the opposite
> side of a boundary that sets it apart from written literature, unites it with
> written literature still more firmly. (1982:15)

The present study has been premised on the dominating centrality
of one quite traditional kind of folklore—the corrido—to written literature, but we have also seen how these writers draw on another kind
of folklore. For even as the Chicano poets turn to Woman as one

countervoice, they do so by evoking the folklore and folklife of the *curanderas* (female folk healers) and the bewitched owls, folk religious activity, and evocatively androgynous imagery of food preparation, roses and weddings. Deeply influenced by folklore, these written poems are, of course, not folk poetry. Rather, in these poems, these powerful gendered folk traditions are joined to a varying education in modernism. The result is a traditionally reinforced "native" conversation with modernism from "below," a conversation that appropriates and revises modernism as much as it revises the strong folk precursors. I turn now to this conversation.

POETICS, POLITICS, AND PATRIARCHS: BEYOND MATERNAL MODERNISM

What has quite rapidly happened is that Modernism quickly lost its anti-bourgeois stance, and achieved comfortable integration into the new international capitalism. Its attempt at a universal market, transfrontier and transclass, turned out to be spurious. Its forms lent themselves to cultural competition and the commercial interplay of obsolescence, with its shifts of schools, styles and fashion so essential to the market. The painfully acquired techniques of significant *dis*connection are relocated, with the help of the special insensitivity of the trained and assured technicists, as the merely technical modes of advertising and the commercial cinema. The isolated, estranged images of alienation and loss, the narrative discontinuities, have become the easy iconography of the commercials, and the lonely, bitter, sardonic and sceptical hero takes his ready-made place as star of the thriller.

These heartless formulae sharply remind us that the innovations of what is called Modernism have become the new but fixed forms of our present moment. If we are to break out of the non-historical fixity of *post*-modernism, then we must search out and counterpose an alternative tradition taken from the neglected works left in the wide margin of the century, a tradition which may address itself not to this by now exploitable because quite inhuman rewriting of the past but, for all our sakes, to a modern *future* in which community may be imagined again.

> Raymond Williams,
> *The Politics of Modernism*

In the poems presented in part 2, the principal sources of counterinfluence are maternalism and modernism. In revising the dominating status of the poetic father, these ephebes recognized and turned to a repressed woman's voice, principally in the form of the maternal. This recognition is one that revises while not wholly rejecting all the cultural complexity associated with patriarchy. Represented in rather conventional imagery in the works of Paredes, Montoya, and Gonzales, this maternally keyed woman's voice acquires a more evocative, suffusing, and thereby more powerful presence in Gómez-Quiñones's "The Ballad of Billy Rivera." In the latter poem, in particular, the evocation of the maternal moves far beyond any antifeminist limiting stereotype of mothering or motherhood.

This choice of a "maternally" keyed poetics by these male poets may not be too surprising in general (Western) and specific (greater Mexican) cultural terms and should not be critically dismissed on essentialist feminist grounds. Julia Kristeva criticizes the easy, though somewhat understandable, repudiation of motherhood as a cultural process "by some avant-garde feminists" (1986:99) and draws our attention to its creative potential even when it constitutes the cultural poetics of men. Further, whatever the power of patriarchy in this greater Mexican culture, the maternal is also heavily endowed with its own poetic power and stands at an even greater distance from the contamination of dominating power and capitalism. For example, consider *la Virgen de Guadalupe* and her socially unifying counterhegemonic meanings for the dominated of greater Mexico in their continual encounters with disrupting powers (Wolf 1958), or consider Mexican state capitalism's recognition of her role and its attempt to incorporate her image (Turner and Turner 1980). Often the dominated men and women of greater Mexico have carried a sign of the *Virgen*, this image of the maternal, into social conflict and, at times, have died in her name. Margarita Melville captures the power of motherhood in Mexican culture, but then diminishes it by severing the domestic from the public through a utilitarian conception of power:

> Motherhood, in Mexican culture, is considered to be the fulfillment of womanhood. To be a mother is to be respected in a way that is unequaled by that accorded to any other role, male or female. It is a respect founded on love and admiration that gives to a mother a degree of domestic power that is seldom fully recognized by outside observers.
>
> Power based on love is intransitive; that is, it extends only to those who love and not to those who love them in turn. Therefore, it cannot be systematized, much like the power of charisma that Weber expounded, and is distinct from economic and political power. Economic power is

transitive, giving one power over one's employees and over their employees as well, if they have any. But the power of Mexican motherhood
extends only to those she loves, that is, to her children. Thus, although
Mexican mothers are universally held in high esteem, it is not a source
of extradomestic power. (1980:11)

But indeed motherhood is such a source of extradomestic power—
and not only in the highly marked politically effective symbolism of *la
Virgen de Guadalupe*. Both in ordinary life, in poems, and in other
forms of symbolic action, motherhood is often inextricably linked with
other forms of power and is powerful in its own behalf. In this instance
we can only agree with Herrera-Sobek: "The Virgin of Guadalupe in
the Mexican ballad . . . is not necessarily perceived as a frail, submissive,
subservient, weak-hearted female . . . she is conceived as a warrior";
hence, "the folk poet, cognizant of this awesome power, interlaces the
corrido lyrics with the luminous image of the Virgin to interject moral
and divine support for the song's hero" (1990:51–52). Moreover, there
is no sharp class distinction between this "working" Virginal Mother
and the working-class mothers of greater Mexico: "For the poor,
women are not pampered dolls but hard-working partners in the common battle for daily survival" (Herrera-Sobek 1990:14).

The second source of counterinfluence, as we have seen, is Anglo-
American modernist poetics, principally Whitman and Eliot. Yet these
two sources of counterinfluence, the maternal and modernism, may not
be separable strategies after all. To better understand the dialectical
relationship of these two tropic figurations to the precursory father-
poem in the ephebes' own poems, we may look to Lentricchia's study
of Wallace Stevens in *Ariel and the Police* (1988).

In the first section of his analysis, Lentricchia identifies a "female"
voice in the early Stevens, a voice that beckons him to the writing of
poetry even as it marks that task as "feminine" and therefore of questionable value in American culture. Bracketed as "feminine," as "lady-
like," poetry becomes a calling of self-doubt for Stevens as he measures
its value against another voice—his father's demand that he prepare
himself for a real career within the world of high capitalism. Complying
with this patriarchally articulated voice of capitalism, Stevens becomes
an insurance lawyer. His poetry is confined to weekends and to an
aestheticizing distance from and repression of the socioeconomic contradictions in American culture. Commenting on Lentricchia's analysis,
Pease notes that for Stevens, poetry

supports rather than subverts the economic sphere. By rationalizing the division between the cultural and the economic as necessary, the poet enforces the boundary line separating the lawyer in Stevens from the poet . . . and this enforced separation of cultural realms produces an answering division in Stevens' capability. . . . Instead of dismantling the logic of the patriarchy, which produces a dominant male who does the commanding and a submissive male who does what he is told, Stevens' poetry naturalizes the difference in modes of cultural production and produces a cultural means of remaining unconscious of the need to overcome their differences. (1988:382)

For Lentricchia, the gender valuations of a capitalist American culture produce a politically debilitating "feminization" of poetry, one clearly keyed on a maternal definition against the patriarch, a "political unconscious" that, in Lentricchia's estimation, keeps Stevens from a critically appointed place in modernism, a political unconscious that, indeed, limits all modernism.

The story of Stevens' early life and career sometimes tells a tale that it doesn't appear to know it is telling, of discontent radical not in the usual senses of left politics but in the etymological sense, "radical" because such discontent is alleviated only by a return to origin, by a son's desire for his mother's breast that would, if granted, simply set aside all of his male obligations in the world of capital. (1988:176)

This debilitation continues throughout Stevens's career, though in his later years Stevens seems to consciously recognize his ultimate failure, despite the growing critical acclaim. What Stevens cannot bring himself to do is to engage society fully and critically through the primary poetic genre available to him in American literary culture: the long—which is to say serious, sustained, and fundamentally political—poem (Lentricchia 1988:200–206). Stevens does not achieve this goal, a goal that, in Lentricchia's idiom of sexuality and gender, would have meant, in our time, a more decided "masculinization" of poetry, a gendered struggle with capitalism on its own terms. It would have meant a phallicization of poetic discourse, a truly radical and needed reappropriation and revision of the category of masculinity from its dominant definitional congruency with economic capitalism. But, for Lentricchia, Stevens's failure is generalizable.

The issue of Stevens' sexual identity as a writer—his effort to phallicize poetic discourse—is not just related to but *is* the canonical modernist issue of poetic authority: the cultural power—or, increasingly, for the poetic modernist—the cultural powerlessness of poetry in a society that masculinized the economic while feminizing the literary. In the context of Stevens' America the nonutilitarian emphasis of aesthetics and literary theory since Kant and the early romantics—initially a badge of honor, a political protest, as Raymond Williams has shown ... increasingly this nonutilitarian emphasis in the modern idea of literature becomes, by the testimony of the modern poets themselves, the mark of poetry's social irrelevance. (1988:168)

If Lentricchia is correct, Western, bourgeois, chiefly Anglo-American culture has rendered paternity, the feminine-maternal, and modernism in such a divisive hegemonic way as to place the latter two as one and in a position of sociopolitical irrelevancy. This irrelevancy more keenly affects poetry but extends to the whole of modernist culture. Given that this debilitating hegemonic gender construction is directly relative to a specific sociocultural formation, that of Anglo-American bourgeois society and culture in our time, Lentricchia's solution is to "masculin-ize" culture. It seems equally logical and not mutually exclusive, how-ever, also to radically alter this bourgeois definition and use of the maternal feminine.

In Lentricchia's understanding, the bourgeois feminine and the ma-ternal can be used as a metaphor to imagine the whole of poetry, the whole of modernist culture. Indeed, the poem that is central to Len-tricchia's analysis, "Sunday Morning," is interpreted as a symbolic state-ment of the "feminization" of modernism: "Complacencies of the peig-noir, and late / Coffee and oranges in a sunny chair." Yet, as Lentricchia also notes, "Sunday Morning," almost against itself, offers another vi-sion, another kind of politics expressing a critically utopian "world of labor, gender, and genital sexuality—now phallically renewed, a world of men (1988:157): "Supple and turbulent, a ring of men / Shall chant in orgy on a summer morn / Their boisterous devotion to the sun." In such lines, Lentricchia says, "The contradictions of Stevens' early life and poetry—work, poetry and nature itself, the conventional realm of female authority—all are reclaimed for a masculine totality, fused in an image of masculine power. Father Nature" (1988:158). But this binary, gendered construction of poetry, modernism, and politics—to be resolved only by the long poem—is no solution, shifting as it does from a conventional "female" capitalist bracketing of poetry, modern-ism, and politics to male utopias, "so astounding, or so absurd ... so seductive" (1988:157), but not whole, sustained, and compelling as symbolic critical action.

This study has suggested an argument for a case of instructive difference. In the poems presented in part 2, especially in Gómez-Quiñones's "Ballad of Billy Rivera," we have seen a literal representation of gender that also metaphorically constitutes a poetic discourse and does so in a way that overcomes the limiting "femininity" of traditional modernism and its occasional male utopian solutions. The difference is one of culture but, as always, culture fundamentally conditioned by *class*, a lesson forgotten or repressed by Chicano formalism and culturalism as well as by Stevens's canonical critics (Lentricchia 1988:204–5).

I have offered a Chicano poetic site with a working-class, culturally distinct inheritance in which folkloric, politically progressive, phallic poetic discourses have an honored place and are available to do antagonistically creative work in the writerly present. But, here also is a site with an equal inheritance of resistive working-class maternal voices, voices "of menudo and familia early / in the morning, on Saturdays / and Sundays," at some social and poetic distance from the "Complacencies of the peignoir, and late / Coffee and oranges in a sunny chair." In such poems these folkloric cultural endowments make relevant a carefully and critically appropriated Anglo-American modernism to produce socially engaged and culturally instructive long poems, poems neither finally "male" nor "female," poems that explicitly speak of class—and race—poems of *our* climate.

We must then speak of a modernism of critical difference. Recently, Paul Gilroy has offered the term "populist modernism" to refer to an important segment of black expressive culture and its artists. "This apparently contradictory term," he says, "suggests that our artists are not just defenders and critics of modernism but that they are at the same time aware of what I regard as their historic responsibility to act as the gravediggers of modernity," that is, as gravediggers for advanced capitalism. Such a populist modernism, Gilroy continues, would be a cultural practice "which exploited instructively and deliberately that quality of perception which DuBois and other people have called 'double consciousness.' " Formally, he adds, such a modernism would "articulate a positive core of aesthetic modernism in resolutely vernacular formats" (Gilroy 1988:45).[3] Houston Baker, Jr., and Henry Louis Gates, Jr., have offered a similar thesis, the former in a more sustained theoretical fashion. Baker (1985) identifies the blues as a rich informing folk text that deeply influences a broad range of African American expressive culture with modernist writing at its center. From this conjunction, Baker generates a theory of vernacular modernism, a deep style, which he continues to trace in *Modernism and the Harlem Renaissance* (1987), showing how Booker T. Washington's oratory also emerges as a key precursor for African American modernism (see also Baker 1988). Gates (1988) locates a powerful informing source for modernism in the vernacular tradition of the "toast" and its central symbolic figure, the signifying monkey.[4]

In all these cases, including my own, strong vernacular traditions—folklore—return to deeply inform and produce a new modernism, one redefining the "best" that has been written in terms of the best that has been said, sung, and signified. The result, it has been suggested, is the reinvigoration of a traditional modernism, now viewed as exhausted in its ability to generate social change. Once bracketed as "ethnic" or "third world," these new emerging literatures seem instead to represent a strong continuation of a critical modernism.

I offer the preceding as a contribution to the debates concerning folklore, new historicist practice, and the evolution of modernism. But this book and I began in the world of greater Mexico, and it is to this world I now return in my final remarks.

THE SIXTIES AND CHICANO
CULTURAL CRITICISM

> I believe it would be an interesting exercise to study the key words and expressions of major conceptual archetypes or foundation metaphors, both in the periods during which they first appeared in their full social and cultural settings and in their subsequent expansion and modification in changing fields of social relations. I would expect these to appear in the work of exceptionally liminal thinkers—poets, writers, religious prophets . . . just before outstanding limina of history, major crises of social change.
>
> Victor Turner,
> *Dramas, Fields, and Metaphors*

In 1977 Joseph Sommers published "From the Critical Premise to the Product," a landmark essay in Chicano metacriticism calling for a critical perspective beyond the formalist and culturalist approaches then prevalent in Chicano literary and cultural criticism. Sommers's argument with formalism lay in its "insistence on separating the text from historical reality or social context"; its disregard of social meaning in favor of a postulation of the text "as occupying 'imaginary space,' as being the created, mental experience which alone can provide an alternative to lived experience, to the chaos, injustice and temporality of the real world"; its "emphasis on consecrated masterpieces as models," which restricts literature to printed texts, valorizes a well-educated middle-class audience, and assigns a relatively "low value to oral literature"; and its "stress on the text as the individual creation of a particular author" who is understood as being engaged in a "private struggle to find a personal voice and to express a personal response" (1977:56).

In explaining the inadequacies of the so-called humanistic-culturalist approach, Sommers faults its "key assumptions," which "not only incorporate a view of culture as static, but also construe race as the controlling element in culture, while positing culture as the central determinant of the people's experience. This line of thought tends to subordinate the idea that culture might be bound up with the social condition of class, as well as the view that cultural forms evolve as a response to the specifics of the historical process" (1977:58). The principal shortcoming of such Chicano cultural criticism, Sommers continues, is its failure to deeply historicize, thus becoming complicit with what Terry Eagleton calls "that rich gamut of idealisms . . . which has served as modern American criticism" (1986:50).

Sommers recommends a third perspective for the successful interrogation of Chicano literature. This perspective

> begins by explaining the singular formal qualities of a text which distinguish it from alternate modes of verbal expression. It must also account for the manner in which a given text rejects, modifies and incorporates features of texts which have preceded it. Analysis, then, includes the notion of intertextuality, the response to literary traditions. Further, since the critic sees literature as a cultural product, the particular text is studied in relation to its cultural ambience, which process in turn means understanding societal structures. (1977:59)

Further,

> Treating critical approaches dialectically, the critic does not reject formalism or culturalist approaches out of hand but tries to incorporate their positive features into a system which transcends their self-con-

structed limitations. Similarly this third approach incorporates into its methodology the concerns of the sociology of literature, which range from analyzing the material conditions and the intellectual climate of literary production to interpreting the reception and impact of a given text. (1977:60)

As a historically evolving practice, Chicano literary criticism has not remained bound to the two earlier constraining sets of premises and has, in fact, moved progressively toward the third. Anticipated by Sommers himself and, as Sommers (1977:60) perceptively notes, by Américo Paredes, a new set of critics is emerging who draw their theoretical energy from the eclectic disciplinary margins of literary and cultural theory. This theory includes Marxism, but it is a Marxism articulated in a poststructuralist critical discourse. This marriage is not without its problems, since contemporary Marxist theorists are sympathetically suspicious of some dominant versions of poststructuralist thought (Chabram 1987; Ros. Sánchez 1987).[5] But in joining these approaches, the new Chicano criticism attempts to rupture the idealistic constraints of mainstream American criticism, including its latest deconstructivist phase, and end up in a subsuming critical position—an ultimate horizon of reading, as Fredric Jameson might say—that, indeed, centrally draws on Jameson as well as other Marxist cultural critics sensitive to the historicity and social fluidity of discourse. The new Chicano critics recognize, as do Lentricchia (1980:206) and Eagleton (1986:62–70), Jameson's work as the prime example of a new kind of American criticism. Yet as they bring these theoretical resources to bear on their interrogation of Chicano literature, they do so critically, by illuminating a literature that brings into question the continuing high canonical— and therefore still quite mainstream—concerns of Marxist cultural criticism itself (Calderón 1983; Calderón and J. Saldívar, 1991; McKenna, in press; J. Saldívar, in press; R. Saldívar, 1979, 1984, 1985, 1990; Ros. Sánchez 1987). Notably, with three fine exceptions (R. Saldívar, 1984; J. Saldívar, 1986; McKenna, in press), poetry has not received as much attention from the new Chicano critics as has prose narrative.

The present study is situated in the new Chicano criticism, though obviously inspired as well by the "native" criticism of Américo Paredes and Joseph Sommers. In order to address the intertextual dimensions of Chicano culture, which have received so little attention, I turned initially to Harold Bloom's theory of poetic influence, and then attempted to "socialize" Bloom by joining his theory of poetic influence to a theory of ideology and society, to a Marxist politics and poetics of culture. By socially imbedding Bloom's "strong" theory of poetry, I was able to examine how the political poetry of one generation, particularly its folk political poetry, powerfully influenced the written poetry of another. Using Bloom's and Jameson's theories of repression, I sought to fulfill Sommers's challenge, to demonstrate "how scholarship concentrating on literary history, rather than being dry and congealed, can point toward deeper understanding and recuperation of a hitherto concealed, even repressed literary tradition" (1977:60).

The epic heroic corrido of greater Mexico furnished a sustaining, largely critical cultural poetics for a dominated people at the turn of the century. Incorporating its influence, Américo Paredes fashioned a more gender-conscious poetry that also spoke critically from the outside toward a centered dominance. Already responding to a greater complexity of the residual and the emergent, the hegemonic and the counterhegemonic, this poetics also incorporated critical emergent aspects of modernism. Independently, and through Paredes, three key Chicano poets from the late 1960s and early 1970s also learned the lessons of the corrido and of modernism. They too struggled to harness the patriarchally charged political energy of the former in the interest of a poetry that needed to be even more responsive to new social and ideological complexities, a response best articulated in modernist poetics. Incorporating the increasingly unrepressed voice of woman as well, this poetry sought to widen the meaning of a community in social struggle.

Following Sommers and Jameson and their injunction to historicize, we can gain additional insight into the social dynamics of this poetry by turning to the anthropology of symbols. This anthropological perspective may also yield a more complex sense of the Chicano movement.

With their socially imbedded quality, these poems and others like them did work as the kind of symbolic action that Victor Turner finds highly operative during those moments of crisis and disharmony that he calls "social dramas." Factions and interests in society generate such action to articulate and press their claims in these moments of conflict (Turner 1974). Turner distinguishes four phases in such social dramas— breach, crisis, redressive action, and reintegration. Of these, the redressive phase is especially noteworthy, for it is here that "the society, group, community . . . is at its most 'self-conscious' and may attain the clarity of someone fighting in a corner for his life" (Turner 1974:41). It is here also that symbolic action proliferates.

Such a social drama occurred in the 1960s among Mexican-Americans. The long Chicano poems of the sixties and early seventies constitute a redressive symbolic action, action by which those in the structural and cultural minority presented their sense of the conflict in rhetorically compelling figurations. Yet the beleaguered group is not wholly homogeneous either ideologically or in terms of the form of its symbolic actions (although Turner sometimes leaves this impression). Unfortunately, literary histories of the Chicano movement have tended to treat the poetic production of this period in ideologically homogeneous terms. Now perhaps we are at a sufficient distance from this period to begin to historicize it in greater detail and complexity.

I have proposed that each of the three long poems examined in part 2 may be taken as a distinctive symbolic representation of a cultural response to the 1960s and to the past. I have identified a perspective of Alienation, best expressed by Montoya's "El Sol y los de Abajo," where the speaker cannot fully come to terms with past and present. Several years later, Corky Gonzales's "I Am Joaquín" exemplifies the spirit of Assertion, closely congruent with a palpable dominant cultural nationalism as much at war with the past as with the present, despite its surface protestations, its seeming "pastness." Finally, the attitude of Reflection, a kind of "final" stage in the classical rite of passage, is the special achievement of Juan Gómez-Quiñones's "The Ballad of Billy Rivera," a ballad in which the poem as a collective representation comes to a richer, more confident, and more politically progressive understanding of past and present.

Thus *within* Turner's redressive phase we have a more classical tripartite temporally phased ritual movement (Van Gennep 1960), a ritual within a ritual. It is as if, once in the redressive and liminal phase, each of these poetic actors "chose" distinct responses relative to a variety of conscious and unconscious factors. In doing so, to draw on yet another symbolic anthropologist (Geertz 1973:93–94), these poets likely became both "models of" culture change and "models for" the production and resolution of change relative to other participants in the movement. Further historical ethnographic work on the culture of the Chicano movement will no doubt speak to these as yet tentative points.

As poetic symbolic action, each of these long poems was generated in social struggle and directly addressed that struggle. Indeed, a commitment to social struggle has been a hallmark of Chicano poetry, and in this commitment Chicano poets have been ably assisted by their mighty precursor, the greater Mexican corrido. In an insight quite germane to our diachronic model of influence and society, Turner also notes that the social dramas and symbolic action in one period can "become objectivated models for future behavior in the history of collectivities" (1974:96). More specifically, the Mexican movement for independence from Spain in 1810, he tells us, was a failure instrumentally, but it "had potent effects on subsequent dramas and revolutionary processes" and established "a new myth containing a new set of paradigms, goals, and incentives for Mexican struggle" (1974:102). Indeed, it might be said that the greater Mexican revolutionary period of the early twentieth century was marked by a social anxiety of influence toward the earlier revolution of 1810, and that this social anxiety of influence was repeated again in the 1960s relative to its strong social predecessor, the revolutionary movement of 1910.

Yet if these poems are instances of a collective symbolic action whereby the movement in some sense also authors them, these long poems also exemplify a new phenomenon in the history of the Mexican people in the United States—the first generation in which a substantial number of young people attend college and university. Through their political involvement and social critique, these poems speak of a male-dominated student generation's efforts to come to terms, culturally and psychoanalytically, with the continuing potent presence of their fathers and patriarchal culture in the context of new demands and desires.[6] Responding to this paternal potency and these new demands and desires, these poems increasingly resolve this seeming contradiction by revealing gradually in themselves the counterinfluential voices of the maternal and of modernism. What they offer is a progressively better, symbolically richer resolution of these various discourses—modernism, woman's voice, and paternal folk tradition—a resolution in the service of their community in their time and in the present.

All theory is text-specific, and ours must be as well. Lest I be misunderstood, I have tried to work through contemporary theories of literature *not* to "apply" them to black texts but rather to *transform* by *translating* them into a new rhetorical realm. . . . It is only through this critical activity that the profession, in a world of dramatically fluid relations of knowledge and power, and of the reemerging presence of the tongues of Babel, can redefine itself away from a Eurocentric nation of a hierarchical "canon" of texts, mostly white, Western and male, and encourage and sustain a truly comparative and pluralistic notion of the institution of literature.

Henry Louis Gates, Jr.,
"Authority (White), Power and the
(Black) Critic"

I would say that the intellectual of working class background, or more broadly of a background outside the social, racial, ethnic, economic, gender-biased, homophobic mainstream, will in effect have to retrieve his outsider's experience, bring it to bear in critical dialogue with the traditional confirmation he has been given.

Frank Lentricchia,
Criticism and Social Change

Epilogue

The case of a Chicano vernacular or populist modernism that I have presented in these pages is an example of a vital and dynamic dialogue between a traditional and powerful folklore and a confirmation of "traditional" modernism. This dialogue, in turn, intersects and poetically defines a crucial period in the history of the greater Mexican people, the years 1965–1972. By attending to the enduring power of the corrido and its countervailing maternal traditions, I have sought to render an active, complex, socially engaged literary history of this period.

Yet these long poems are themselves literary histories of the period—that is, histories cast in literary form. Though written and circulated in oral, manuscript, and rough published form during the Chicano movement period, the poems did not appear in their definitive published form until 1972. Thus, as I argued in my concluding chapter, they become symbolic representations of the period and one way of understanding that period and its contributions to critical modernism.[1] Nonetheless, these poems are not "period pieces." They and their powerful precursors still speak as vehicles of a critical modernism, especially since other postmodern modes of cultural critique are so wanting. If read with interested intercultural understanding, these poems provide us with historically engendered critiques of the present. And unlike most American long poems, these truly sacerdotal Chicano poems speak to a large social grouping, not merely to an alienated cult in the manner of traditional modernism (Walker 1989). But if these poems are to reach readers other than Mexican-Americans, it will be because the Mexican-American intelligentsia has first read and made use of them.

Chicano poetry has, of course, continued to develop since the movement and into our own time. As I suggested in chapter 4, the seventies and eighties might be termed the epoch of Chicana poetry, whose history, in terms of influences, regions, and ideologies, remains to be fully written. To read these fine lines from Lorna Dee Cervantes (1981:25),

> My sense of this land can only ripple through my veins
> like the chant of an epic corrido.
> I come from a long line of eloquent illiterates
> whose history reveals what words don't say

is to know the continuing influence of the epic balladry of greater Mexico for a new generation.

Beyond its assistance to writers and critics, this study has been an analysis of a poetry deeply imbedded in social conflict and change. Many pressing social questions continue to confront the Mexican-American community, among them the education and future of its intelligentsia.

The specific site of struggle is the contemporary American university, which each year enrolls more young Mexican-Americans, the leadership of the future. The first task of these Chicano long poems, these examples of vernacular modernism, will be to assist in preventing the emergence of alienated cults among these young Mexican-Americans, an alienation generated by a gender and class division in this population.

As I was writing a draft of these pages in May 1988, I took a break, picked up the *Stanford Daily*, the student newspaper, and read the following:

> One of the fastest growing minorities in the country, and at Stanford, Mexican-Americans often face cultural difficulties that other students here would not encounter. "Some people confused me for one of the Mexican food service workers," said one freshman about his first week at Stanford. The student, a Mexican-American who wished to remain anonymous, said that the assumptions fellow-students made about him "really hurt."

I am not as concerned about the assumptions that Anglo students or staff made about this young Mexican-American student as I am about those assumptions he is making about himself and the Mexican food service workers. I am less concerned about his hurt feelings than I am about the deeper hegemonic injuries he has incurred before even arriving at Stanford. I do not know if he is representative or more honest than most Mexican-American students today. I do know that a community beset by externally generated problems (education, health, political representation, unemployment) is now also contending with a growing internal class alienation. This young man is the representative site of struggle upon which all of our texts have to bear. For an effective struggle to overcome socioeconomic problems will require a clear consciousness of our proper relationship to our community among those who will be direct agents of change for that community. A complex literature of social change, read in terms of its empowering historical antecedents and its full critical dialogue with the present, has a decisive role to play in this formation and struggle. Such is the power of literature as symbolic action. If this book assists in the artistically sensitive, yet political reading of such a literature, I will feel I have done my small part in reconstituting the sign of community, as I did twenty-five years ago with that rain-soaked sign on the West Mall of the University of Texas: Mexican • American • workers • students • meeting. *Una mano no se lava sola.*

APPENDIX A

Harold Bloom:
An Exposition and Left Critique

Frank Lentricchia approvingly acknowledges that "no theorist writing in the United States today has succeeded, as Harold Bloom has, in returning poetry to history." For Lentricchia, this return to history constitutes a much needed and important break with "both the New-Critical concern with the isolated, autonomous monad" and the more contemporary, equally ahistorical "poststructuralist tendency to dissolve literacy history into a repetitious synchronic rhetoric" (1980:342). Nonetheless, Lentricchia also notes the political limitations of Bloom's contributions. Here, I want to discuss the way in which Bloom's central concept of poetic influence returns poetry to history, the severe limitations of that return, and the theoretical basis for its critical elaboration toward a truly historical and social poetics. If such an elaboration is vitally necessary for a richer understanding of any poetry, it may be more so for modern Mexican-American poetry, a poetry generated in sociohistorical conflict and change.

But why, in the examination of such a social poetry, use Bloom at all? Why not immediately employ a strict sociohistorical criticism rather than elaborate Bloom's ideas into such a criticism? My answer is that even as it stands, Bloom's theory of poetic influence is of invaluable assistance in closely explicating the relationship between poems past and present in this particular culture. I note four important related reasons.

First, Bloom's theory offers a way to dynamically and chronologically historicize the cultural poetry of this population, a task that has been largely ignored. Second, as we shall see, Bloom's theoretical interest in the psychodynamics of poetical patriarchy and the authoritative role of the father figure certainly speaks to a social group with these general cultural investments. Third, as Bloom himself has begun to note, ultimately, the greatest and most influential master poems in Western culture may be those formed in an oral tradition. I propose that we may here have such a case, given Mexican-Americans' well-documented adherence to oral tradition. Finally, even as these writers adhere to their Mexican oral tradition, they also fall under the influence of the Anglo-American modernist poetics in which they were schooled; hence, their susceptibility to a "canonical" criticism.

However, I do not want to treat these questions of modernism, patriarchy, and oral tradition separately from the sociohistorical. Rather I wish to offer an expanded but integrated theoretical framework, one that is keyed to the sociohistorical, including the prime consideration of ethnicity, class, and gender.

Bloom has indeed returned poetry to history, but in a way that at first glance might seem fairly orthodox and superficially chronological. His general contention that poets are influenced by earlier poets is initially neither interesting nor controversial, given an Anglo-American scholarly industry devoted to identifying echoes and allusions. Were we to follow this simple concept of influence, we would rest content with identifying formal and imagistic echoes of the Mexican corrido in contemporary Chicano poems. However, Bloom quickly rejects this mundane sense of influence and elaborates a far more radical, dynamic understanding of what influence means in poetic relations.

At the core of Bloom's theory is the proposition that poetry is about other poetry and little else: "Poems . . . are neither about 'subjects' nor about 'themselves.' They are necessarily about *other poems*; a poem is a response to a poem, as a poet is a response to a poet, or a person to his parent" (1975a:18). There is, however, a historical dimension to these relationships. A poem is a response usually to a temporally distant precursor poem whose influence on the later work springs from its artistic—rather than merely chronological—priority. This is the status that my study accords to the epic heroic corrido of greater Mexico. But to the considerable degree that Bloom really means "father" when he says "parent," his theory analogizes from the father-son relationship in the Freudian Oedipal complex. This brings us to the influential presence of Freud in Bloom's theory.

Since Bloom posits that any cultural product can be construed as a poem (1975a:70), inevitably he thinks of himself and Freud as poets of a different kind, and in a telling essay he speaks of "wrestling with Sigmund" (1982b:85–117). This particular relationship of influence merits its own analysis in Bloom's terms, but that is for another time and place. To fully understand Bloom's theory, nonetheless, we do need to account for Freud's presence in the theory, if only in a more mundane sense of influence, although from time to time I briefly note Bloom's active revisionary struggle with Freud. Indeed, this accounting may also have special pertinence to the explication of my particular Mexican cultural case with its special patriarchal emphasis.

The concept of the father is the first of three places in Bloom's theory where Freud is quite evident. If "a poem is a response to a poem [as] a person to his parent" and such responses take the form of a struggle, we soon find ourselves thinking about the specific struggle between father and son for the affective control of the mother: the Freudian Oedipus complex. Bloom is almost fully explicit in analogizing poetic and Oedipal relations: "*Only a poet challenges a poet as poet*, and so only a poet makes a poet. To the poet-in-a-poet, a poem is always *the other man*, the precursor, and so a poem is always a person, always the father of one's Second Birth. To live, the poet must *misinterpret* the father, by the crucial act of misprision, which is the re-writing of the father" (1975a:19). And, later: "poets differentiate themselves into strength by troping or turning from the presence of other poets. Greatness results from a refusal to separate origins from aims. The father is met in combat, and fought to at least a standoff, if not quite to a separate peace" (1975a:80).

To complete this Oedipal analogy, the younger poet must, of course, be as a son. Yet—and for reasons I do not understand but which may constitute part of Bloom's revisionary struggle with Freud—Bloom nowhere names the third term of the complex—the mother—or its poetic analogy, except to say: "Beyond the pleasures of poetry lies the maternal womb of language out of which poems arise, the literal meaning that poems both evade and desperately seek" (1975a:92).

The son's Oedipal struggle with the father is, according to Freud, motivated simultaneously by the desires for the mother's sole love and for the father's death, both aspects of Freud's concept of the drive or instinct, that is, Eros and the death wish. In the realm of poetic relations, Bloom interprets Eros to mean that the ephebe generates his poem as an assertion of his own living creative existence as a poet. However, Bloom denies that the death wish exists in the poet as poet: "by definition no poet, *as poet*, can wish to die, for that negates poethood" (1975a:91). Rather than having both instincts at war, poets deal with only one: "Literally, poems are refusals of mortality. Every poem therefore has two makers: the precursor, and the ephebe's rejected mortality. A poet, I argue in consequence, is not so much a man speaking to men as a man rebelling against being spoken to by a dead man (the precursor) outrageously more alive than himself" (1975a:19).

Paradoxically, however, he who is now dead and past is nonetheless always present—"outrageously" alive—in the ephebe's poetic consciousness, much as the son always partakes a great deal of the father even as they struggle. In the attempt to write his own presumptively "autonomous" poem, the young poet, always unconsciously aware of the precursor, struggles and defends against the latter's influence and does so in the very writing of the poem. Here we come to the third Freudian contribution—the concept of defenses. Bloom acknowledges and then appears to rewrite Freud's basic proposition: "A defense then is a psychic operation or process directed against *change*, change that might disturb the ego as a stable entity. Defense is set against internal movements from the id, movements that must appear as *representations* (desires, fantasies, wishes, memories)" (1975a:92). In Bloom's terms, defenses are generated and set against representations from the id, although throughout it must also be the case that defenses are also generated against representations from the father. Bloom is not fully clear and explicit on this defensive double thrust, although we have already noted that "every poem . . . has two makers: the precursor and the ephebe's rejected mortality."

There is ample charter for this dualistic movement in classical Freudian theory, which corresponds well to Bloom's conception of the poetic drive and the precursor's dominating influence. In the standard Freudian formulation, the father is understood as superego, the ego's source of the normative, the lawful, the authoritative. To keep a sense of its own healthy developmental autonomy, the ego must offer successful defenses against the authoritative domination of the father who stands as a restricting antithesis to the id's rebellious claims. As Fenichel notes: "All the defense mechanisms usually employed in the fight against instincts may also become directed against the "anti-instincts" originating in the superego. In such cases, the ego develops a countercathexis, one against the instincts and another one against the superego" (1945:132).

Having introduced the concept of defense into his theory, Bloom continues his revision of Freud by analogizing and elaborating the concept into a literary hermeneutics. Defenses, which are always generated against the id and superego, are, more specifically, for Bloom, mounted against *representations* from these linguistic images. That is, like poets and critics, the ego cannot know instinctual essences beyond language; the ego can know them only as images, figurations in language, and its defenses are generated accordingly. In Bloom's revision, all defenses take the form of a *trope*, "a word or phrase used in some way that is not literal," which is to say, fundamentally, poetic language (1975a:93). Bloom understands poems to be, in whole or in part, antithetical tropic responses to equally tropic representations from the past, the precursors. Furthermore, each poem or portion of it operates as what Bloom calls a "revisionary ratio" with respect to precursory poems. He takes *ratio* to mean "thought," poetic thought cast as imagistic figurations. These again, Bloom sees as attempts to address the power of the past poem, to ward off its dominating influence by revising it in one's "own" words and thus responding in an illusory fashion to the instinctual drive for poetic immortality. To summarize thus far, in Bloom's own words:

> An antithetical practical criticism must begin with the analogical principle that tropes and defenses are interchangeable when they appear *in poems*, where after all both appear only as images. What I have called "revisionary ratios" are tropes and psychic defenses, both and either, and are manifested in poetic imagery. A rhetorical critic can regard a defense as a concealed trope. A psychoanalytic interpreter can regard a trope as a concealed defense. An antithetical critic will learn to use both in turn, relying upon the substitution of analogues as being one with the poetic process itself. (1975a:88–89)

To teach us how to be such antithetical critics, Bloom has elaborated a complex model in which images, tropes, and defenses are aligned in what he calls a "map of misprision," a set of revisionary ratios (see Bloom 1975:84). Through these strategies, or revisionary ratios, the son-poet tries to cope with the influence of the strong precursor. The defenses principally take the form of images that exhibit at once both the later poet's influence and difference in relation to the master poem. The six ratios may appear only in part and in any sequence in any particular poem, although Bloom has carefully noted that all six in the particular sequence shown in his map appear in "a remarkable number of poems" (1975a:105); indeed, "all . . . can be at work in really comprehensive and ambitious poems, however long or short" (1975a:96).

The later poet's experience of the precursor's superior artistic power, together with the knowledge that the precursor has come *before*, is the origin of what Bloom calls "the anxiety of influence," the anxious feeling that everything poetically worthwhile has already been said, leaving little room for subsequent greater poetic effort. If he is to succeed, the younger poet—the *ephebe*, or young man in training, to use Bloom's terms—must try to forge his own poem so that, paradoxically, the precursor becomes the source of new creativity.

In an effort to create his own poetic being, the ephebe develops his own poetic powers to the imagined point of being a wholly new creative self. This imagined act of poetic selfhood necessarily entails a fundamentally antagonistic and antithetical relationship with the precursor poem (or poems). The ephebe's imagined achievement lies in the attempt to negate the precursor's primacy by replacing it with his own: "Poetic strength comes only from a triumphant wrestling with the greatest of the dead, and from an even more triumphant solipsism" (1975a:9). Yet by the very terms of this struggle, the precursor's influence marks the ephebe's poem even as the ephebe attempts to come to terms—his terms—with this influence. For the ephebe must write his poem in a way that takes in yet conceals this influence while ostensibly creating a "new" poem. This strategy of acknowledgment and concealment in the fashioning of the later poem, Bloom calls variously "rewriting," "revision," "misinterpreting," and "misprision." In principle any poem can and should be interpretively read in these terms, according to Bloom, for there is no other way to read: "there are *no* texts, but only relationships *between* texts" (1975a:3).

To say that a given poem is a direct result of and is shaped by its antagonistic relationship with a precursor poem is at once to say too much and not enough. It is too much because Bloom's analytical practice is generally restricted to those he repeatedly calls "strong" poets, and he concentrates on post-Enlightenment poetry from the Anglo-American literary tradition. For Bloom the strongest of these poets are Milton and Emerson, on their respective sides of the Atlantic; subsequent strong poetry in this Anglo-American tradition takes its shaping influence ultimately from these two figures, though mediated along the way by others (e.g., Whitman), who assume their own precursory status in relation to later poets (e.g., Stevens).

We also need to say more concerning Bloom's concept of poetic influence, beginning with his perhaps startling revelation, noted earlier, that it extends to activities not properly "poems" and, conversely, that anything can be construed as a poem. "Contact, in a poem," he tells us, "means contact with another poem, even if that poem is called a deed, person, place or thing" (1975a:70). Thus the precursor poem might be a piece of "strong" critical writing: "As literary history lengthens, all poetry necessarily becomes verse-criticism, just as all criticism becomes prose-poetry" (1975a:3).

HISTORY AND THE SOCIAL IN THE POET

We can now begin to appreciate why Lentricchia initially compliments Bloom for returning poetry to history, in contrast to the New Criticism's insistence on the poem's location and status as an ahistorical aesthetic monad. In Bloom's theory the poem is no longer a temporally isolated artistic construction but rather an artistic process whose making occurs in a dialectical and revisionary relationship to history, conceived as a master great poem, and to precursor poets. Yet even as Lentricchia praises Bloom for this return to history, he ultimately argues that Bloom has returned the poem to such a thin sense of history that Bloom is simply a "neo" new Critic (1980:331).

Lentricchia strongly objects to Bloom's essentialist definition of *poet* and *poem* and his restriction of influence, and therefore of history, to relations between poems. "That even the strongest poets are subject to influences not poetical is obvious even to me," says Bloom, "but again my concern is only with *the poet in a poet*, or the aboriginal poetic self" (1973:11). This formulation, Lentricchia tells us,

> is shrewd, disarming and also question-begging and evasive. What about those "influences not poetical"? And what is the poet in a poet? Something isolate and impregnable to all externally originating influences except those literary in character? The unspoken assumption is that poetic identity is somehow a wholly intraliterary process in no contact with the larger extraliterary processes that shape human identity. (1980:326)

Thus Bloom has opened the poem to history, but only to a purely literary history. Therefore, Lentricchia cautions, Bloom "has not evaded what he believes to be the central error of New Critical doctrine," namely that, "poems are created by the poetic faculty; the poetic identity is somehow ontologically severed from human identity" and "all those forces outside of poetic history as Bloom narrowly conceives it, have no bearing upon the discourse of poetry." Lentricchia rejects this narrow view of history, for in it "the psychic and social life of the poet as a man in the world count for nothing" (1980:331). For Lentricchia, a final unacceptable implication of Bloom's negation of the social is that poetry and poetic relations are cast in a willful, individualistic capitalist idiom of competition, language as poetic commodity, and poetic personal profit.

Yet "having said that against Bloom's theory," Lentricchia does not wholly reject it as a partial basis for a poetic literary history, for "there is nothing in the theory of influence that would prevent it from being modified and broadened so as to take into account those criticisms." Bloom's sense of poetic history is narrow and aestheticist only because

> he has not cared to see the restrictive family romance of literary language within an encompassing context of a larger cultural family of writing which would draw it into context with the discourses of other disciplines. [He] privileges major writers and their dynastic wars only because he has not cared, to this point, to take into account the many sibling minor writers and a whole series of *contemporary* networks of repression from which strong writers must wrest their identities at perilous points in their development. (1980:344)

Lentricchia recommends Foucault's theory of genealogy, discourse, and power as a way of modifying and broadening Bloom.

Notwithstanding Foucault's affinities with critical Marxism (Lentricchia 1988:29–102), however, I am interested in a more specifically Marxist cultural criticism that nonetheless incorporates Foucauldian poststructuralist thought. Indeed, beyond his own recommendation in *After the New Criticism* and *Criticism and Social Change*, Lentricchia also seems to have this more specific Marxism in mind as the most effective critical practice. He proposes a Marxist perspective conceived of as rhetoric in the best sense of this term: "the kind of Marxist theory that I am urging is itself a kind of rhetoric whose value may be measured by its persuasive means and by its ultimate goal: the formation of a genuine community" (1983:11–12). As cultural criticism, this kind of theoretical practice consists of

> the production of knowledge to the ends of power and maybe social change ... the kind of activity that a Marxist literary intellectual preeminently engages in ... the activity of interpretation ... [that] constructs a point of view in its engagement with textual events, and in so constructing produces an image of history as social struggle, of, say class struggle, an image that is not "there" in a simple sense but is the discovery of the active intellectual soul. This sort of interpretation, when worked through the traditional texts of the humanities, will above all else attempt to displace traditional interpretations which cover up the political work of culture. (1983:11)

To this same general end, the Marxist literary critic Fredric Jameson has offered a specific critical program for reading texts as "images of social struggle," to use Lentricchia's phrase. For Jameson, all cultural texts may be read in terms of what he calls "the political unconscious." Like Bloom, Jameson relies on and revises Freud, but his revisionary mode is directed toward radical ends. For Freud, of course, cultural texts may encode hidden, repressed meanings in disguised symbolic form for an individual, but in Jameson's Marxist revision, such symbolic structures and their meanings refer not to an autonomous individual psyche, but rather to a collective experience in history, an experience of social antagonism, conflict, and change. Drawing on but subsuming other strategies for textual reading—the psychoanalytic perspective, poststructuralism, Northrop Frye's archetypal criticism, and Althusserian Marxism—Jameson develops his own trilevel hermeneutic for interpretively uncovering a text's range of meaning in a historical field of domination, conflict, and repression.

Jameson's first level is that of "political history, in the narrow sense of punctual event and a chronicle-like sequence of happenings in time" (1981:75). This first-level reading must go beyond examining the text merely as a record or mirror image of historical "facts," even facts of social struggle in some manner of "socialist realism." Taking the notion of social contradiction as a key tenet, Jameson tells us that even at this first level, the cultural text is to be read as a socially symbolic act that symbolically both represents and resolves particular and local social contradictions in imaginary form. These contradictions cannot be presented and resolved in real social life because they have been repressed by a collective psyche that cannot fully and clearly articulate its needs in a specific local social context.

At the second level, the text is seen as a single utterance that can be more fully understood only when set in a larger field of antagonistic class discourses. Here, "the individual utterance or text is grasped as a symbolic move in an essentially polemic and strategic ideological confrontation between the classes" (1981:85). To read at this level, however, requires a wider and richer understanding of the class-antagonistic character of other discourses that constitute the specific historical context of the chosen text. Against and through this context, the symbolic act is again viewed as a presentational resolution of a repressed localized social contradiction, but this time, however, the contradiction is "in the form of the dialogical as the irreconcilable demands and positions of antagonistic classes" (1981:85).

Finally, Jameson would have us read the text in the context of history conceived "in its vastest sense of the sequence of modes of production and the succession and destiny of the various human social formations" (1981:75). That is, the text is interpretively placed by the way it speaks to the conflicts between distinct modes of production (feudalism, capitalism, etc.) as these change and overlap in time and constitute distinctive social formations. The text will speak to "that moment in which the coexistence of various modes of production becomes visibly antagonistic, their contradictions moving to the very center of political, social, and historical life" (1981:95). A text may speak to these relatively long-term antagonisms within a given social formation, antagonisms generated by

> vestiges and survivals of older modes of production, now relegated to structurally dependent positions within the new, as well as anticipatory tendencies which are potentially inconsistent with the existing system but have not yet generated an autonomous space of their own. (1981:95)

At the two lower levels, reading focuses on a text's symbolic "contents," but at this third level, Jameson places interpretive emphasis on a text's *form*, but form apprehended as ideology. Here it is necessary to grasp "formal processes as sedimented content in their own right, as carrying ideological messages of their own, distinct from the ostensible or manifest content of the works" (1981:99). It is in the ideology of form, rather than traditional "content," where Jameson locates the possible contradictions and conflicts between distinct cultural modes of production as these overlap in any given social formation.

I opened my discussion of Jameson by introducing him as an example, perhaps the best current example, of Lentricchia's ideal Marxist literary critic who "in the activity of interpretation ... constructs a point of view in its engagement with textual events, and in so constructing produces an image of social struggle" (1983:11). However, Jameson's trilevel interpretive construction of texts in terms of social struggle conceives of "struggle" in a very particular manner. For Jameson, a cultural text engages society in a dialectic that must be interpretively grasped simultaneously. One side of this dialectic consists of a text's symbolic critique of the present social order of domination. At the same time and perhaps more importantly for Jameson, cultural texts can also be symbolic projections of a repressed human desire for community and non-alienation, a state of social life that presumably characterized "primitive communism" (either in historical reality or as a critically useful image) and that will also characterize a future utopian social order not yet in existence. Under conditions of domination long extant in human history, the purpose of cultural texts is to record in repressed symbolic form the traces of that past and the anticipations of a utopian future. This dialectic of positive projections and negative critique is always, Jameson would insist, not on the surface of the text but in its unconscious deep structure. The purpose of a Marxist criticism is to see how, at the level of the repressed unconscious, a cultural text may be understood as a dialectical utterance in a fundamental human history, namely, "the collective struggle to wrest a realm of Freedom from a realm of Necessity," the latter a synonym for the repression that has long affected humankind (1981:19): "It is in detecting the traces of that uninterrupted narrative, in restoring to the surface of the text the repressed and buried reality of this fundamental history, that the doctrine of a political unconscious finds its function and its necessity" (1981:20).

Until, Jameson might add, such a utopian time when repression ceases to exist and the distinction between texts and life is creatively blurred. Until then, a Marxist cultural criticism can reveal to us the repressed historical traces of a utopian social order and its anticipations in our cultural acts. Such a criticism, to return to Lentricchia, will present us with images of social struggle as models for the creation of this future.

Yet if Jameson's Marxist methods for reading closely yet widely help us to "socialize" the reading of a poem, they do not help us to historicize our readings longitudinally. That is, Jameson can help us to understand *Lord Jim* or "I Am Joaquín" with reference to their synchronic historical moments. However, little that he says is of analytical assistance in grasping dynamically the chronological intertextual relationship of such works as socially symbolic acts to their respective past literary cultural traditions also understood as socially symbolic acts.

Here we may be able to press to our service Raymond Williams's Gramscian-inspired concepts of the dominant hegemonic culture against which a Chicano poem may be seen as an instance of the counterhegemonic, as an instance of an emergent culture in opposition to the dominant hegemony. This opposition is both construable in Jameson's terms of the political unconscious and measurable in its effectiveness in those same terms. However, Williams also lends himself toward a historicizing of Bloom's thin sense of poetic relationships. For it is also the case that what in an earlier period is an emergent oppositional culture can, at a later period, become a "residual" tradition (Williams 1977), still active in Bloom's sense of an anxiety of influence, but always a social anxiety of influence.

APPENDIX B

Juan Gómez-Quiñones, "Canto al Trabajador"

CANTO AL TRABAJADOR
a Juan Gómez Duarte

I

Doy la mano
al que lucha
canto
    a los arrieros y vaqueros
    a los rieleros y mineros
        moledores de nueces y
        lechugueros y betabeleros
Canto
    a los piscadores
    a los steelworkers y los del auto
    a los mecánicos y plomeros
también
    a los electricistas, carpinteros
    a los lavadores y a las operadoras
    a todos los trabajadores.
Canto a los trabajadores
Todos los meses son crueles
    y la semilla queda aunque arranquen la mata
todos los meses son crueles
    para ellos de las manos esculpidas.
Siento los pies de Cuauhtémoc
    último soberano y primer rebelde
    mártir de la conquista
    primer sabor de lo amargo y la rosa.
Cantaremos a los trabajadores
y con la ayuda de los compañeros
echando un pie con el pueblo será
Canto a los trabajadores.

II

My father's holy hand is etched
    in holy grime.

I remember my father's hand
        etched in cries and sweat.
Huddled on the corner
I have seen
        the men who work.
What I know I learned
        from my father's worker's hand
who is we and who are they
        of right and wrong
    who has built the cities
and wherefrom came the riches.
I have seen the workers scattered
        like rosary beads across fields.

Rain flooded streets
sweat the work, dry the wire, change the tire
wounds from clashing steel
a care away from injury and death

the put down stare
exaggerated patience
ridicule the English

You learn
eating at trocaderos
filled with Mexicanos and drunken foremen

On cold windy days
your hands bleed and your hands can hardly hold a wrench
no books or street demagogues teach
we learn from bitterness and broken bodies.

My father's hand is etched in time
Canto a los trabajadores.

APPENDIX C

Juan Gómez-Quiñones, "The Ballad of Billy Rivera"

THE BALLAD OF BILLY RIVERA

Huey Tlatoani
Tloque Nahuaque
Quetzal
Erase que Era.

Antes que hubiera el hombre
estaba la tierra
Y de todo fue primero el espíritu
Y la naturaleza habla, el espíritu habla
    ellos-él toman forman
10   el espíritu renace
       habla y toma forma
   florece el espíritu

Sabes que
from the dispossessed
from the despised, from those who lived at the edge
came the flame
the land had been water by tears enough.
this sentence served.
In 1965 the campesinos
20   struck the fields of Delano

La leona parrió, La concha se movió
    entre gritos de rabia se pelió
    abandonados de los dioses
    el que no luchó lo apedraron
    la muerte cobró su día
    en esos meses cuando se acabó el mundo
      pueblo de cantares y guerreros
Ay Tenochtitlán, sobrevivimos.

Por las calles de mi barrio
30   pasan los dioses antiguos
Viento de llanto su voz
    llamando a su pueblo
Por las calles de mi pueblo

llaman los antiguos dioses
lloran por su pueblo
llamas en brote

Silk and Satin, southern comfort-pepsi cops
hustle the last set
stone red todos alivianando
40   to johnnies
cordovan mirrors straight kaki
It begins somewhere in Texas winds through to California

Vuela, vuela Palomita
Madre mía de Guadalupe
Por tu religión me van a matar

de allí
De donde está la
Bodega de Tormentas
de donde se almacenan
50   los vientos.
de allí se regresó.

Se empezó la caminata
por garzas y carrizales

Entre ríos, plata y sembrados
Por las parras del
Florido y Nazas
de allí se empezó.

Sólo en la danza
hay unión

60 Sólo en la danza
Se une
espíritu, alma y ser
por eso nos gusta

Sólo en el canto
se regala de verdad
papalotear Raza

La revancha es nuestra
Adiós mis amigos queridos
Adiós los falsos quereres.

70 later.
tierra, tierra, tierra.

There is only one relevant demand.
freedom.
once you get over fear
the road is open

later.
you never saw so many fucken pigs.
We left LA around 1 in the morning
3 meetins, usual shit and a demonstration tomorrow.
80   near fresno, we took a wrong turn

    R . . . , went past in a blue station wagon.
de colores, de muchos colores
at 9, can you believe it. At 9 we
    were fed menudo, by masc people.

At 12 noon the demonstration
You never saw so many fucken pigs
    in your whole life.
tripping, just tripping
en mil novecientos sesenta y ocho
90   empezaron nuestras avanzadas
pueblo maldecido y bendecido por
    sus dioses. Que vivan los mejicanos.

I just want to feel high again
Que lejos estoy del pueblo donde nací
México lindo y querido
porque no morir
Por una mujer casada
    loco y apasionado
ando en el movimiento
100 has dejado sólo amargos sentimientos
me encorporé a las filas por
    una mujer bonita
Soy soldado de la levita, de esos
    de las filas del movimiento
Soy soldado de levita, de esos de botón,

corre, corre maquinita,
triste cantan los sinsontes,
    de la sierra y de abajo
    van los hombres formando cuarteles
110   Ay Celaya

The river flowed around the
    hill
He saw the dust become the troop
    gritó, tomen las alturas al otro lado del río
tuvo tiempo de recordar cuando
    habían desfilado por las calles de la capital
hace tres días los vecinos de Sencillo
    had made barbacoa, hung streamers, shouted
    Viva Villa

120 El mayor ordenó que desensillaran la metralla
    al cabo que de aquí no salían.

porque era inocente

le cortaron la cabeza para ejemplo de la chusma

Al son del rezo antiguo
se comienza a labrar
los dioses olvidados han vuelto

AZTLAN vive.
por los montes y los llanos
sembrados de mi raza.
130   —Por Vida—

Vino el remolino y los levantó
Vendrá el viento y nos levantará

Pueblo rencoroso, da el grito.
Esperanza triunfa sobre la experiencia.

Otra vez se oyen las Torcazas
y los poetas cantan su visión de
Anáhuac.
los realistas, los sin fe han tenido su hora
pueblo:
140   Juez
testigo
víctima.
Sentencia servida.

Cantares de poetas
Utopías de sacerdotes.

En verdad se puede ser libre y bello.
Grito de Joaquín
de los peones de Tejas
de los repatriados

150   In .... Mexicans on ....
were repatriated, but they came back.
Today the migra makes sweeps
through the barrio.
arreando el mar.

Montes y llanos sembrados de la Raza
por pueblos y mercedes
en barrios y por muelles.
Sembrados de mi raza.
—Por Vida—, clavamos en paredes.
160 Clavos de amargura dejan llagas de
esperanza.
¿Cuál futuro? ¿Cuál pasado?
Sabes.
Yesterday two weeks after the
blowouts, 2 buildings were burnt.
Today or was it last week? or May last year, next year
En Coachella two growers signed contracts.

Ya pasó.
Sabes.
170   Have you ever walked the streets of
            East L. A.
    have you ever seen them shine.
    Early in the morning the air smells
            of menudo and familia, early
            in the morning, on Saturdays
            and Sundays.
    Sometimes the cars are covered with paper roses.
    rosas de papel,
                    y
180   hasta en eso raza,
    Recordamos, los campos y las flores.
    AZTLAN, ha de ser tierra de rosas.
            tierra de un pueblo de rosas.
    Sometimes, the cars are covered with
            charming paper maché
                roses.
    When *these* people get married.
    Sabes.
    Have you seen the streets of East L. A.,
190   Been in Denver cold in Winter
        En Tejas es donde calienta el sol.
        Roses are Rosas.

    Saturday
            and easy afternoons seeping beer
                stuttering conversations of bold
                    secret lives once led and never shared
            car washing, clothesbuying, body sprucing
                pepsicola-cops and paper-maché dances
            torn dresses and southern comfort breath
200   Sunday morning mass
            tired mornings that lead to tired evenings
                and then once again.
    Sabes que Billy o. d.
            they found him thursday dead two days
    BILLY RIVERA'S WAKE WILL BE
        at guerra & holman mortuary
        1724 e. florence avenue
        today 2-2-58
        from 12 p.m. to 12 a.m.
210   FUNERAL WILL BE SAT. 2-3-58
                at 8:30 a.m.

Notes

CHAPTER I

1. The Battle of Celaya was actually two major battles fought on April 6–7 and 13–15, 1915. Villa said that he lost some six thousand men in the battle—a conservative estimate, one would assume (Quirk 1969; Knight 1987:323–325).

2. Yet, as my colleague Renato Rosaldo reminds me in a personal communication, the medieval Spanish romance, at least in Castilla, sometimes did deal with border conflicts between Moors and Christians.

3. For a corrective, though fundamentally not wholly revisionary, literature concerning Paredes's gemeinschaft sense of border society, see Montejano 1987:15–37 and Rosaldo 1987.

4. Cortina 1984 offers a very compressed review of corrido scholarship focusing mostly on matters of origins, form, and distribution. In a brief review he understandably does not take up sociohistorical or theoretical considerations. His last questions and proposed research concerning the displacement of the traditional corrido by forces of commercialization are addressed by me later in this chapter and in Limón 1983a.

5. See Linderman 1987 for a comparable discussion of the tension between honor, manhood, and courage and the emerging industrial mass violence of the American Civil War.

6. But let us note Fredric Jameson's sense of the critical character of modernism's "ideology of form" and "the Utopian vocation" of its "newly reified sense, the mission of this heightened and autonomous language of color to restore at least a symbolic experience of libidinal gratification to a world drained of it, a world of extension, gray and merely quantifiable" (1981:63).

7. I find only six references to the treacherous woman in Mendoza's collection (1954) and none at all in Paredes's collection of border corridos (1976), while images of the maternal appear in at least thirteen corridos in Mendoza's collection. The bulk of Herrera-Sobek's evidence for the treacherous woman image appears to come from post-1930s corridos (Herrera-Sobek 1990:71).

8. A parallel example is the relationship of the blues as a residual culture to Afro-American literature and as an emergence (Baker 1985).

9. While I am restricting my study of the corrido's influence to written poetry, we must continue to keep before us its continuing, if attenuated, presence today as a folk corrido, whether sung or printed; see Fernandez 1983, Fuentes 1973, and Heisley 1983.

CHAPTER 2

1. Personal communication from Américo Paredes, in which he also furnished the text of the corrido.

2. Appendix A provides a more detailed exposition and critique of Bloom's ideas.

CHAPTER 3

1. All page references to *With His Pistol in His Hand* are to the 1958 edition published by the University of Texas Press. The 1971 reprint has identical pagination.

2. For a discussion of social terror experienced by proletarian women in Mexico as a primary genitive source for their prolific legendry concerning men, witchcraft, and insanity, see Limón 1986b.

3. In 1985 I overheard several young men sitting in García's Lounge in eastside Austin, Texas, after just having listened to a corrido by a local singer. I imagined what men sitting around a campfire in 1901 would have said about the ballad and juxtaposed my version of their campfire conversation with my notes from the bar:

Who Was Gregorio Cortez?

1901	1985
Era un hombre muy valiente. (He was a brave man.)	He sure blew that *gringo* away!
Era de por aquí. (He was from around here.)	You shoot the *man*, you go to jail, *bro.*
Yo conocía su papa. (I knew his father.)	Corridos are like fairy tales, man. That stuff didn't really happen!
Eso pasó. Era un hombre decente de familia. (It happened. He was a decent family man.)	Limón says it happened in Karnes City just like the corrido says.
¿Quién sabe? (Who knows?)	What does Limón know?
	El bato la cagó. (The guy "screwed up.")
Hizo mal, quizás. (Perhaps he did wrong.)	Se estaba defendiendo, *ese!* (He was defending himself, man!)
Hombre valiente.	¡Le sobraban huevos! (He had extra balls.)

4. Our understanding of the years between "Guitarreros" and *With His Pistol in His Hand* awaits the publication by Arte Publico Press of a selection of Paredes's verse from this period.

5. Yet as I speak of "metaphor," we should always be aware of continuing "incidents" like the following. It occurred in 1972 in Dallas during a police investigation of an alleged petty burglary of a soft-drink machine by two Mexican-American boys, ages twelve and thirteen.

> The oldest boy, David, was put in the back seat with officer Darrel Cain; the younger, Santos, was in the front seat . . . Cain began questioning the Rodriguez brothers about the burglary attempt, but both boys denied any knowledge of the incident. Cain then took his 357 Magnum revolver from his holster, spun the cylinder, and pointed it at the back of Santos' head . . . the boy repeated that he knew nothing; the gun clicked, but did not fire. Again, Cain demanded information. Santos said, "I am telling the truth." Cain squeezed the trigger a second time, and the revolver fired, instantly killing the twelve-year-old boy with a massive head wound. (Achor 1978:262)

Both little Santos and a grown Irishman who had also died in Dallas of a massive head wound ten years earlier were the subjects of corridos.

6. For my discussion of *With His Pistol in His Hand* as an experimental ethnography see Limón 1986c.

CHAPTER 4

1. On earlier militant labor activities organized by Mexican-Americans in Texas, see Nelson-Cisneros 1975 and Zamora 1986.

2. For an extended analysis of the term *chicano* and the general problem of ethnic nomenclature for this group, see Limón 1981.

3. With the exception of a booklength study by Muñoz (1989), the Chicano movement of 1966–1972 is only now beginning to draw extended scholarly attention. We all look forward to Juan Gómez-Quiñones's forthcoming book on this subject.

4. However, Rivera, Bruce-Novoa, and his editors make a common mistake by saying *With a Pistol in His Hand* rather than *With His Pistol in His Hand*. For the corridista and for Paredes, the difference is crucial, for the latter more clearly suggests that Cortez was self-empowered to defend his honor and his right.

5. While the long poems of the Chicano movement are shorter than such classical American long poems as *Leaves of Grass* and *Paterson*, these Chicano poems meet Walker's (1989) definition of the genre in that they "include history" (Ezra Pound's phrase) but do so in a suasive rhetorical manner toward a defined public.

6. For extended treatments of Alurista, Sergio Elizondo, and Ricardo Sánchez, see Bruce-Novoa 1980, 1982. Raul Salinas's longish poem, "Trip Through the Mind Jail," has not received the extended, detailed attention it deserves, and we await Raul Villa's forthcoming treatment as part of his study of Chicano prison poetry.

CHAPTER 5

1. "La Jefita," which appeared in *El Espejo* in 1969, is reprinted by Valdez and Steiner (1972:266–68) and by Epringham (1982:20–24).

2. "El Sol y los de Abajo" appears in Montoya's *El Sol y los de Abajo and Other R.C.A.F. Poems* (1972) and is reprinted by Hernandez (1991:65–68).

3. This is precisely the task taken up by the Chicana poets of the post-movement period (M. Sánchez 1985).

4. "El Louie" appears in Valdez and Steiner (1972:333–37) and is reprinted in Epringham (1982:58–65). "Los Vatos" first appeared in *El Espejo* in 1969 and is reprinted almost in full by J. Saldívar (1986:11–12). These poems, as well as the others discussed in this chapter, will probably appear in Montoya's forthcoming *In Formation: The Selected Poems of José Montoya / The RCAF: A Retrospect*, to be published by Chusma House.

5. In ambivalent fashion, Saldívar (1986:13) also views Benny as "anti-hero" and the poem as a "radical alteration of hero and world" in comparison to the corrido ethos.

6. Cf. Hernandez's reading of this concluding section of the poem:

> Attempting to maintain the dignified tone of the *corrido*, the poet seems suddenly to realize the discrepancies between past and contemporary history and feels that he must stop, after apologetically attempting to rationalize his present condition. He seeks to compare his father's historical experience with his own, half-heartedly arguing that circumstances have changed ("En las mismas situaciones / Diferentes condiciones"). He brings his ballad to an abrupt halt by addressing himself and his peer group with a single negation—an emphatic and meaningful *caló* term: "¡Chale!"—as a dramatic recognition that the language of the urban underworld can provide contemporary Chicanos with the rhetorical means by which to convey an epic stance.
>
> "El corrido de mi jefe" represents a masterful structural depiction of the psychological process that the poetic voice undergoes in attempting to reconcile his present and his past. The next stanza brings to full consciousness this fundamental conflict. It involves no less than the son's image of his father's exemplar masculinity and his own apprehension ("me faltan los huevos de mi jefe") at achieving a heroic level "worthy of the ballads." The use of Spanish signals to an in-group audience, with a sense of urgency, the need to develop a renewed epic awareness, now inhibited by psychological oppression ("the gava's yugo de confusión").
>
> In the last stanza, the poetic voice draws from the ancient Mayan tradition ("Chilam Balam's prophetic / Chant") to reaffirm the vision that has been revealed through the journey into the past. The redemption is granted by the claim to a pre-Columbian spiritual heritage which legitimizes the historical experience of Chicanos and transcends that of the mestizo—expressed in the interplay of English and Spanish: the languages of the conquerors. In this context the consciousness of the poet announces triumphantly that only through such a process of self-discovery will Chicanos achieve their aesthetic and historical liberation. (1991:75)

I differ with Hernandez's otherwise supportive reading on three key points: "the father's exemplar masculinity" and the poetic son's "apprehension . . . at achieving a heroic level" are actually present from the beginning; a single "Chale!" hardly constitutes recognition of the epic possibilities of the urban underworld; and, finally, Hernandez seems too uncritically accepting of the poet's final "vision."

7. For Montoya's admiring acknowledgment of the corrido, see Montoya 1980c.

CHAPTER 6

1. From the *San Francisco Daily Herald* (April 18, 1853), quoted in Castillo and Camarillo (1973:47–48).

2. Acosta collected this corrido-like song in southern Arizona in May 1948, but he provides no information concerning the song's origins or likely compositional history.

3. Bruce-Novoa makes a further paradoxical comparison: "The woman equals the *corridos*, and both equal the poem. They are all passive faithful sources of culture" (1982:64–65).

CHAPTER 7

1. Teresa McKenna is currently preparing an annotated edition of "The Ballad of Billy Rivera," and I am deeply indebted to her for her perceptive commentary and conversation on the poem.

2. "Garzas" (herons) and "carrizales" (reeds) are also common Hispanic surnames. The trek of the farmworkers was thus made by *garzas* and *carrizales*, in two senses.

3. *Aztlán* is the mythic northern ancestral homeland of the Aztecs before they began their journey southward to conquer and settle south-central Mexico. Said to be in what is now the southwestern United States, this alleged origin point for this "great" civilization acted as its own mythic symbolic validator for some in the Chicano movement who wanted to claim a historical primacy in the Southwest.

4. Here, I refer to Whitman's "Song of Myself": "Have you reckon'd a thousand acres much? have you reckon'd the earth much?" On Whitman's modernity see Pearce 1987:5; for his close affinities with T. S. Eliot, see Pearce 1987:303–5.

CONCLUSION

1. Regarding the reasons for this repression, one must consider the hierarchical and colonialist implications of the term *folklore* itself for Anglo-American and European critics; the exclusion of folklore from most graduate programs in literature; and, finally, the discipline of folklore's almost willful, defensive self-exclusion from current discussions in cultural criticism.

2. Yet in another context Lentricchia hints at the enabling power of folklore. His recounting of an anecdote concerning his Italian grandfather and the latter's critical folk appraisal of Americans includes a tentative definition of folklore, though he uses the word "stories": "Soon this will be an anecdote for me alone because soon it will have no claim whatsoever to being what all we anecdotalists want our stories to be—a social form which instigates cultural memory: the act of narrative renewal, the reinstatement of social cohesion" (1988:4).

3. I am grateful to Raul Villa for leading me to Gilroy's work.

4. Another comparative case may be found in Anglo-Irish literature. Lloyd (1987), in his excellent study of James Clarence Magnan and his role in nineteenth-century Irish nationalist literature, analyzes Magnan's struggle with the father and his indebtedness to Irish balladry, his critical anticipation of modernism and evocation of the androgynous through the assumed role of the dandy,

and his equivocal attitude toward nationalism in favor of a larger political cultural sphere. Lloyd also turns quite specifically to concepts of hegemony and counterhegemony and to a political analysis of colonialism.

5. Angie Chabram has published an admirable metacritical survey of Chicano criticism (1987). My only complaints concern her commentary on what she calls the "Austin circle" of criticism inspired by Américo Paredes, a scene I know well. On this topic Chabram relies heavily on conversations with Raymund Paredes and on his article-length literary history (1982). While "a group of students trained at UT Austin [were] heavily influenced by Américo Paredes' work," we were not primarily trained in formal literary studies as R. Paredes implies (Chabram 1987:60–61). Rather, with the exception of R. Paredes himself, we were all trained in anthropological folklore studies. This point is instructive on three counts. First, Chabram misses the opportunity to examine the work of the Austin group's anthropological folklorists (Richard Flores, Manuel Peña, Olga Najera-Ramirez, Suzanne Seriff), and she thereby misses the chance to introduce folklore into her literary scholarship. Second, our training in anthropological folklore brought us into close contact with Marxist and poststructuralist perspectives. Third, the misunderstanding leads Chabram to oversimplify in defining a San Diego circle that carried on "dialogues with the works of Eagleton and Jameson" and confining the Austin circle to "the writing of literary histories which draw from folklore and a cultural studies methodology" and which "surface[d] largely as a result of the appearance of seminal literary histories" (1990:60).

6. These insights may be borne out—or not—by further historical ethnographic work on this student generation in relation to that of their parents and grandparents. For my own ethnographic work on this population, see Limón 1982a; 1982b.

EPILOGUE

1. See Cantor 1990 for a perceptive definition of the 1960s as a time of critical modernism before the onset of the cynical postmodernism of the present moment.

References

Abrahams, Roger D.
1963   *Deep Down in the Jungle: Negro Narrative from the Streets of Philadelphia*. Chicago: Aldine.
1972   "Folklore and Literature as Performance." *Journal of the Folklore Institute* 9:75–94.

Achor, Shirley
1978   *Mexican Americans in a Dallas Barrio*. Tucson: University of Arizona Press.

Acosta, Vicente S.
1951   "Some Surviving Elements of Spanish Folklore in Arizona." Master's thesis, University of Arizona.

Acuña, Rodolfo
1981   *Occupied America: A History of Chicanos*. 2d ed. New York: Harper & Row.

Alurista
1976   *Timespace Huracán*. Albuquerque: Pajarito Publications.
1980   "From Tragedy to Caricature . . . and Beyond." *Aztlán* 11:89–98.

Anzaldua, Gloria
1987   *Borderlands / La Frontera: The New Mestiza*. San Francisco: Spinsters / Aunt Lute Book Co.

Baker, Houston A., Jr.
1985   *Blues, Ideology, and Afro-American Literature: A Vernacular Theory*. Chicago: University of Chicago Press.
1987   *Modernism and the Harlem Renaissance*. Chicago: University of Chicago Press.
1988   *Afro-American Poetics: Revisions of Harlem and the Black Aesthetic*. Madison: University of Wisconsin Press.

Bakhtin, M. M.
1981   *The Dialogic Imagination: Four Essays by M.M. Bakhtin*. Trans. Caryl Emerson and Michael Holquist; ed. Michael Holquist. Austin: University of Texas Press.
1986   *Speech Genres and Other Late Essays*. Trans. Vern W. McGee; ed. Caryl Emerson and Michael Holquist. Austin: University of Texas Press.

Barrera, Mario
1979   *Race and Class in the Southwest: A Theory of Racial Inequality*. Notre Dame: Notre Dame University Press.

Bauman, Richard
    1975   "Verbal Art as Performance." *American Anthropologist* 77:290–312.
    1982   "Conceptions of Folklore in the Development of Literary Semiotics." *Semiotica* 39:1–20.
Bloom, Harold
    1973   *The Anxiety of Influence*. New Haven: Yale University Press.
    1975a   *A Map of Misreading*. New York: Oxford University Press.
    1975b   *Kabbalah and Criticism*. New York: Seabury Press.
    1976   *Poetry and Repression: Revisionism from Blake to Stevens*. New Haven: Yale University Press.
    1982a   *Agon: Towards a Theory of Revisionism*. New York: Oxford University Press.
    1982b   *The Breaking of the Vessels*. Chicago: University of Chicago Press.
    1984   " 'Before Moses Was, I Am': The Original and Belated Testaments." *Notebooks in Cultural Analysis: An Annual Review* 1:3–14.
Brown, Norman O.
    1959   *Life Against Death: The Psychoanalytical Meaning of History*. New York: Random House.
Bruce-Novoa, Juan
    1980   *Chicano Authors: Inquiry by Interview*. Austin: University of Texas Press.
    1982   *Chicano Poetry: A Response to Chaos*. Austin: University of Texas Press.
Cabral, Amilcar
    1973   *Return to the Source: Selected Speeches of Amilcar Cabral*. New York: Monthly Review Press.
Calderón, Héctor
    1983   "To Read Chicano Narratives: Commentary and Metacommentary." *Mester* 11:3–14.
Calderón, Héctor, and José D. Saldívar, eds.
    1991   *Criticism in the Borderlands: Studies in Chicano Culture, Literature, and Ideology*. Durham: Duke University Press.
Candelaria, Cordelia
    1986   *Chicano Poetry: An Introduction*. Westport, Conn.: Greenwood Press.
Cantor, Jay
    1990   "The Patriarchs." *Tikkun* 5:11–14, 87–92.
Castillo, Pedro, and Albert Camarillo
    1973   *Furia y Muerte: Los Bandidos Chicanos*. Los Angeles: UCLA Chicano Studies Center.
Cervantes, Lorna Dee
    1981   *Emplumada*. Pittsburgh: University of Pittsburgh Press.
Chabram, Angie
    1987   "Chicano Critical Discourse: An Emerging Practice." *Aztlán* 18:45–90.

Clifford, James, and George E. Marcus, eds.
  1986   *Writing Culture: The Poetics and Politics of Ethnography*. Berkeley and Los Angeles: University of California Press.
Cline, Howard
  1969   "The Neo-Bourbons" [1953]. In *Revolution in Mexico: Years of Upheaval, 1910–1940*, ed. James W. Welkie and Albert Michaels. New York: Knopf.
Cobb, Jonathan, and Richard Sennett
  1973   *The Hidden Injuries of Class*. New York: Random House.
Cockcroft, James
  1983   *Mexico: Class Formation, Capital Accumulation, and the State*. New York: Monthly Review Press.
Cortina, Rodolfo J.
  1984   "Research on the Corrido: The Questions of Origin, Toponymy and Persistence—A Review Essay." *Studies in Latin American Popular Culture* 3:203–9.
Davidson, Cathy N.
  1984   *The Experimental Fictions of Ambrose Bierce*. Lincoln: University of Nebraska Press.
De Colores: A Journal of Chicano Expression and Thought
  1980   Special issue, "Contemporary Chicano Literary Criticism" (5, nos. 1–2).
de la Garza, Rodolfo O., Frank D. Bean, Charles M. Bonjean, Ricardo Romo, and Rodolfo Alvarez, eds.
  1985   *The Mexican American Experience*. Austin: University of Texas Press.
de Leon, Arnoldo
  1982   *The Tejano Community, 1836–1900*. Albuquerque: University of New Mexico Press.
  1983   *They Called Them Greasers: Anglo Attitudes Towards Mexicans in Texas, 1821–1900*. Austin: University of Texas Press.
Delgado, Abelardo
  1969   *25 Pieces of a Chicano Mind*. Denver: Barrio Publications.
di Bolla, Peter
  1988   *Harold Bloom: Towards Historical Rhetorics*. New York: Routledge.
Dickey, Dan William
  1978   *The Kennedy Corridos: A Study of the Ballads of a Mexican American Hero*. Monograph no. 4. Austin: University of Texas, Center for Mexican American Studies.
Dundes, Alan
  1969   "The Devolutionary Premise in Folklore Theory." *Journal of the Folklore Institute* 6:5–19.
Eagleton, Terry
  1986   *Against the Grain: Essays, 1975–1985*. Cambridge: Verso Books.

Elizondo, Sergio
    1980   "Sergio Elizondo" [interview by Juan Bruce-Novoa]. In *Chicano Authors: Inquiry by Interview*, by Juan Bruce-Novoa, pp. 67–82. Austin: University of Texas Press.
Epringham, Toní, ed.
    1982   *Fiesta in Aztlán: Anthology of Chicano Poetry*. Santa Barbara, Calif.: Capra Press.
Fenichel, Otto
    1945   *The Psychoanalytical Theory of Neurosis*. New York: Norton.
Fernandez, Celestino
    1983   "The Mexican Immigration Experience and the *Corrido Mexicano*." *Studies in Latin American Popular Culture* 2:115–30.
Fischer, Michael M. J.
    1986   "Ethnicity and the Post-Modern Arts of Memory." In *Writing Culture: The Poetics and Politics of Ethnography*, ed. James Clifford and George E. Marcus, pp. 194–233. Berkeley and Los Angeles: University of California Press.
Fite, David
    1985   *Harold Bloom: The Rhetoric of Romantic Vision*. Amherst: University of Massachusetts Press.
Flores, Richard
    1987   "Revolution, Folklore, and the Political Unconscious: 'Los Sediciosos' as a Socially Symbolic Act." Paper read at the 1987 meetings of the American Folklore Society, Albuquerque, N.M.
Foley, Douglas
    1977   *From Peones to Politicos: Ethnic Relations in a South Texas Town*. Austin: University of Texas, Center for Mexican American Studies.
Foucault, Michel
    1980   *Power/Knowledge: Selected Interviews and Other Writings, 1972–1977*. Ed. Colin Gordon. New York: Pantheon Books.
Fuentes, Rumel
    1973   "Corridos de Rumel." *El Grito* 6:3–40.
García, Alma
    1989   "The Development of Chicana Feminist Discourse, 1970–1980." *Gender and Society* 3:217–38.
García, Richard A.
    1991   *Rise of the Mexican American Middle Class: San Antonio, 1929–1941*. College Station: Texas A&M University Press.
Gates, Henry Louis, Jr.
    1987   "Authority (White), Power and the (Black) Critic: Or, It's All Greek to Me." *Cultural Critique*, no. 7, pp. 19–46.
    1988   *The Signifying Monkey: A Theory of African-American Literary Criticism*. New York: Oxford University Press.
Gates, Henry Louis, Jr., ed.
    1984   *Black Literature and Theory*. New York: Methuen.

Geertz, Clifford
1973   *The Interpretation of Cultures: Selected Essays by Clifford Geertz.*
         New York: Basic Books.
1980   "Blurred Genres: The Refiguration of Social Thought." *American
         Scholar* 29:165–79.
Geijerstam, Claes Af.
1976   *Popular Music in Mexico.* Albuquerque: University of New Mex-
         ico Press.
Gilroy, Paul
1988   "Nothing But Sweat Inside My Hand: Diaspora Aesthetics and
         Black Arts in Britain." In *Black Film, British Cinema*, ed. Kobena
         Mercer. London: ICA Documents, no. 7, pp. 44–46.
Ginzburg, Carlo
1982   *The Cheese and the Worms: The Cosmos of a Sixteenth-Century
         Miller.* New York: Penguin Books.
Goldman, Shifra M., and Tomás Ybarra-Frausto
1983   *Arte Chicano: A Comprehensive Annotated Bibliography of Chi-
         cano Art, 1965–1981.* Berkeley: Chicano Studies Library Publi-
         cations Unit, University of California at Berkeley.
Gómez-Quiñones, Juan
1973   *5th and Grande Vista (Poems, 1960–1973).* New York: Colección
         Mensaje.
1979   *Mexican Students Por La Raza: The Chicano Student Movement
         in Southern California, 1967–1977.* Santa Barbara: Editorial La
         Causa.
Gonzales, Rodolfo
1972   *I Am Joaquín: An Epic Poem* [1967]. New York: Bantam Books.
Gonzales-Berry, Erlinda
1980   "Perros y Antiperros: The Voice of the Bard." *De Colores* 5:45–68.
Greenblatt, Stephen
1980   *Renaissance Self-Fashioning.* Chicago: University of Chicago Press.
1988a   Introduction to *Representing the English Renaissance*, ed. Stephen
         Greenblatt. Berkeley: University of California Press.
1988b   *Shakespearean Negotiations: The Circulation of Social Energy in
         Renaissance England.* Berkeley: University of California Press.
Harris, Charles H., and Louis R. Sadler
1978   "The Plan of San Diego and the Mexican-United States Crisis of
         1916: A Reexamination." *Hispanic American Historical Review*
         58:381–408.
Heath, Shirley Brice
1972   *Telling Tongues: Language Policy in Mexico. Colony to Nation.*
         New York: Columbia University Teachers College Press.
Heisley, Robert Michael
1983   "Corridistas de la Huelga." Doctoral dissertation, University of
         California at Los Angeles.

Hernandez, Guillermo E.

1980   "On the Theoretical Basis of Chicano Literature." *De Colores* 5:5–
18.

1991   *Chicano Satire: A Study in Literary Culture.* Austin: University of
Texas Press.

Herrera-Sobek, Maria

1990   *The Mexican Corrido: A Feminist Analysis.* Bloomington: Indiana
University Press.

Hoggarth, Richard

1961   *The Uses of Literacy: Changing Patterns in English Mass Culture.*
Boston: Beacon Press.

Howe, Irving

1976   *World of Our Fathers.* New York: Harcourt Brace Jovanovich.

Huerta, Jorge A.

1982   *Chicano Theater: Themes and Forms.* Ypsilanti, Mich.: Bilingual
Review Press.

Jameson, Fredric

1981   *The Political Unconscious: Narrative as a Socially Symbolic Act.*
Ithaca: Cornell University Press.

1984   "Postmodernism, or the Cultural Logic of Late Capitalism." *New
Left Review,* no. 146, 53–93.

Jimenez, Francisco, ed.

1979   *The Identification and Analysis of Chicano Literature.* New York:
Bilingual Review Press.

Kaplan, Abraham

1980   "The Jewish Argument with God." *Commentary* 70:43–47.

Knight, Alan

1987   *The Mexican Revolution.* Vol. 2, *Counter-Revolution and Reconstruction.* New York: Cambridge University Press.

Kristeva, Julia

1986   "Stabat Mater." In *The Female Body in Western Culture,* ed. Susan
Rubín Suleiman, pp. 99–118. Cambridge: Harvard University Press.

Kushner, Sam

1975   *The Long Road to Delano.* New York: International Publishers.

Latin American Literary Review

1977   Special Issue of Chicano Literature (5, no. 10).

Lamadrid, Enrique

1990   "Juan Gómez-Quiñones." In *Dictionary of Literary Biography:
Chicano Writers,* ed. Francisco Lomeli, 82:285–90. Detroit: Gale
Research Publications.

Leal, Luis

1982   "Mexican-American Literature: A Historical Perspective." In *Mod-
ern Chicano Writers: A Collection of Critical Essays,* ed. Joseph
Sommers and Tomás Ybarra-Frausto, pp. 18–30. Englewood Cliffs,
N.J.: Prentice-Hall.

1987   "México y Aztlán: El Corrido." *Aztlán* 18:15–26.

Lentricchia, Frank
  1980   *After the New Criticism.* Chicago: University of Chicago Press.
  1983   *Criticism and Social Change.* Chicago: University of Chicago Press.
  1988   *Ariel and the Police: Michel Foucault, William James, Wallace Stevens.* Madison: University of Wisconsin Press.
Limón, José E.
  1973   "Stereotyping and Chicano Resistance: An Historical Dimension." *Aztlán* 4:257–70.
  1974   "El Primer Congreso Mexicanista de 1911: A Precursor to Contemporary Chicanismo." *Aztlán* 5:85–117.
  1981   "The Folk Performance of *Chicano* and the Cultural Limits of Political Ideology." In *"And Other Neighborly Names": Social Process and Cultural Image in Texas Folklore*, ed. Richard Bauman and Roger D. Abrahams, pp. 197–225. Austin: University of Texas Press.
  1982a   "El Meeting: History, Folk Spanish and Ethnic Nationalism in a Chicano Student Community." In *Spanish in the United States: Sociolinguistic Aspects*, ed. Lucia Elias-Olivares and Jon Amastae, pp. 301–32. New York: Cambridge University Press.
  1982b   "History, Chicano Joking and the Varieties of Higher Education." *Journal of the Folklore Institute* 19:141–66.
  1983a   "The Rise, Fall, and 'Revival' of the Mexican-American Corrido: A Review Essay." *Studies in Latin American Popular Culture* 2:202–7.
  1983b   "Western Marxism and Folklore: A Critical Introduction." *Journal of American Folklore* 96:34–52.
  1986a   "La llorona, the Third Legend of Greater Mexico: Cultural Symbols, Women and the Political Unconscious." In *Renato Rosaldo Lecture Series Monograph* 2, ed. Ignacio M. Garcia, pp. 59–63. Tucson: University of Arizona Mexican American Studies and Research Center. [Also appears in *Between Borders: Essays on Mexicana/Chicana History*, ed. Adelaida R. Del Castillo. Los Angeles: Floricanto Press, 1988.]
  1986b   *Mexican Ballads, Chicano Epic: History, Social Dramas and Poetic Persuasions.* Working Paper no. 14. Stanford: Stanford University Center for Chicano Research.
  1986c   *The Return of the Mexican Ballad: Américo Paredes and His Anthropological Text as a Persuasive Political Performance.* Working Paper no. 16. Stanford: Stanford University Center for Chicano Research.
  1989   "A Southern Renaissance for Texas Letters." In *Range Wars: Reflections on Texas Literature*, ed. Tom Pilkington, pp. 127–39. Dallas: Southern Methodist University Press.
  In press "Barbarians, Christians, and Jews: Three Narrative Scenes in the Sociolinguistic Legacy of the Mexicans of Texas." In *The Mexican*

Legacy of Texas, ed. Robert O'Connor. College Station: Texas A&M University Press.

Linderman, Gerald F.
1987   *Embattled Courage: The Experience of Combat in the American Civil War.* New York: Free Press.

Lloyd, David
1987   *Nationalism and Minor Literature: James Clarence Magnan and the Emergence of Irish Cultural Nationalism.* Berkeley: University of California Press.

Lukács, Georg
1974   "On the Nature and Form of the Essay" [1910]. In *Soul and Form,* trans. Anna Bostock, pp. 1–18. Cambridge: MIT Press.

McDowell, John H.
1972   "The Mexican Corrido: Formula and Theme in a Ballad Tradition." *Journal of American Folklore* 85:205–20.
1981   "The Corrido of Greater Mexico as Discourse, Music, and Event." In *"And Other Neighborly Names": Social Process and Cultural Image in Texas Folklore,* eds. Richard Bauman and Roger D. Abrahams. Austin: University of Texas Press.

McKenna, Teresa
In press *Parto de Palabra: Studies on Chicano Literature in Process.* Austin: University of Texas Press.

Marcus, George E., and Michael M. J. Fischer
1986   *Anthropology as Cultural Critique: An Experimental Moment in the Human Sciences.* Chicago: University of Chicago Press.

Melville, Margarita, ed.
1980   *Twice a Minority: Mexican American Women.* St. Louis: C. V. Mosby.

Mendoza, Vicente T.
1939   *El Romance Español y el Corrido Mexicano: Estudio Comparativo.* Mexico City: Universidad Nacional Autónoma de México.
1954   *El Corrido Mexicano.* Mexico City: Fondo de Cultura Económica.

Meyer, Doris L.
1975   "Anonymous Poetry in Spanish-Language New Mexico Newspapers, 1880–1900." *The Bilingual Review / La Revista Bilingue* 1:259–75.

Meyer, Michael C., and William L. Sherman
1979   *The Course of Mexican History.* New York: Oxford University Press.

Miller, James
1986   "C. Wright Mills Reconsidered." *Salmagundi,* nos. 70–71, pp. 82–101.

Montejano, David
1987   *Anglos and Mexicans in the Making of Texas.* Austin: University of Texas Press.

Montoya, José
   1969a   "La Jefita." In *El Espejo (The Mirror): Selected Mexican-American Literature*, ed. Octavio Romano, pp. 188–89. Berkeley: Quinto Sol Publications.
   1969b   "Poetry." In *El Espejo (The Mirror): Selected Mexican-American Literature*, ed. Octavio Romano, pp. 180–92. Berkeley: Quinto Sol Publications.
   1972a   "El Louie." In *Aztlán: An Anthology of Mexican American Literature*, ed. Luis Valdez and Stan Steiner, pp. 333–37. New York: Knopf.
   1972b   "El Sol y los de Abajo." In *El Sol y los de Abajo and Other R.C.A.F. Poems*, pp. 34–40. San Francisco: Ediciones Pocho-Che.
   1980a   "Interview." In *Chicano Authors: Inquiry by Interview*, by Juan Bruce-Novoa, pp. 115–36. Austin: University of Texas Press.
   1980b   "Russian Cowboys, Early Berkeley and Sunstruck Critics / On Being a Chicano Writer." *Metamorfosis* 3:48–53.
Mukarovsky, P.
   1977   *The Word and Verbal Art: Selected Essays by Mukarovsky*. Trans. and ed. John Burbank and Peter Steiner. New Haven: Yale University Press.
Muñoz, Carlos
   1989   *Youth, Identity, Power: The Chicano Generation*. London: Verso Books.
Najera-Ramirez, Olga
   1987   "Greater Mexican Folklore in the U.S.: An Annotated Bibliography." *Ethnic Affairs* 1:64–115.
Nelson-Cisneros, Victor
   1975   "La Clase Trabajadora en Tejas, 1920–1940." *Aztlán* 6:239–65.
O'Connor, Richard
   1967   *Ambrose Bierce: A Biography*. Boston: Little, Brown.
Ong, Walter J.
   1982   *Orality and Literacy: The Technologizing of the Word*. New York: Methuen.
Ortega, Adolfo
   1977   "Of Social Politics and Poetry: A Chicano Perspective." *Latin American Literary Review* 5:32–41.
Ortner, Sherry B.
   1973   "On Key Symbols." *American Anthropologist* 75:1338–46.
Ostriker, Alicia
   1983   *Writing Like a Woman*. Ann Arbor: University of Michigan Press.
Owens, Craig
   1983   "The Discourse of Others: Feminists and Postmodernism." In *The Anti-Aesthetic: Essays on Postmodern Culture*, ed. Hal Foster, pp. 57–82. Port Townsend, Wash.: Bay Press.
Paredes, Américo
   1958a   "The Mexican *Corrido*: Its Rise and Fall." In *Madstones and*

Twisters, ed. Mody C. Boatright, Wilson M. Hudson, and Allen Maxwell, pp. 91–105. Dallas: Southern Methodist University Press.

1958b   *With His Pistol in His Hand: A Border Ballad and Its Hero.* Austin: University of Texas Press. Reprint, 1971.

1963   "The Ancestry of Mexico's Corridos: A Matter of Definitions." *Journal of American Folklore* 76:231–35.

1964a   "Guitarreros." *Southwest Review* 16:306.

1964b   "Some Aspects of Folk Poetry." *Texas Studies in Language and Literature* 6:213–25.

1967   "Estados Unidos, Mexico y el machismo." *Journal of Inter-American Studies* 9:65–84. [Reprinted in translation in *Journal of the Folklore Institute* 8(1971):17–37.]

1976   *A Texas-Mexican Cancionero.* Urbana: University of Illinois Press.

1978   "On Ethnographic Work Among Minority Groups." In *New Directions in Chicano Scholarship*, ed. Ricardo Romo and Raymund Paredes, pp. 1–32. La Jolla: University of California Chicano Studies Program.

1980   "Versos Varios." Unpublished manuscript of poetry with author's commentary.

Paredes, Raymund

1982   "The Evolution of Chicano Literature." In *Three American Literatures*, ed. Houston Baker, Jr., pp. 33–79. New York: Modern Language Association.

Patterson, Tim

1975   "Notes on the Historical Application of Marxist Cultural Theory." *Science and Society* 39:257–91.

Pearce, Roy Harvey

1987   *The Continuity of American Poetry.* Middletown, Conn.: Wesleyan University Press. [Originally published in 1961.]

Pease, Donald E.

1988   "Patriarchy, Lentricchia, and Male Feminization." *Critical Inquiry* 14:379–85.

Peña, Manuel H.

1982   "Folksong and Social Change: Two Corridos as Interpretive Sources." *Aztlán* 13:13–42.

Porter, Carolyn

1988   "Are We Being Historical Yet?" *South Atlantic Quarterly* 87:743–86.

Portillo, Estella, ed.

1973   *Chicanas en la literatura y el arte / Chicanas in Literature and Art.* Special issue of *El Grito* (4, no. 1).

Quirarte, Jacinto

1975   *Mexican American Artists.* Austin: University of Texas Press.

Quirk, Robert E.

1969   "Battle of Celaya." In *Revolution in Mexico: Years of Upheaval,*

1910–1940, ed. James W. Wilkie and Albert L. Michaels, pp. 107–11. New York: Knopf.

Rivera, Tomás

1980   "Interview." In *Chicano Authors: Inquiry by Interview* by Juan Bruce-Novoa, pp. 137–62. Austin: University of Texas Press.

Robinson, Cecil

1977   *Mexico and the Hispanic Southwest in American Literature.* Tucson: University of Arizona Press. [Revised from *With the Ears of Strangers: The Mexican in American Literature.* Tucson: University of Arizona Press, 1963.]

Rodriguez, Juan

1974   "Acercamiento a cuatro relatos de 'Y no se lo trago la tierra.' " *Mester* 5:16–24.

1979a   "La Búsqueda de identidad y sus motivos en la literatura chicana." In *The Identification and Analysis of Chicano Literature,* ed. Francisco Jimenez, pp. 170–78. New York: Bilingual Press.

1979b   "Notes on the Evolution of Chicano Prose Fiction." In *Modern Chicano Writers: A Collection of Critical Essays,* ed. Joseph Sommers and Tomás Ybarra-Frausto, pp. 67–73. Englewood Cliffs, N.J.: Prentice-Hall.

Romano, Octavio I. V.

1968   "The Anthropology and Sociology of the Mexican Americans: The Distortion of Mexican American History." *El Grito* 2:13–26.

Romano, Octavio I. V., ed.

1969   *El Espejo (The Mirror): Selected Mexican-American Literature.* Berkeley: Quinto Sol Publications.

Rosaldo, Renato

1985   "Chicano Studies, 1970–1984." *Annual Reviews of Anthropology* 14:405–27.

1987   "Politics, Patriarchs, and Laughter." *Cultural Critique,* no. 6, pp. 65–86.

Said, Edward

1983   "Opponents, Audiences, Constituencies and Community." In *The Anti-Aesthetic: Essays on Postmodern Culture,* ed. Hal Foster. Port Townsend, Wash.: Bay Press, pp. 135–59. [Originally published in *Critical Inquiry,* September 1982.]

Saldívar, José David

n.d.   "Our America and the Canon: Genealogy, Politics and Literary History." Unpublished manuscript.

1986   "Towards a Chicano Poetics: The Making of the Chicano Subject, 1969–1982." *Confluencia* 1:10–17.

1991   "Chicano Border Narratives as Cultural Critique." In *Criticism in the Borderlands,* ed. Héctor Calderón and José Saldívar. Durham: Duke University Press.

Saldívar, Ramón

    1979   "The Dialectics of Difference: Towards a Theory of the Chicano Novel." *Melus* 6:73–92.

    1984   "*Korean Love Songs:* A Border Ballad and Its Heroes." In *The Rolando Hinojosa Reader: Essays Historical and Critical,* ed. José David Saldívar, pp. 143–57. Houston: Arte Publico Press.

    1985   "Ideologies of the Self: Chicano Autobiography." *Diacritics* (Fall), 25–34.

    1990   *Chicano Narrative: The Dialectics of Difference.* Madison: University of Wisconsin Press.

Salinas, Raul

    1980   *Un Trip through the Mind Jail y Otras Excursions.* San Francisco: Editorial Pocho-Che.

Sánchez, Marta

    1985   *Chicana Poetry: A Critical Approach to an Emerging Literature.* Berkeley and Los Angeles: University of California Press.

Sánchez, Ricardo

    1976   *Hechizo Spells.* Los Angeles: Chicano Studies Center, University of California at Los Angeles.

Sánchez, Rosaura

    1983   *Chicano Discourse: Socio-historic Perspectives.* Topsfield, Mass.: Newbury House.

    1987   "Postmodernism and Chicano Literature." *Aztlán* 18:1–14.

San Miguel, Guadalupe

    1987   *"Let Them All Take Heed": Mexican Americans and the Campaign for Educational Equality in Texas, 1910–1981.* Austin: University of Texas Press.

Simmons, Merle E.

    1957   *The Mexican Corrido as a Source for the Interpretive Study of Modern Mexico (1870–1950).* Bloomington: Indiana University Press.

    1963   "The Ancestry of Mexico's Corridos." *Journal of American Folklore* 76:1–15.

Sommers, Joseph

    1977   "From the Critical Premise to the Product: Critical Modes and Their Applications to a Chicano Literary Text." *New Scholar* 6:51–80.

Sommers, Joseph, and Tomás Ybarra-Frausto, eds.

    1979   *Modern Chicano Writers: A Collection of Critical Essays.* Englewood Cliffs, N.J.: Prentice-Hall.

Tinker, Edward Larocque

    1961   *Corridos and Calaveras.* Trans. Américo Paredes. Austin: Humanities Research Center, University of Texas.

Tovar, Ines

    1975   " 'Roses are Rosas': Juan Gómez-Quiñones—A Chicano Poet." *Mester* 5:95–100.

Turner, Victor
   1974   *Dramas, Fields, and Metaphors: Symbolic Action in Human So-ciety*. Ithaca: Cornell University Press.
Turner, Victor, and Edith Turner
   1980   *Image and Pilgrimage in Christian Culture*. Oxford: Basil Black-well.
Vaca, Nick C.
   1970   "The Mexican American in the Social Sciences. Part II: 1936–1970." *El Grito* 4:17–51.
Valdes, Luis, and Stan Steiner, eds.
   1972   *Aztlán: An Anthology of Mexican American Literature*. New York: Knopf.
Van Genep, Arnold
   1960   *The Rites of Passage*. Trans. Monika B. Vizedom and Gabrielle L. Caffee. Chicago: University of Chicago Press.
Walker, Jeffrey
   1989   *Bardic Ethos and the American Epic Poem: Whitman, Pound, Crane, Williams, Olson*. Baton Rouge: Louisiana State University Press.
Webb, Walter Prescott
   1935   *The Texas Rangers*. Cambridge: Houghton Mifflin.
White, Hayden
   1973   *Metahistory: The Historical Imagination in Nineteenth-Century Europe*. Baltimore: Johns Hopkins University Press.
   1978   *Tropics of Discourse: Essays in Cultural Criticism*. Baltimore: Johns Hopkins University Press.
Williams, Raymond
   1977   *Marxism and Literature*. Oxford: Oxford University Press.
   1989   *The Politics of Modernism: Against the New Conformists*. London: Verso.
Wolf, Eric
   1958   "The Virgen of Guadalupe: A Mexican National Symbol." *Journal of American Folklore* 71:34–39.
   1969   *Peasant Wars of the Twentieth Century*. New York: Harper & Row.
Womack, John, Jr.
   1968   *Zapata and the Mexican Revolution*. New York: Knopf.
Ybarra-Frausto, Tomás
   1978   "The Chicano Movement and the Emergence of a Chicano Poetic Consciousness." In *New Directions in Chicano Scholarship*, ed. Ricardo Romo and Raymund Paredes, pp. 81–110. La Jolla: University of California at San Diego, Chicano Studies.
Zamora, Emilio
   1986   *El Movimiento Obrero Mexicano en el Sur de Texas, 1900–1920*. Mexico City: Secretaria de Educación Pública.

Index

Compositor: Impressions, A Division of Edwards Brothers, Inc.
Text: 10/13 Sabon
Display: Sabon
Printer: Edwards Brothers, Inc.
Binder: Edwards Brothers, Inc.